Game Changer

Game Changer

Cora Staunton
with Mary White

TRANSWORLD IRELAND

TRANSWORLD IRELAND
Penguin Random House Ireland, Morrison Chambers, 32 Nassau Street,
Dublin 2, Ireland
www.transworldireland.ie

Transworld Ireland is part of the Penguin Random House group
of companies whose addresses can be found at
global.penguinrandomhouse.com

First published in the UK and Ireland in 2018
by Transworld Ireland
an imprint of Transworld Publishers

A CIP catalogue record for this book
is available from the British Library.

ISBN 9781848272590

Typeset in 11.5/17 pt Sabon
by Integra Software Services Pvt. Ltd, Pondicherry

Printed and bound in Great Britain by Clays Ltd, Elcograf S.p.A.

Penguin Random House is committed to a sustainable
future for our business, our readers and our planet. This book
is made from Forest Stewardship Council® certified paper.

1 3 5 7 9 10 8 6 4 2

To a special lady in heaven

Contents

1

Getting Addicted

FOR MY ELEVENTH BIRTHDAY MY GODFATHER, COLM, GAVE ME A cerise pink Nike T-shirt. The tomboy in me overlooked the colour because it was my first Nike anything, and within six months, I'd worn it ragged. I reckon I slept in it the night before my first All-Ireland final – the 1993 Community Games in Mosney. I was playing with the U13 Carra ladies football team, and the four-hour bus journey to Meath made it feel so much more monumental. If they'd told us we were going to the Olympics, we'd have believed them.

We were tied with a crowd from Kerry with just a few minutes to go in the final. They were handy out, but we were putting it to them. I loved it; breaking tackles and firing over points. Michelle McGing set everything up down the middle, and between the two of us, we thought we had them. Michelle, however, got a bad knock to her elbow when she was burrowing her way through midfield. She was on the ground, holding the elbow, and I knew it was bad. I thought to myself, *If I could just get one more ball, I could kick the winner.* But the odds now of getting my hands on the ball with Michelle off the field were slim. We'd been playing football together since we made our Holy Communion, and Michelle could read me like a book.

I looked across to the sideline. Our coach, Eamonn Chambers, was whispering words of inspiration into the ear of one of our gang, and patting her on the back. *He's about to send her on! You're joking me? We've an All-Ireland to win, and we're not going to do it with her on!*

I didn't get the ball again, and they went down the other end and scored the winner. It was my first-ever big loss, and I couldn't cope. From there on out, things were never going to be the same for me again.

Eamonn did the rounds, consoling us. 'Hard luck, Cora. Hard luck.' I couldn't reply. I couldn't get the words out, because in my head, I was roaring at him. Roaring.

You cost us the game, ya feckin' eejit!

It wasn't even that it was an All-Ireland he'd cost us, I was just thinking that he cost us a game. One game, for God's sake. To be fair, Eamonn had only a panel of twenty or so. And, it wasn't like we were a fully fledged football squad either. But the girl he brought on to replace Michelle, well, football wasn't really her thing. And I thought his decision cost us the game. For that, I could barely forgive him.

The same girl's mother – or was it her father? – had sadly passed away a few weeks beforehand, and Eamonn was just being a good person, a good coach. I didn't see it like that, however. Winning that game, and winning a gold medal, was all that mattered to me. *What was he thinking? There was no time for sympathy. He cost us a medal!*

I know it probably meant the world to her to come on. If just for a few minutes, Eamonn's gesture made her forget all the grief in the world, but I couldn't empathize. I couldn't understand. I'd lose my own mother four years later and would come to realize the importance of such support, but in that moment, I couldn't reason why Eamonn did what he did. How could he let his heart rule his head? I know I sound ruthless, and it's hard to comprehend, but that's who I was. It's who I am.

It's not a selfish thing. It's just in my psyche. It's always been in my psyche. A game of cards, a board game, anything really. I have to be the best. I have to win. Call it what you want – tunnel vision, passion, an obsession, an addiction ... because that's what it was, an addiction. I craved winning, and I'd been like that since day dot.

I was born stubborn. On 13 December 1981, I arrived four weeks premature, having grown restless from all the hanging around. It was a Sunday and my mother, Mary, was cleaning up the breakfast dishes before Mass. Even with a few weeks to go she was still fluttering about the place, tidying and organizing, and I decided it was time.

I was the second youngest of eight – four girls and four boys – and I was sandwiched between the four boys. Dad met Mam, Mary Summerville, at a dance in Ballinrobe. She had been to a wedding in Killawalla, and afterwards her friends Mairtín and Mary dropped her to Ballinrobe for the dance. She joked with us, years after, that she also had accidentally set up a date with another fella for the same night, but she decided that whoever came along first would win. And Michael Staunton was bang on time.

That was Mam: always practical, with a great sense of humour. She used to say, 'You should never run after a man or a bus, because there's always another one following behind.'

They married in September 1972, and the following May, my eldest sister, Sheena, was the first to arrive. In ten years, they managed to raise us all in Castlecarra, a mile outside the village of Carnacon in the county of Mayo on the west coast of Ireland.

My parents had a lot in common. They were both raised on small rural farms – Dad was from Castlecarra and Mam from Clonbur in Galway – yet they were also very different. Dad's a very shy man. He has no airs and graces, and has a good word for everybody. It was Mam who brought out his sociable side. When they did go out, Dad would order a Guinness, and a vodka or a Martini and white for Mam, and they'd dance the night away with friends. That was their thing, socializing on a Friday or a Saturday night at whatever local pub was holding a dance, and with eight children at home, God knows they needed the release.

They were both serious workers. Before Dad met Mam, he worked as a labourer on building sites in England with his younger brother. Being the eldest, he'd send home the few bob to my grandparents to keep them and the farm going. He moved home in 1969, aged twenty-five, when he inherited a small dairy farm on 50 acres of land from his uncles Pete and Walt. Ever since, he has farmed cattle, and the odd few sheep.

Mam was just as hard-working, organizing and budgeting for a household of ten. She ran a tight ship, and she was strict and very direct – which she had to be to keep us all in line. If you wanted something, you didn't go to Mam. Dad was the softer touch, but they were equally as loving. Family meant the world to them, and it's only looking back now that I realize how hard it must have been for them to rear us all.

They first lived in the house they inherited from Dad's uncles – a two-storey country farmhouse with two bedrooms and no bathroom. There was a downstairs toilet, but no bath, so it was a case of washing themselves and us the old-fashioned way with a warm basin of water and a towel. As for the sleeping arrangements, everyone piled into two beds.

In 1983, they got enough money together to build their own house. Mam was the decision-maker and the driver in terms of getting things done, and she insisted that the workmen complete the bathroom first. The new house was built only a few feet away, and every Saturday night, Mam carried each of us across the yard to have our weekly wash in the new bath. On the first night we moved in, she didn't even go to bed. She was on a mission to clean and get our new home ready, and if that meant missing out on a night's sleep, then so be it.

Financially, things were tough. I could tell at times that we were stuck for money because I'd hear my parents talking about it. Sometimes, when I passed the kitchen late at night, I might have picked up on a conversation. Either way, I'd have sensed it. The only source of income was from the farm. You'd only get a milk cheque a few times a year, so Dad had to go to Social Welfare to keep things going. Sheena, the eldest, was more aware of it than the rest of us. For her twenty-first birthday, Mam told her that she could have money for a twenty-first outfit or an interview outfit, as the money wasn't there for both.

We didn't have a lot, but others didn't either. It was the eighties, and there were a lot of families like us, just doing their best to get through. I wasn't even conscious of the hand-me-downs; all I cared about was having a pair of football boots. Mam bought my first few pairs in the second-hand shop in Claremorris, and it didn't bother me that they were someone else's before me. It was just how things were. However, for Christmas, my parents always pulled a rabbit out of the hat. They always got me something sporty – a dartboard, a Scalextric race car track, a bike – and my youngest brother Brian and I would play together for hours on end.

I was in fifth class when Mam got a part-time job as a catering assistant in Mayo General Hospital in Castlebar. I remember standing at the gate, waving her off. She was obviously going because money was tight, but I'd like to think she enjoyed it too. She worked for Campbell Catering on the maternity ward, and she went above and beyond to look after the new mothers, being a mother of eight herself. If there was any extra tea or toast floating around, Mary Staunton made sure they got it.

Even now, Mam's former colleagues would say how she insisted on perfection. She wasn't the greatest cook, but if there was salad being prepared for the patients, and the tomatoes weren't cut to her standards, she'd return them to the kitchen. She was extremely caring, but there was a perfectionist in her too, and I gather that's where I get it from.

We were lucky to have a Ford Cortina to get around, but try fitting ten people into a Ford Cortina. There were major scraps to see who would sit beside the window. It was survival of the fittest just getting into that car, never mind getting a seat next to the window. It was dog eat dog – and you ate what you were given too, because if you didn't, someone else would eat it for you.

We didn't have family holidays. We might have had a day out around the grounds of Ashford Castle for one of our Communions or Confirmations, but that was the extent of it. Sometimes there was a trip to Salthill in Galway in the summer for a 99 ice cream and a walk along the pier.

I spent most of my time running around the farm causing trouble with the boys. Myself, Brian, David and Michael were always outside, jumping off walls, climbing up trees or getting scratched by briars on some thick ditch we hiked. There wasn't anything else to do back then in rural Ireland. There were no mobile phones or iPads. We had no choice but to make our own fun around the farm.

When it came to helping out, Brian and I got away with it the most. There were enough of the older ones there to work, and all we might be asked to do was stand in a gap when Dad was moving cattle. Every summer, we all helped out in the bog. We'd head out 5 miles over the road on the tractor, Dad driving and us lot on the trailer behind. Mam would have packed a mountain of sandwiches for us, and we'd turn the turf, foot it and bag it, until the sun came down. Even now, that's Dad's favourite pastime, footing the turf and puffing on his pipe packed with Mellow Virginia tobacco. Only these days he has the grandkids heading off with him instead of us.

There's a mix of everything in Carnacon. People keep to themselves in one regard, but there's a big community spirit too. It has grown over the years with eight hundred of us now holding the fort. It's fairly central. We're 10 miles from Castlebar and Ballinrobe, and it's 12 miles, give or take, to Claremorris. The village sits on the shores of Lough Carra, whose peaceful setting could be on any postcard boasting the rural beauty of the west of Ireland. We've a church, a national school, a community centre, a shop and two pubs. There's a row of houses about a mile long that start at the graveyard, and our farm is in among that row. The farm was small enough back in the day when Dad inherited it – as I said, 50 acres or so – but my brother Michael took it over and has breathed a bit of life back into it in recent years. It's 80 acres now, and Dad is still working alongside him, pipe still in hand.

Sheena lives in Foxford with her family, about thirty-five minutes away. Peter, the eldest of my brothers, lives down the road with his wife and two boys, and works in my brother David's plumbing business. Collette is the third eldest and she's the brains of the family. She works as a solicitor in Dublin, raising her family there, and we'd like to think that she's the poshest of the lot! Then there's Kathleen who lives over the road, about five minutes away, with her husband and three kids. She's three years older than me, and growing up we shared a bedroom. Kathleen does everything for everyone, a bit like Dad. She can't sit still either, but a lot of us would be made that way. David is the entrepreneur – he owns his plumbing business. We were in the same year in school, but we barely saw each other. He was a terror because he didn't want to be there. Every day at 4 p.m., I knew what was coming down the line – a phone call home, or a note of some description. When he wasn't breaking teachers' hearts, he was breaking Mam's, running miles back the field so he wouldn't have to go to school, and she bounding after him. Now he's probably the most successful out of the lot of us.

The baby of the family is Brian, a civil engineer, who moved to Australia a number of years ago. He's now living in Sydney with his wife and two young sons, and despite the distance we're the most alike, in looks and in personality. Like me, he's mad about sport, even though he doesn't play much, and there's a bit of Dad's shyness and generosity in each of us too.

Dad's the kind of man who'd head off across the field to the neighbours to give them a bit of kindling he had collected, or the head of a cabbage or a lettuce that he grew himself. Carnacon is rural enough like that, but I love it. It's home.

A few years ago, I bought a house a mile or two away down by the lake. It was an old bungalow owned by a couple I knew who wanted to move closer to town. So, I bought it and did it up with the help of my brothers. There's a small bit of work to be finished outside in the garden, like seeding the lawn and putting in a few flower beds, but, the location is perfect – close to family, and to football.

Carnacon is a special place, and it's probably written in the stars that it's where I'm from.

There are a few stately homes and ringforts dotted around the back roads – there's so much history wrapped up in the place. The Mayo flag originated in one of the stately homes, Towerhill, and down the road from my house, the remains of Moore Hall overlook Lough Carra. Burned down during the Irish Civil War, it had been owned by an aristocrat called George Moore, who made his fortune in the wine and brandy trade in Portugal. The story goes that when the Penal Laws were relaxed, he built Moore Hall, and the likes of the famous Irish poet W. B. Yeats were known to have partied there into the early hours of the morning.

During the height of the Famine in 1846, George entered a horse called Coranna in the Chester Gold Cup. He won £17,000 from the bets he'd laid and he used his winnings to import thousands of tons of grain to feed his tenants in and around Carnacon. He also gave each tenant a cow from his winnings. I'm not sure if my parents named me after the winning horse, or even if they knew about that story at all, but I like to think there's a connection.

Either way, that's what we're all about up here – looking after each other, and winning.

My earliest memory of really getting into the buzz of playing football involves a bicycle. We had a two-wheeler with Harley Davidson-style handlebars and a long three-seater banana saddle. Brian and I would hop on and cling to each other while David pedalled with all his might, wobbling us the 3 miles to the school pitch in Ballyglass.

Had it not been for that three-seater, football might never have become a part of me. David and Brian would cycle to training with the Ballintubber boys team, and with the extra seat, it was just as easy for me to tag along. Mam was delighted, too, to have her youngest three out of the way.

I was just seven and a whippet of a thing, all bone. None the less, I was able to take on a batch of young fellas, stitched together from places like Carnacon, Ballintubber, Ballyglass and Killawalla. We'd a handy U14 team with the likes of Alan Dillon, his brother Gary, and John Carter, and we won numerous local juvenile competitions.

I also wasn't the only girl playing with Ballintubber. Michelle McGing and I would change into our jerseys in the girls' toilets, and our Mikasa-gloved little hands would tuck in the oversized jerseys as far as they would go. Down the hall, we could hear the lads chattering away in the dressing room. Out on the pitch, no boy would want to mark us. A girl, making a show of them? It didn't go down too well.

Our coach, Seán Hallinan, would always get me or Michelle to mark the best boy on the opposing team. 'Cora, go in there now and take up number nine. Don't let him get near the ball.' His thinking was that it would hurt the young fella's pride and quench his appetite to score. But Seán soon found out that we weren't afraid of putting it up to any of the boys. It had the opposite effect in fact, because it brought the best out of myself and Michelle.

Any tackle that came my way, I made a point of bracing myself, and then redirecting the player's force right back at them. I was small, but I learned quickly how to make a tackle, and how to break a tackle. The drive to prove myself deepened one day during an U10 blitz game against Castlebar Mitchels. I came in for some special treatment from a young fella who had no problem playing it rough. Any chance he got, he'd puck me, or try to put me off. The tears were close, but I didn't want to let him win. I bit my tongue. Every bump he gave, I gave back twice as hard. I don't know why it upset me, because I should have been happy he was taking me on. He was challenging me. And, once I saw that, I realized that regardless of who it was doing the thumping, I needed to be better than them. I *had* to be better than them.

Our own team didn't think twice about me and Michelle playing. Each of us was just one of the lads. Seán would fit as many of us as he could into his car, including myself and Brian, and he'd drive us to every pitch in the county for matches. More often than not, we'd win, so there was never an issue. Every year, Mam made sure I wrote a thank-you card to Seán, and I would Sellotape it to the top of a blue box of Roses to acknowledge his endless lifts to games.

If I wasn't playing in the garden, or with the Ballintubber boys team, I was banging footballs off the freshly painted walls of the community hall adjacent to Carnacon National School. A narrow 10-foot archway separates the two buildings, and at 12.30 p.m when the bell rang, a herd of us would run through there. It was a small, rural school back in the day, with a hundred pupils or so drawn from surrounding parishes to make up the numbers, and just two teachers. We were a close-knit group, but the principal, Art Ó Súilleabháin, was key to making it work. Every September he'd declare 'Blackberry Week' open, and instead of homework, you had to pick 250 grams of blackberries. The following morning, outside the classroom, we'd measure our batches. We'd then swap berries from jar to jar to make sure that we all made the cut. It taught us teamwork, and it taught us to look out for one another, and we did.

There were fourteen in my class – seven boys and seven girls – yet I was the only girl who ever enjoyed battering those freshly painted walls. Every September, on the first day of school, I waited in line to be picked for our lunchtime kickaround. Butterflies flying.

'Noel.'

'Paul.'

Ah come here … I'm wayyyy better than Paul!

'Donal.'

'Darren.'

'Cora.'

I was in their world now. I made up the numbers, but they accepted me because I could play as well as any of them.

For the rest of the school year, it was Manchester United versus AC Milan. Every day for four years, from second class to sixth, I weaved in and out of fellas who were gradually growing into themselves, and I into myself. They didn't hold back, and neither did I. Every goal was accounted for, and by the year's end, the scoreline could easily read Manchester United 343, AC Milan 338. It was magical.

Art, the principal, was sports mad. Any chance he got, he shipped us off to a competition – basketball, soccer, Gaelic, handball, racquetball, rounders, unihoc, you name it. More often than not, I was still the only girl playing. Every day I'd pester him to let us out into the yard to play. Before asking, I'd always have my work done so that it would be harder for him to refuse us. 'Cora, maith an cailín … off you go!'

I loved the taste of competition. Getting roiled up. Proving myself to the lads. I lived for it. If I wasn't playing soccer, then I was playing basketball or handball in PE class, and both sports honed my hand-eye coordination. We had a glass-backed handball alley in the school, and during the summer of fourth class, Art and Seán Hallinan painted the floor in the baking heat. Their efforts paid off when a year later I won the Connacht Primary Schools Girls' Handball Championship. For the finals, it meant a trip to Croke Park, and it was my first time not only being there, but being in Dublin. It was the first All-Ireland I'd win there too, aged eleven, and I can still remember the big smile on my face when Art stopped on the drive back to Mayo to treat us to a bag of celebratory chips. I got such a kick out of coming home with a medal in my pocket to show Mam and Dad.

There was also a trip to Castlebar for a schools soccer tournament, and I thought I'd made it then too. The excitement of

heading off on the bus, the adrenalin, pitting myself against unfamiliar faces, new competition, new rivals. I was hooked. Nothing
else mattered in our little world but ourselves and sport. But then
in sixth class, when I was twelve years of age, the reality of life hit
us like a bolt out of the blue.

The McGuinness brothers, Paul and David, lived over the road,
just a stone's throw from the graveyard. Paul was in my class, and
David, his younger brother, was two years behind us in fourth.
Every lunchtime we did battle together in the hall, and after school
we'd do it all over again, either in their back garden or ours. Lough
Carra is close to their home. It's the largest marlstone lake in Ireland, and its peacefulness draws you in. Even now I sometimes
take a walk on the shoreline, or relax in one of the secluded spots
on the lake that only the locals know about.

One day, David and a friend took to the lake on a raft, but
David never came home. Somehow he had fallen into the water,
and never came back up. It was a huge tragedy, and it was the
first time I sensed what it felt like to have sorrow descend over
our community. It felt heavy on our little shoulders, even though
we didn't truly understand the enormity of it, or the suffering that
David's family were going through. As the adults comforted us,
all we could do was watch the new community centre where we
played football together every day be transformed into a shrine for
one of our own.

It was one of the first funerals to take place in the centre, and I
remember soccer jerseys from every corner of the world hanging
on the walls. It felt like a celebration of David's ten years with
us. He had the potential to be a great footballer, and it struck me
that it was a lovely way to honour him. He was laid to rest in the

graveyard next to his home, and the proximity of it all made it that little bit harder to deal with. It was the first time, too, that I understood the meaning of community. The people of Carnacon came together in a way I'd never seen before. The adults called into neighbours more often than usual to have cups of tea, and the children – Paul's classmates – made sure he never felt alone. It was all we knew, this togetherness. Our parents led the way, and we followed. We were young, but that sense of unity really struck me.

Playing ball in the community centre kept us going. It was normality, and I was living for football by then. Every Christmas, Santa delivered a new football. Not the training type, but the real deal – the shiny one that slipped out of your hands if you didn't grip it correctly. Thumb to thumb, and index finger to index finger. For the next year, I'd kick the thing to death up and down the garden, and most evenings Mam would have to haul me in to go to bed.

I was a complete tomboy, and every now and then, Mam would try to get me interested in something other than sport. One year, she dragged me to the Feis Maitiú in Castlebar to watch Kathleen recite a poem. Thankfully, I never had to suffer the pain of a Feis myself, because she learned from the time I ran out of my first, and last, Irish dancing class that I had no interest in anything other than sport.

I was, however, forced to wear a dress.

'Cora, we're not leaving until you put on that dress.'

'I'm not wearing it!'

'You are. Now, put it on!'

It was maroon with a red robin on the front, and it matched my black tights and patent shoes perfectly. Mam was strict, and there was no getting out of it. She bundled us into the Ford Cortina, red robin and all, and I was cranky for the rest of the day. I cried all the way to my Communion too. But I did eventually learn to stand my ground. By the time my Confirmation came around, I was wearing a trouser suit!

When I turned thirteen it was time to step away from playing with the Ballintubber boys. There was now a ladies team in Carnacon, which Jimmy Corbett – the father of one of the girls – and Beatrice Casey, a former club player, had set up. They were my first club coaches, and I'm sure they'll be my last.

Beatrice and I go a long way back. When I was three or four, and still in a cot, Beatrice would babysit myself, David and Brian. For years I'd kick the football out the back garden with her, so when she and Jimmy set up the club there was only one place I was going. For the next few years, Beatrice and Jimmy took me across the breadth of Mayo to watch matches with them. Afterwards, we might stop in a remote pub. I'd sip from a glass bottle of Coca-Cola, munching on a bag of Tayto cheese and onion crisps, and all the while I'd listen to them talk football.

They taught me how to observe a play, and how to analyse it. How to break it down, and how to make it better. Right there was where I got my football brain – sat between the two of them, debating and dissecting games for hours. They're two of the shrewdest people I've ever met. Even now, twenty-plus years later, we'll go to the Drum Inn for a drink after a match and run through every detail. Up until then I'd only ever thought about catching a ball, and kicking it between the posts. I didn't see the bigger picture: the need for having a unified style of play, the importance of impact substitutions, how to read a game when you're in the thick of it, and how to analyse a game when the whistle has blown. Where was it won? Where was it lost? Where could we improve? What did we need to change the next day? That constant questioning and searching for answers as to how to get better was instilled in me over and over again. It also kept me grounded. Even though I had the talent, Jimmy and Beatrice never differentiated me. No matter who you were, or how good you were, you had to work hard. And so, with every Coca-Cola came a new lesson, and I soaked it all up.

I was just eleven when Jimmy and Beatrice first judged that my slight frame could handle the rough and tumble of junior club football. There was never any doubt in their minds that I'd be up to it in the forward line. After those matches, the conversations with Jimmy, in a pub in Ballintubber, were always educational. I remember after one game he asked me how much I had scored. I figured it was 2–5, but then Jimmy asked if I knew the player who was marking me. I didn't have a clue. I was so busy figuring out how I would squirm around my defender, I hadn't even looked at her face. I missed the point. Jimmy didn't care how much I'd scored, he just wanted me to realize who I'd pocketed 2–5 off. It turned out it was Bernie O'Neill, the full-back for the Mayo ladies football team at the time. I didn't realize how big a deal it was because I was just in awe of the older players on my own team that I was lining out with – the likes of Beatrice, her sister Helen Casey, Helen Malone, Katherine Kelly, Imelda and Bernie Jordan, and my cousin, Maria Staunton.

I was playing against women double my age, and double my size. But when I got my hands on the ball I ran with it as fast as my 5ft-nothing legs could carry me. There was an urge within me to prove myself to them. I wanted them to accept me. However, I sensed very quickly that they were protecting me. Any little shoulder bump or jersey tug, they had my back. In those sixty minutes of my first league game, I realized what it felt to be part of a team, and what playing for Carnacon was all about. The older ones looked out for me that day, and it's the very reason I now go out of my way to make sure younger players are OK when they come into either the club or county set-up. It was what was done for me, and it's what I've done for others during my career.

Shortly after my junior debut, I also experienced the thrill of winning the U14 All-Ireland final with Mayo. A year later Carnacon went on to win the 1995 U14 Féile A final. That Féile final was the first time I stepped out on to the turf in the old MacHale Park, and the width of the place blew my mind. I remember that game solely for the bet I'd made with my friend Caroline Brennan's father.

'I'll give you a five-pound note for every goal you score in the final,' he said after we won the semi-final.

Fair enough!

Later that day I went home not only with a medal, but £15 better off. Gerry Brennan sadly passed away a few years ago, but I'd say he's still looking down, cursing me with a wink.

They were my first two All-Ireland titles, and by then I was well and truly addicted.

2

Mam

I HATED SECONDARY SCHOOL. I DIDN'T MIND THE ACADEMIC SIDE of things, but it just wasn't for me. I didn't like being cooped up inside all day, staring at four walls. Study just wasn't my focus. All I cared about was football. Winning made me feel happy. I knew I was a good player too, and that sucked me in even more.

The biggest decision I had to deal with back then was what secondary school I was going to go to. Sheena, Collette, Peter, Kathleen and Michael all went to Balla before me, but I wasn't going to follow the crowd. I wanted to play football, and win, and Ballinrobe CS were winning.

So, when I approached Mam one evening in the kitchen, she gathered my mind was already made up, and she knew me better than anyone. Mam and Dad both knew they'd be wasting their breath convincing me otherwise. Mam was all about us getting a good education, but at the end of the day her concern was more that we would be good people with strong life skills, that we were streetwise, independent and knew right from wrong. In that sense, Mary and Michael Staunton did a fine job raising us.

I could have applied myself a little better, but in truth, I don't look back fondly on my time in secondary school. I had come from a national school with a hundred pupils where everyone knew everyone into a throng of eight hundred hormonal teenagers, and I never felt comfortable there. Socially, I was awkward. I was shy, and not very confident in who I was, or how I looked. I was just a normal, self-conscious teenager with a little strain of rebel in me.

Out the back of the principal's office there was a skip, and that's where you'd find the so-called 'troublemakers'. Some days I'd be there in the middle of the 'countries', sharing cigarettes with the 'townies', and other days not. I could tell the principal disapproved of who I was hanging out with. But they were good people, just teenagers being teenagers. I never mitched or skipped class, I wasn't brave enough. I knew Mam would kill me if I ever got caught, so the odd cigarette by the skip was as much as I got up to.

Around that time I won a few sports awards, and sometimes recognition can turn the tide against you. It's an Irish thing, because people feel the need to take you down a peg or two. I was only just into my teens, but even then I could sense that people had an opinion of me. It's something I've lived with most of my life – people's preconceptions. The first thing people ask my friends is, 'What's Cora really like?' That's been the question since day one because people want to know the real me. They've watched me on television roaring at a teammate and they presume I'm the same person off the field. But that's not the case. It's been hard to deal with people's preconceived opinions, even though they might never have met me. In recent years, social media has taken that to a whole new level. But, I coped. I compartmentalized. Football became my refuge. Inside the white lines, my football did the talking, and once I did that, then to hell with what people thought.

A few weeks after starting first year, I tried out for the junior school team. My aim, however, was to make the senior team. I wanted to win at the next highest level, and the level after that, and the level after that. The environment in Ballinrobe CS encouraged that kind of thinking, and that's why they had won four Senior A Schools All-Ireland titles in a row between 1991 and 1994. I wanted a piece of it.

The man who built the foundation of that success was Richie Bell, the former PE teacher. Unfortunately, I never met him. He had died suddenly the year before I started secondary school, and by the time I came in, my soon-to-be business studies teacher Gerry Fahy was in charge. At that stage, the team nearly ran itself. Bell's own work ethic and desire to win had rubbed off on his players – the likes of Christina and Marcella Heffernan, Denise Horan and Sinéad Costello, who would go on to make history by winning Mayo's first senior All-Ireland title in 1999.

I was the only first-year to make the cut for the senior school team, and those players taught me how football should be played. We trained two or three evenings a week. Sometimes we'd train in the morning before class, on the makeshift pitch out the back of the school, and I killed myself trying to impress them. I wanted to prove that my intensity and hunger matched theirs. They recognized this pretty quickly, too, and off the pitch, they looked out for me. Denise minded me, and Sinéad made sure I was never left sitting on my own on the bus.

Before big games, we trained on the Ballinrobe GAA pitch, and you always knew things were getting serious when you ventured through the gates. In the spring of 1995, the work paid off. We won a senior and junior All-Ireland schools title, beating St Joseph's of Spanish Point in the senior, and St Joseph's College of Kilkee in the junior. For Christina and Denise, this was their fifth Senior A Schools All-Ireland title in a row, a feat that has not yet been surpassed.

Between school, club and county football, nothing else in my life got a look-in. I was fanatical about it. Seven days a week, I played and trained, and when I wasn't doing that I was probably dreaming about doing it. The dream, of course, was to play senior football for Mayo. There were a few players in my age group around at the time who were miles better than me – the likes of Catherine Kelly from Ballintubber was an amazing footballer, with a midfield engine that would test the best of them – but like so many girls, they dropped off.

There wasn't any fear of that happening to me. Especially not when I got called up to the Mayo seniors shortly after our schools All-Ireland win.

So it was the spring of 1995 when the house phone rang, and Jimmy Corbett was on the other end. He had been chatting to Gerry Feeney, Willie Joe Padden and the late Mattie Casey, who were members of the senior Mayo ladies management team, and they told him they wanted me to tog out. Jimmy had been involved in underage teams with Mattie Casey, so it was just a case of 'Cora, sit in the car, we're going'. I was only thirteen years old, 5ft-nothing and no more than 7 stone. Mam was anxious. She was concerned about how rough it might be given how light I was, but at the same time, herself and Dad weren't going to stop me.

Funnily enough, as much as I had dreamed about it, I wasn't anxious or afraid. I had played with the boys, most of whom thought they were better than me, when I knew otherwise. I also played with Ballinrobe CS where the players were more experienced than me, so all I could do was give it my best shot.

My debut came in the autumn of 1995 during a Division 1 National League game against Monaghan. I scored ten points from corner-forward, but we lost. I don't remember much else about that day other than I wasn't fazed, by the seniority of my teammates or the occasion. I was fifteen years younger than our own Fiona McCarthy, who was a manager with Dunnes Stores, and I hadn't even sat my Junior Certificate, but I quickly became adjusted to wearing the Mayo jersey. It felt good. I didn't have a worry in the world – only how I would improve for the next game.

But that summer, off the pitch, life proved to be much more challenging.

It was the August bank holiday weekend, and the sky was spotless. Dad was off about the farm somewhere, and Mam was working in the hospital. Usually they'd have headed off to the Galway Races for the weekend but, for some reason, they decided not to go. Kathleen and myself were stuck to the couch watching television when we heard Mam come through the front door, and the minute she saw us sat there, she went daft.

'It's scorching outside and ye're in here watching telly, and not a bit of housework done!'

She was right to be mad, but instead of making her usual cup of tea, she headed straight down to bed, which wasn't like her. She said she had a bad cold and we had no reason to believe otherwise, but it didn't add up. It went on for two days. Mam in bed, and us confused about why she hadn't got up yet.

Eventually on the Monday, the doctor was called. Mam had guessed she had cancer for a good while – a year or more, since finding a lump, or two, on her breast, and she was right too. She admitted to us that she had gone to the doctor's surgery on two occasions and sat in the waiting room. However, before her name was ever called, she'd stood up and walked out.

Deep down, I think Mam feared what the future might hold. She probably sensed too how serious it was, but she didn't want it to rock our worlds, so she didn't say anything.

Do I regret she did that? No. She was protecting us. It was her decision, and at the time she felt it was the right thing to do. We didn't need to know, the younger ones anyways. Of course, it would have been better for herself had she told someone and sought treatment sooner, but she didn't want to worry us. That was Mam. She never put herself first, ever. It shows her tenacity, too, her determination and her 'just get on with it' attitude, but she got to the point where she was so ill that it was no longer possible to hide it.

That August day when the doctor was called to the house, he told Dad to bring Mam to the hospital as soon as possible. I remember sitting in the back of the car, the silence between the two of them, but I was just thinking that I was going for the spin. I sat in the waiting room, flicking through magazines, while they both went in to see the consultant. Mam had apparently told Dad that she had known she had cancer, and the doctor ate the head off him for it. My father's a gentle soul, and when they came out of the room I knew by his face that things were serious.

The nurses settled Mam into a ward to carry out some tests, and Dad and myself headed home. I sat silently in the passenger seat and he kept his eyes glued to the road. How he drove that night, I'll never know. The man was shaking.

The same night, my brother Peter rang Sheena, who was living in Dublin at the time, to tell her that Mam had been brought to hospital with suspected pneumonia. That's what we had been told earlier in the day, but Sheena had previously worked in the hospital, so she rang the ward to check on Mam. An abrupt nurse answered the phone and asked who she was. Sheena told her that she was Mary Staunton's daughter, to which the nurse replied, 'Well, you'd better get here quick. Your mother's very sick. She's got cancer.' That's how Sheena found out. It wasn't the way Mam wanted her to find out, but it was just a case of 'This is it, now let's get on with it'.

Sheena immediately made her way to the hospital, and she remembers seeing a packet of ten Silk Cut Purple cigarettes placed neatly in Mam's bedside locker. 'Take them home before I smoke them,' she said, and Sheena did. Mam loved her cigarettes. She wasn't a chain smoker, but it was an escape of sorts with eight small children running around the place. Having a cigarette was a quiet moment to herself, and she enjoyed that.

I was none the wiser as to what was going on. I still thought it was pneumonia, though I sensed it was something more serious. The next day we got up for breakfast, and Dad went across the road to talk to his brother's wife, Margaret – Mam's best friend. We could see everything from the kitchen window, and we watched the two of them crying out on the road. The older ones protected myself and Brian, but we eventually found out what was going on. Back then, in the nineties, there was no mention of stage one, or stage four. It was just a case of 'Mam has cancer'. We knew that was serious, but we never thought about prognosis or recovery. Cancer was something that affected 'older' people; all we knew was that Mam was sick, so we took the journey as it was. The good days with the bad days.

At the time, Sheena had a friend whose uncle was the main oncologist in the Mater Private Hospital in Dublin, so Mam went up to see him. It cost a fortune, in petrol money, consultant fees and prescriptions. We didn't have private health insurance, so eventually Mam had to get a Medical Card. It was an obvious financial drain on the home, but Kathleen was working part-time and that helped. She could afford to buy Mam a touch lamp. It sounds like a small thing, but it was massive for us, and for Mam. She was so weak at times, and this meant that she could reach out, barely touch the lamp, and turn it on or off herself.

Looking back, I do sometimes regret that we didn't have the money to buy her more things. To treat her, or make her a little more comfortable. We made do, but it would have been nice to have been in a position where money didn't come into it.

Four weeks after Mam had been to see the consultant in Mayo General Hospital, she was admitted to St Luke's Radiation Oncology Centre in St James's Hospital in Dublin. She stayed there for a month and a half, and during that time we only got up to see her once. We visited on a Sunday, and driving to Dublin back then was a big deal. Brian and I were delighted with our day out, loaded with sweets, still not comprehending the gravity of it all. When we got there, it was a different story. I remember seeing people whose legs were hanging off, and hearing the distinct croaking sound of the voice box of a throat-cancer sufferer echoing in the hallway. My senses overloaded, and I was afraid to touch the stairs. That's my main memory. Mam looked the same, thank God, and that made it easier to deal with visiting what was a strange, new environment.

When Mam went for radiotherapy in Dublin, it meant she was away for weeks on end. Those times were tough, but we got used to it. That trip became the routine for the next three years. In and out, up and down, going for bouts of treatment. And through that time it was football that kept me in check, kept me going.

Friends and family were great. A far-out cousin, Vincent Keane, gave me a job working in his pub, the Carra Lodge. I was fourteen and in second year in school, but even then I knew he was giving me the hours to help out with things at home. Vincent was a character and a half, and he never drank himself until he took over the pub. He played for Ballintubber back in the seventies and eighties, and was a mountain of a man. He knew his football, and everyone knew him. If ever a customer in the bar asked me how a game had gone for Carnacon or Mayo, Vincent would jump straight in there. 'You know Cora learned everything there is to know about football from me? She did, she did . . .'

He was a gas man.

When Mam was feeling up to it, herself and Dad would drop me to work on a Saturday night and stay for a drink or two, chatting to Vincent and their friends. Later, I'd head away home with them. On Sunday mornings I'd walk back to the pub, or take the bike if the lads hadn't already taken it, and I'd open up. I'd work all day collecting glasses and emptying ashtrays, and in the evening someone would usher me home to get ready for school the following day.

I loved it, chatting to everyone. Back then, I was nobody. Now I'm uncomfortable because people recognize me. They didn't treat me any differently in Carra Lodge. Back then, I was just Cora. There was no such thing as closing time and there was a belt of smoke everywhere. The customers partied all night, and anything would go. It was a great source of money, and Vincent always gave me a little more than he had to. A few years back he passed away, but I'll never forget those gestures by Vincent and his wife, Sally.

Work and football made life more normal. I was captain of the U16 Mayo team and was also playing minor while heading off to club games with Beatrice and Jimmy every other night of the week. The amount of football I was playing was insane. This will give you an idea of how mental it was. Over the course of seven days in September 1996, we lost three major games: on the Saturday an U16 All-Ireland final to Waterford; on the Sunday a senior All-Ireland semi-final to Laois, after extra-time; and the following Saturday a minor All-Ireland final to Waterford. In the semi against Laois, I scored 1–10, but it was my missed penalty in extra-time that cost us a visit to Croke Park. That might have affected another player at such a young age – the weight of the county on scrawny shoulders – but I relished the challenge. From day one I had pressure on me, and I was used to it. I was Cora. I was expected to score, and score a lot; pressure was just part of the deal. It's the losing that haunts you. But, as brutal as those three defeats were, things got a lot worse for me and my family in the coming months.

At the start of 1997, Mam was doing relatively OK. Thankfully she kept her hair, which was a huge relief for her because that was the one thing she couldn't have coped with. It was jet black, and she was very much a lady in how she looked. Slowly, she started putting on weight due to the build-up of fluid in her body and all the medication she was on, and her right arm was twice the size it should have been. There was also a lot of fluid around her waist, her chest and her tummy, and it bothered her. She started to wear tracksuit pants, which she'd never have done, but the looser waist-band helped take the pressure off.

That September it was Mam and Dad's twenty-fifth wedding anniversary, and Mam was out of hospital at the time. To mark it, we went to her hometown of Clonbur for Mass, and then we had a meal in the local pub in Ballintubber, across from the abbey. The Carnacon community was once again brilliant at this time too. They came together and raised a couple of hundred pounds to send Mam and Dad to Lourdes, not only because of Mam's illness, but so they could also celebrate their anniversary. Mam had never been out of the country, so Kathleen took it upon herself to go to the passport office in Galway to get a copy of Mam's birth certificate for her passport application. After a few days of trying she'd had no luck in tracking it down, so she rang Mam to tell her.

'They can't find your birth certificate, Mam. You'd swear you were adopted!'

'I am,' Mam replied.

There wasn't much else said during the conversation, and straight away Kathleen rang Sheena to tell her what Mam had just said. The following day, Sheena visited the adoption agency in Dublin, where she found a copy of Mam's adoption certificate, which allowed her to get a passport in time to travel to Lourdes.

Again, us younger ones were oblivious to all of this. The timing wasn't right to talk about it. Mam had enough to do trying to get on with the present.

That winter and into the following spring, her health began to deteriorate. She lost her appetite and barely had the energy to lie on the new pull-out bed we had bought to make life a little easier for her. I had decided to do Transition Year, so I could stay at home and help out, and I ended up missing a lot of school. When I was able to go, I walked the mile home from the bus stop, but if I was lucky enough Dad would collect me in the tractor from the end of the road to bring me the rest of the way home. Then it was a case of housework, then homework. I had to kick into gear. We had been expected to do our bit before, absolutely, but I was now the only girl at home so I had to look after Mam, Dad and the boys. And if Mam needed lifting in and out of bed, I did that too.

I was never one to cook, so Kathleen prepared the week's dinners at the weekend when she was home from college, while I ran the household and did the chores during the week. There was also Margaret Mannion, a neighbour who lived a mile down the road, who was Mam's home help. She was a godsend, and was in fact the aunt of the Tyrone footballer Cormac McAnallen who died suddenly in 2004 of an undetected heart condition. The care Margaret gave Mam in her last few months meant so much to us, and we can never thank her enough for making things a little easier.

My elder brothers and sisters realized a lot sooner than Brian and I that Mam was dying. It was in April 1998 when things really started going downhill. There were times when Mam was contrary because of all the medication she was on, and we knew by the start of the summer that the chances of her pulling through were slim. I never gave up hope that she was going to get better though, even in her final weeks. It just didn't feel real, the possibility of her not being around.

On 9 July 1998, the doctors rang Dad and told him there wasn't much time left, and that we should make our way to Mayo General Hospital in Castlebar. We stayed there for two days, rotating between Mam's room and the corridor. We didn't want her to be on her own when she went so we made sure someone was by her side all the time. I remember it was late on a Friday night, and my eldest brother, Peter, drove Brian, myself and my cousin Sandra down to Supermac's on the Westport Road because we hadn't eaten all day. It was 2 a.m., the nightclubs had just emptied, and there were drunken bodies falling through the doors for a late-night snack. The novelty and carnage of it kept us entertained. And then the phone rang.

'Peter, ye need to come back.'

An hour later, at 3 a.m., Mam passed away. We were all in the room, by her bedside. Eventually, at 5 a.m., we left the hospital. The rising sun and fresh air dried our tears. At home, in the sitting room, we assembled Mam's pull-out bed. And there, five of us curled up and cried ourselves to sleep.

On the morning of the funeral I found out that my mam, Mary Staunton, had been adopted. Myself and Brian overheard someone say it in passing in the kitchen. But I didn't think anything of it. I was just trying to cope with Mam's passing, full stop. Mam never talked about it to me, but what we do know is that she was adopted legally at the age of ten by Michael and Kate Summersville in Clonbur. We think she was with the family as early as five, but I have no huge desire to find out any more than that. Mam had told her friends that she didn't want to know who her real parents were, so why would I want to know? That was her decision, and I'm going to respect that.

Standing at the graveside on the day of the funeral, I remember the coffin being lowered down. Vincent Keane was by my side with his giant arms wrapped around me. Like Beatrice and Jimmy, Vincent and Sally Keane were a huge support at that time. It was lovely to have people around, and I needed them. I was so confused. I was angry, and I was numb. We all were.

It was Sheena, Collette and Kathleen who carried the family in the aftermath of Mam's passing. Kathleen left college to mind myself and Brian. As a family, we were a mess. It took us well over a year to get any sort of structure back in our lives, and even then there was still a void that we all tried to fill by keeping busy. 'Don't cry when I'm gone,' Mam used to say. We tried, we really did, but it was an impossible ask.

Mam was dead twenty years on 11 July 2018, and Dad is still as bad as ever. For two decades he's been both our mother and father, and he's done an incredible job. We don't talk about that, or about Mam all that much, but you remember the good times, and you just keep going. I was angry with life. And, to an extent, I was angry that sport had dragged me away from Mam at a time when I could and should have been spending more time with her. That feeling made me resent football, and to a point resent myself. I started drinking and smoking, and hanging around the community centre, not giving a shit. It was hard to get my focus back because I didn't see the point.

When I returned to school that September, a lot of the kids didn't know my mam had died because they weren't from my locality. I went into fifth year grieving, and the vice-principal, Sister Brenda, was the only one I really remember who got it. She was as strict as anything, but maybe she was more at peace in dealing

32

with death than the rest of us. It was difficult because I always felt like people were looking at me differently. I could sense the pity off them, and it hovered over me for months on end. I kept to myself. I didn't talk to people about how I felt, and I didn't go to counselling. There's no right or wrong way to grieve, but that's how I coped. Yes, I got lonely, but I just got on with it.

Mentally, did that make me a stronger person? I think it did.

Have I dealt with it? I'll never really know.

All I know is, life moved on, and I went with it.

3

Glory Days

THREE DAYS AFTER WE BURIED MAM, I PLAYED IN A CLUB GAME. Beatrice and Jimmy conspired to get me out as soon as possible. There's compassion, and then there's mollycoddling. They knew I'd run a mile from the latter, so they pretended that they were in dire need of players, and it worked. My boots were never too far away, and I switched to autopilot. The game was a blur, yet for sixty minutes, the numbness went. Just the simplicity of running after a ball, catching it and kicking it made things bearable.

Three weeks later, we lost the 1998 minor All-Ireland final to Monaghan, and for the first time ever the misery of defeat didn't enter my head. At that time football was an escape, but it no longer consumed me the way it had before. It was a shred of normality in a world turned upside down.

In late autumn I captained Carnacon to our first Mayo Senior Club Championship title. I was sixteen, and I can remember it as clear as day. It was against Hollymount, our biggest rivals. If we could have stabbed each other in the back, we would have. The hatred ran that deep. They were just a fifteen-minute drive away through Robeen, a townland that divided the clubs. They had an excellent team with the likes of Christina Heffernan and Sinéad Costello, with whom I had won schools All-Ireland titles. That was then, and this was now. Carnacon only won the Junior A county title the year before, and Hollymount were going for four senior titles in a row. But we weren't pussy-footing about the place. We were out to rattle them.

The scene was Knockmore, near the shores of Lough Conn. It was a neutral venue, an hour or so from both of us. As soon as the ball was thrown in, I heard a distinct voice coming from the sideline. I looked across to see a man shouting excitedly into a microphone, hanging on to it as if his life depended on it. It was the great Willie 'The Shoe' McNeely, who was broadcasting the game live on Midwest Radio. He was literally in the thick of it with us. Willie 'The Shoe' was Mayo GAA. For years he commented on Mayo football and wrote articles for the sports pages of the *Connacht Telegraph*, and he was a huge character. It was like watching a game on television, only you were in the midst of it yourself. Time stood still every time you flew by him.

'And 'tis Staunton now with the ball. She's hugging the sideline. Off she goes ...'

Jesus, Willie, get out of my way!

'Staunton comes in on the inside, swings the right leg at it, and 'tis over the barrrrrr! It's a point for Cora, and it's a point for Carnacon!'

I was so driven to get that win that I pushed myself every second to get on the ball. After three minutes I had the ball in the back of Margaret Tierney's net, but Hollymount had also raised a green flag of their own. We wasted a few chances, but defensively Maria Hayes, Michelle Corbett, Niamh Lally and Aisling McGing were

35

doing well. Midway through the first half I buried my second goal, and Caroline Hession added a third to give us a comfortable half-time lead (3–3 to 1–2). Regardless, I was going for the jugular, and within a minute of the restart I registered my third goal. Hollymount have character, and guts. They came back by moving their goalkeeper, Tierney, into an attacking role, and that threw us. We kept plugging away and put six points over the bar just before the final whistle to win 4–10 to 3–5.

Lifting the trophy was special. Yet, in that moment, beating our rivals Hollymount was equally satisfying. We celebrated that first senior county title in style, but I had yet to return to the county set-up despite it being a few months after Mam's passing. I just wasn't ready for it.

That first Christmas without Mam was tough. As a family, we were still adjusting. Sheena, Collette and Kathleen carried the rest of us, and Dad too, but there was an emptiness to that Christmas. Kathleen suggested to Dad that he get myself and Brian a PlayStation to distract us, but I'm not sure it ever did. To be honest, I don't know if it ever got easier, missing Mam. When my nieces and nephews started to come along, some of the pain did go away. It's like your new memories soften the pain of older ones, and you just go with it.

Come January 1999, I was ready to show my face again for Mayo. If anything, playing more football meant less time studying, and that suited me grand. My first day back, we played Laois in the opening round of the Division 1 National League. I sat on the bench, itching to get on, but it wasn't happening. John Mullin and his son Jonathan, who were in charge of the team, had brought in a new coach, a guy called Finbar Egan from Athlone. He had coached Diane O'Hora with Clann na nGael in Roscommon, and it was Diane who mentioned to John that she knew a lad who could whip us into shape. He's the best coach I've ever had, but he also consumed my life. When you were training, you were training, and when you weren't, you were talking to Finbar. It was like he occupied his own space in my brain.

Laois came from behind to beat us, and I believed that if I had come on I could have helped. As I squelched off the pitch in my tracksuit, I made sure Finbar could hear me.

'There's no point in me coming back if I'm not going to get a game,' I complained.

Slowly, he turned around.

'You're dead right,' he said. 'There's absolutely no point in you coming back. How would I know if you're any good if I haven't seen you at training?'

I just shrugged my shoulders, pretending not to care, but I got the point.

'One thing is certain,' Finbar continued as we made our way out the gate. 'When I'm involved, if you're not going to train, you're not going to play!'

And that was that. I went gung-ho to prove this fella wrong. Over the next six years, I missed just three training sessions. First, it boiled down to ego and proving Finbar wrong. But, over time, missing training just went completely against my belief system and I grew to love everything about it. There were no two ways about it, I did it to survive. I could also see how committed Finbar was to the team and that rubbed off. He spent eighteen hours of his week just driving to and from our sessions; not to mention the time he put in on the pitch, or late at night at home watching footage. We could see that he was giving it his all. That changed us as a group and created a culture of commitment.

At the start of 1999, Mayo football was hanging on by a thread. We had just about enough players to make a team. That said, we were a committed bunch. We wanted to work together, and by God did Finbar make us work. He didn't pander to anyone. He was a headstrong, tactical genius, and I lapped it up. He could always convince us to see things from his point of view. I took his word as gospel. I don't know how he did it, but he got you to believe in everything he said.

What made him a good coach? He was pragmatic, and he could communicate to us exactly what he wanted us to do. Every drill had a purpose, and he made us think about the decision process behind every move we made. Why are you running there? What other options do you have? Why do you think we want to push up on their wing-backs? After one of our very first training sessions, I latched on to one of Finbar's most famed questions – 'Why are you running there?' It made me think. I couldn't go through the motions any more, none of us could. We had to think, we had to learn, and we had to deliver. Not for Finbar, but for ourselves.

The top pitch in MacHale Park is what broke us in Finbar's first year, but it also made us. Legend had it that the pitch was the same size as Croke Park, and if we were to come anywhere near the then reigning All-Ireland champions, Waterford, we would have to cover every blade of grass on it a thousand times over. They were bigger than us, but if we could outrun them, we'd have a chance.

In his twenty-five years of coaching, Finbar never flogged a team harder than he did us that year. He'd tell you that himself. The burning stench of vomit up through your nostrils was a common sensation. You took as little time as possible to hurl up your dinner because you had to get back in line for the next sprint. You'd train on a Wednesday, and you'd be dead after it. Then you'd spend Thursday dreading Friday's session. On Saturday, you'd repeat the process all over again. Hating it, then craving it.

His speciality was his 'Up and Downs'. We had to line up on the end-line – twenty-seven women, all levels of fitness, holding hands. He'd blow the whistle and we had to sprint from one end of the pitch to the other. We were allotted a time of between forty-five and seventy seconds. That was it, and if the chain broke, we started all over again. Sometimes we had to do up to twenty of them in a session, and it didn't take us long to learn that we needed one another. It's a little bit of a cliché, I know, but during those drills we really strengthened as a team.

Finbar was a psycho for football. A complete psycho. It was all or nothing, and he knew how to get into your head too. I could be curled up on the couch in my pyjamas on a Monday night and the house phone would ring at 11 p.m. It would be Finbar looking to talk about my performance at the weekend. Mine and everyone else's. It might have been a school night, but I'd spend the next hour and a half hanging on his every word, my ears burning on the earpiece. Dad, Kathleen and Brian didn't think anything of it. They knew I was just as obsessed about football as Finbar, and he did that with a lot of players. It wasn't just me. He'd listen to your comments and then he'd form his own opinion. His decision, however, was final, and there wasn't a hope in hell you could influence him once he'd made up his mind. Finbar Egan was far too stubborn for that.

*

Things went well that spring. We reached the Division 1 National League semi-final against Waterford, and it was a sign that we were coming. But, when it mattered most, we imploded. The game was level after normal time, so it went to extra-time. In the seventy-third minute, Diane O'Hora nailed a goal to put us ahead by a point. We thought we had it won. But, Jesus, Waterford hadn't even started with us. The green flag was like a red rag to a bull. Geraldine Ryan came on and popped over four points as if she were doing it in her sleep. Then Rebecca Hallahan blew the ball past Denise Horan, and they sauntered away eight points the better. In the space of a few minutes they turned the game, and us, into sitting ducks. By God, did that teach us a lesson.

We were cocky in the very moment we shouldn't have been, and it would never happen again. Since that day, I'll never think a game is over until I hear the whistle. Never.

For the next four months, Finbar laid into us four nights a week. He flattened us. Praised us a little, then flattened us again. He not only wanted to build our physical stamina, but our mental stamina too. We were young, we were raw, and we had a hell of a way to go. Finbar running us into the ground in the aftermath helped build us back up again.

Our next competitive game wasn't until the senior All-Ireland semi-final against Meath in September, but we prepared for it as if it was the All-Ireland itself. The day before the game, we bundled on to the bus and drove two and a half hours to Maynooth University in Kildare. There was a big cheer when Claire Egan hopped on because she chose us over playing soccer for the Irish U18 team. She was the final link of our 'Up and Downs', and we needed her for her fighting spirit.

The atmosphere was relaxed, considering the fact that we were trying to reach our first senior All-Ireland final. That night we watched Pat Comer's documentary *A Year 'Til Sunday* which followed the 1998 All-Ireland-winning Galway football team. Twelve months earlier those lads had been where we were now, and that inspired in us a sense of what could be. In their coach, John O'Mahony, they had a man who believed in them. We had the same in Finbar and in our managers John and Jonathan Mullin, who left no stone unturned back west.

After three years of travelling the same route to Dublin to see my mother undergo chemotherapy in St James's Hospital, this was a new journey. I watched the police escort turn off Collins Avenue and into Parnell Park in Dublin, and I thought of Mam, and how she should have been there to see me.

I was in such a trance I barely noticed the RTE television rig outside the ground which was there to broadcast the station's first-ever ladies football All-Ireland semi-final. It was history in the making, but that fact didn't matter to us. We were in the zone. As part of the warm-up, Finbar designed a drill that had us standing on the halfway line, staring down the pitch at Meath. We wanted them to know that we didn't consider ourselves inferior. They were the favourites, and we knew no one had given us a chance, but we were quietly confident.

At half-time we were four points down yet the dressing room was ultra-calm. We had been there before. The question now was, could we keep our heads if we went ahead? We did, and we could. Diane O'Hora, Sinéad Costello, Christina Heffernan, Helena Lohan, Orla Casby and sixteen-year-old Sabrina Bailey made sure of it. I was nervous in the first half, tense, but I loosened up, scoring a total of 1–4 from corner-forward. The others settled too, and we outscored Meath 3–10 to 1–3 in the second half and were now headed to Croke Park for the first time in Mayo's history.

Kerry and Waterford had dominated the landscape for the previous decade, with Monaghan dipping in every now and again, but this was a new era – for us and the sport. We could sense it, that we were part of something. Not a movement, but a change. It was an exciting place to be. By 2017 I had played in twenty-one All-Ireland finals between club and county during my career, seven of which were in Croke Park, yet the feeling of getting to your first is never surpassed. The closest I can describe it is like walking on air. I was so happy that we had actually got ourselves to Croke Park that I wasn't even thinking of the final itself. But, we had to think. We had to focus.

A week after beating Meath, ten of us had to line out in the minor All-Ireland final against Monaghan. I was captain, and we didn't want the Farney side to beat us for the second year running, but they did. My psyche took a big hit, and I'm sure the other girls felt the same. Just seven days earlier we were it, on the best journey of our lives, and just like that, we had nothing. My emotions were all over the place, but we had to get a grip. The senior All-Ireland final against Waterford was what mattered now. Maybe it was no harm to have lost that minor All-Ireland. It hurt, and defeat meant that doubt started to creep in.

Will we have the bottle for it the next time?

What if it all falls apart again?

But that made us hardier, and Diane O'Hora wasn't long telling us to cop on either. Aged twenty-two, she was the second oldest member of the team and the right choice as captain. Diane had served in the Lebanon with the Irish Army and had a lot more life experience than the rest of us. I suspect that if her time in the army taught her anything, it's not to feel sorry for yourself. So we parked the minor All-Ireland final loss and returned to training with the seniors.

The buzz around Mayo that year was mighty. There was bunting nearly hanging off cattle, and every auld fella with a cap was reading about us from a bar stool. This level of support was only ever rolled out when the Mayo men got to Croke Park. They had returned empty-handed twice out of the last three seasons, so the fuss was about us redeeming ourselves as a county more than anything.

We were a glimmer of hope for people. And that's when it dawned on me what playing for Mayo was really about. We were giving people something to believe in. Before, I was just a teenager putting a green and red jersey on over my head, hoping I played well. Now, I knew the meaning of those colours, and how deep the dye ran. I realized that I was representing something much bigger than myself. Some say that brings added pressure, but I only ever saw it as a privilege. And, whether it was Mayo or Carnacon, the passion always boiled at the same temperature for me. Club is your bread and butter. It's who you are. Yet, that's balanced by the honour of playing for your county. So when the reality of what it meant to run out in Croke Park wearing a Mayo jersey hit, the day couldn't come fast enough.

Seven days out, we trained in Ballinrobe. It was the last time any of us had a chance to impress Finbar. In those A v. B games someone was always on the edge of rejection or a spot on the team. Their year could amount to nothing, or it could amount to something. For fifty minutes we went a hundred miles an hour. No one came up for air. I was on the dugout side of the pitch, tucked into the corner, when a ball came in low. Claire Egan had the same idea, and as we collided I heard a loud cracking sound followed by a sharp shooting pain in my shoulder. Immediately I knew it didn't feel right. I had snapped my collarbone. My shoulder slumped, with nothing there to hold its frame in place, and Claire looked on in shock as the lads ran over.

The thought of missing the All-Ireland final hadn't yet entered my head. That's until I caught sight of a few of the girls. Their faces said it all. It was bad. In my head I started to panic, and cry. My cousin Maria Staunton and Niamh Lally drove me to A&E in Mayo General Hospital. I sat in the back seat, and I remember watching them, the tears running down their cheeks. When we got there, Dad and Kathleen were already waiting for me. The last time we were all there together was the night Mam died. The last fourteen months of football with Mayo had distracted us all. Getting to the All-Ireland senior final was a new beginning for all of us. The team was winning. Parents had gotten to know one another, and Dad enjoyed getting out to games. Going back to play with Mayo after Mam passed away had also made me cop on. I'd realized it was just Dad now and I didn't want to cause him any more trouble. Yet, there I was landed in A&E.

A nurse ushered me around the corner into a cubicle to get an X-ray. I could tell she was cranky. She snapped at me to take off my jersey, but I couldn't manage to lift my arm. She saw me struggling, which agitated her even more, and with her two hands she caught the bottom of my jersey and yanked it up over my head. I let out a roar with the pain of it, and the tears didn't take long to follow. I've never understood why she couldn't have just cut the jersey off me. I still see that woman in the hospital today, and I can't even look at her!

Outside, Dad, Kathleen and the girls heard the scream, and when I came back out I could see Dad's eyes filling up. He was devastated for me. He had seen how hard I had worked over the last few months, and here I was with yet another blow to deal with. When we got home I locked myself in my bedroom. I didn't come out for hours. I was numb. It was almost how I felt when Mam died. Not that I cried a lot. I just sat there trying desperately to make sense of it all.

For the next few days I hid away. Beatrice Casey called over to see me, and I could see the hurt in her face for me too. She didn't pretend to be able to relate to what I was going through, which I appreciated, but she put perspective on it. I was young, and there were still plenty of All-Ireland finals to come my way. She joked too that if Mayo didn't win it for me, then she'd shoot the lot of them! That brought a smile to my face. Beatrice always knew the right things to say, and she was one of only a few I would let in. If the house phone rang, I wouldn't answer it. Unless it was Finbar. Like Beatrice, he knew not to throw pity my way. That only made me worse. I could only cope with those who didn't mollycoddle me.

Monday and Tuesday were taken up with trying to figure out if I could play. Finbar brought me to physios here, there and everywhere, and we all hoped one of them would be mad enough to tell us what we wanted to hear, but there was no hope. Finbar asked me to put on a brave face and to be positive for the girls. It was the year after my mam died, and when you're seventeen, you're thinking, *Why the hell is everything going wrong for me? Why don't I have the right to be pissed off?* I questioned everything, but I knew Finbar was right. The girls were so upset. Claire was probably suffering the most, and I know she cried a lot that week too. But it wasn't Claire's fault and I never held it against her. It was an accident.

That still didn't stop me feeling sorry for myself. Obviously, the preparations continued at full pelt, but I felt a little isolated from the group. It had nothing to do with the girls, I just didn't feel like I was in the thick of it. I was on the outside looking in. I was the missing link in our 'Up and Downs' and that was difficult for me.

Just like we had done for the All-Ireland semi-final, we stayed the night before in Maynooth University in Kildare. Maria and myself roomed together, and just before we headed to the Glenroyal Hotel for dinner there was a knock at the door. It was Finbar. He sat down in a chair in the corner of the room as if he was just coming in for a chat, and then out of the blue he told me that I was starting on Sunday. They would leave me on for the first thirty seconds, and then I'd make way. I couldn't believe it, but he was deadly serious. He had even spoken to Michael Ryan, the Waterford coach, to make sure that his players knew not to nail me in the opening minute. Hearing that news took my mind off everything. I was back on the inside, and I would finally get to wear the green and red of Mayo in Croke Park.

Looking back, I'm sure Finbar was only doing it to help me. In the previous months we'd built up a bit of a relationship and he had learned what I'd gone through at home with Mam. By letting me start, it was his way of easing some of the pain for me.

On the day of the final, 3 October 1999, there were 15,101 people in Croke Park. Waterford were favoured to win, even though they were without Rebecca Hallahan. Hallahan was one of Waterford's best players but she was serving a three-month ban for an alleged striking incident that happened in their semi-final win over Monaghan. At least I was getting the chance to walk out on to the pitch. It was a long road from Carnacon's home pitch, Clogher, to Croke Park, and I was so grateful to get to start.

As I followed the Artane Band around the pitch in the pre-match team march, my right arm dangled limply. I didn't want to wear a sling because that would show weakness. When the whistle blew, I cherished what turned out to be the next forty-seven seconds at corner-forward. I took in the rush. I took in the Hill and the sound of the crowd, before Finbar called me and sent in Orla Casby to the half-forward line. She already had the slip of paper ready to pull from her sock and when she came on, everyone knew to rotate in the forward line. As a result, Michael Ryan spent the next five minutes reshuffling his own crew.

It was horrible to have to watch the game from the bench. I felt helpless, and every now and then I snuck out of the dugout and wandered down to the sideline. I had to get closer or I would have lost my mind. We started slowly when it came to getting scores. Once settled, we got in a rhythm, and points from Diane O'Hora, Sabrina Bailey and Christina Heffernan saw us lead by a point at half-time (0–5 to 0–4).

In the dressing room, we didn't think we had it won but we believed in ourselves. Less than a minute after the restart, Diane and Christina both fired over frees, and Imelda Mullarkey, our corner-back, added another point from play. We were in the zone, but Waterford were going for a possible sixth title in a decade, and Michael Ryan instructed his players to throw everything at us in the final quarter. They did, but we managed to keep them three points adrift.

In the last ten minutes the 'Up and Downs' kicked in, and Waterford started to cramp. It was happening, and we were out-running them, with Sinéad Costello picking off a vital point to widen the gap to four points (0–12 to 0–8). For the first time ever the countdown clock was used in Croker, and as the seconds ticked, the crowd lifted. A section of fans behind our dugout started to sing 'We Are The Champions' before the whistle went, then suddenly, we had done it.

As the substitutes ran on, a reporter grabbed me for a word. And, let's just say I made a fool of myself. 'We've done what the Mayo men couldn't do!' I shouted down the camera lens. It was my first interview on television, and it was a fierce stupid thing to say. It's one of a few regrets I have in my career, because I should have known how hard it was to bloody win one. The lads had given it everything, and more, and in my moment of madness I forgot that. Thankfully there wasn't a big deal made out of it in the after-math. I feared that there would be, but Mayo people understood the emotion that was involved and all they were interested in was celebrating with us.

Diane O'Hora became the last captain to lift an All-Ireland cup on the Hogan Stand before it was demolished and rebuilt. Marcella Heffernan didn't want to leave the place. 'I don't want to go home. I want to stay here for ever!' she said as we walked out from under the stadium.

If she could have, she would have too, because there's no better place to be than in the winning dressing room on All-Ireland final day. We sang, and the girls hugged. I could still only manage slight contact but I was beaming, as were Finbar, John and Jonathan Mullin. We all knew we were part of something incredibly special, and we felt it too, especially when we were all back on the bus together, in our own space, as one.

That night we attended the Ladies Gaelic Football Association's victory function at Jurys Hotel in Ballsbridge. We enjoyed the celebrations, and the next morning, when I lifted my head off the pillow, a smile shot across my face. I know I only featured for all of forty-seven seconds but I had put in as many 'Up and Downs' as the rest of them. That's what made us, the savagery of those sprints. If you asked me, 'Would you do it all over again?' Absolutely. Vomit and all!

The homecoming west to Mayo was one of the best nights of my life. We crossed over the Galway border into Shrule on Monday evening, and our bus driver, Eoin Cronin, probably put down the toughest shift of his life. We went on to Kilmaine, The Neale, Ballinrobe, Tourmakeady, Hollymount, Claremorris and Knock before finally landing in Ballyhaunis at 2 a.m. Every town we hit was wedged, and Midwest Radio broadcast the procession live. The majority of us crashed in Yvonne Byrne's three-bedroom house in Ballyhaunis, and there wasn't a bit of flooring to be seen.

Yvonne – or Crazy as she was known to us – was a solid centre-back who played her club football with Hollymount. Her mother, Margaret, was the County Board treasurer and she was only de-lighted with life that we had gone and won the Brendan Martin Cup. She loved the banter and minding us all too. By the time I surfaced the next day, she already had our jerseys washed and ironed, and her sister-in-law, Joan, had even come over to help make us all a bite to eat.

Fed and watered, we took off again, but first, a few of us popped around to one of Crazy's neighbours with the cup. Katie Johnson was a hundred years old and a proud Mayo woman. She had seen a lot in her lifetime – two world wars and a civil war – but she had never seen the Brendan Martin Cup coming back to her home county. Seeing the glint in her eye made me realize just how rare it was to win, and the joy it brought to others.

Mam wasn't there to witness it, and I missed out on that. But all I needed to do was look down and read the crest on the Mayo jersey to know that she was there.

It read: Dia is Muire Linn. God, and Mary, be with us.

I think she was.

4

Growing Up

MY FRIENDSHIP WITH YVONNE 'CRAZY' BYRNE HAD BEGUN DURING a training game ahead of the 1999 All-Ireland final. She got the nickname for being the joker in the bunch, forever making the rest of us laugh. We ended up marking each other at county training, and when the ball was down the other end of the field, we watched Finbar's big head following the play. Crazy saw a window of opportunity, as she typically did, and she just came out with it.

'So, do you drink?'

'Yeah. Do you?'

'I do.'

And there and then we plotted to buy a bottle of red After Shock to celebrate if we got to the All-Ireland final. That's how our friendship began – in the middle of a pitch in Castlebar, talking about After Shock.

Twenty years on, Crazy is still my closest friend. She is someone I completely trust. She's loyal and can go with the flow when I don't know how to. Over the years, I'd bring her as a shield to award ceremonies, so I didn't have to make small talk. She'd make craic in a hole, so having her there made everything much more painless.

Back in the day, I didn't want to step outside my comfort zone. I didn't want the hassle of being in the spotlight, and Crazy got that. She protected me from people, and probably myself too. I was happy to stand back and not engage. In the last number of years I've embraced myself a bit more in that regard. I realized it was OK to be good at what I did. Not only that, I realized that I could genuinely influence young players or guide them on to the right path. I suppose as I matured, I grasped that. But it took a long time, and it wasn't easy either.

During my career I was spoken about in a way that I never saw myself. I would go to awards and think to myself, *What the hell am I doing here?* I was so uncomfortable with the whole thing. The MC would be about to introduce me and I could feel the awkwardness coming on. I could see everyone else noticing it too, and that made it worse. I just wanted to hide from it all, and the attention drove me further into myself. Compared to how confident I was on the pitch, in those situations I was the complete opposite.

That's where Crazy came into her own. And it wasn't just her, it was her entire family. It was her father, Pat, and mother, Margaret, who treated me like I was one of their own. You see, when I didn't have a mam, Margaret Byrne was there for me. When I broke my jaw in college, it was Margaret who spent most of her Sundays liquidizing dinners to send back with me to Athlone IT, to make sure that I had something nutritious to eat for the week. If Mam had been around she'd have done the same and, deep down, Margaret knew that, even though they had never met. It was her maternal instinct, and in a way I was Margaret and Pat's 'other' daughter.

So, when Crazy and myself filled in our CAO applications for college, we both put down Sport and Recreation in Athlone IT. Over the next four years we grew up to be adults in the real world and we learned even more about each other. A lot of the other Mayo players opted to study at NUI Galway or UL, but personally, Athlone was a better fit for me. For a start, Finbar was living there. I knew then that I wouldn't venture too far outside the football bubble, and that suited me perfectly.

Every year between July and October, drink was strictly off-limits during the height of championship. There was one exception, however: the week we finished our Leaving Cert. One night we ended up on a pub crawl around Ballyhaunis with Crazy's friend Martin, and a few others. The lads were killing me with vodka and Red Bull, and we ended back in Martin's house, a few miles outside the town, for a party. Crazy wasn't drinking because she was on antibiotics, and she knew we had to be home before Margaret and Pat woke to open the shop they ran from the family home. That, and so they wouldn't know we'd been out until all hours of the morning.

As the house party faded, Crazy put me to bed to catch a few hours of sleep then woke me at 6.30 a.m. to get me back to Ballyhaunis before her parents surfaced. She bundled me into Martin's car and delivered me back to her place. Then she loaded her bicycle into the boot and returned the car to Martin before cycling back home. There were two problems, however. One, time was running out before our cover was blown; and two, Crazy was conscious that she would be spotted. You see, her uncle was a postman, and she knew that there was no way he'd not see a mad woman pedalling home at that hour of the morning when he was doing his round. So, with Martin's to her back, Crazy took off out the road. Not long into the journey she heard a car coming in the direction of Ballyhaunis. Off the bike she jumped and threw it, and herself, behind a hedge, just in case it was the uncle. Thankfully, it wasn't. She arrived back with about a minute to go, launched the bicycle back into the shed, ran up the stairs and into bed before her parents woke. I'm telling you, she's some woman!

We started our lives as college students in September 2000, and moved into a three-bedroom house in Willow Park, across from Athlone IT, with three others. On a Sunday, Kathleen or Dad would drop me to Ballyhaunis and Crazy and I would raid Margaret and Pat's shop for supplies before heading off.

In the first year, we were finding our feet. It was an entire new experience, living with people other than your family, and it took some adjusting. Over the years we lived with Aisling McGeehan from Donegal, Crazy's second cousin Avril Robinson, and Mayo's Triona McNicholas and Michelle McGing. For me it was challenging because of my OCD. Well, I've never been officially diagnosed, but I wouldn't need to pay someone to tell me that I have some form of it.

This is how it goes. Everything must be clean. I can't handle a dirty house. I've been known to eat my dinner and clean at the same time. Even if I go to Kathleen's house, I could be watching telly but at the same time I would be cringing inside at the thought that the playroom next door might be untidy. If there's a dirty cup on the table, I can't cope. It must be washed and put away before I can sit down and relax. And God help me when my nieces and nephews call over. I love them to bits, but part of me can't wait until they go so I can hoover up the crisp crumbs that might be on the floor. I've even been known to come home after a night out, throw my clothes in the washing machine and wait until they're done to hang them up. It could be 3 a.m. or 4 a.m. in the morning, but I have to get it done. There's a process to that too. You wash the clothes. Then you fold them. And then you hang them out on the line. People can never get their heads around why I fold the clothes first. Well, by doing that, it takes out all the creases. What's not to get?

Any awards I've won are in Dad's house. They're better off there too because I'd be dead from polishing anything shiny. I sometimes hoover twice, three times a day, and mop the floor once a day. I'm guessing that when I die, the two things they'll bring up to the altar are a mop and a hoover! I get these habits from Mam. She was so house-proud. Even with the ten of us, the place was always spotless. She used to handwash all the white nappies, and they'd be whiter than white, dazzling my aunt through her kitchen window across the road.

So you can see why it might have been a little difficult to live with me. Crazy and my other housemates over the years accepted that it was part of my genetic make-up, but I'm sure I drove them mad at some point when it came to my cleaning habits.

By the time I went to college I had gone through a lot of stuff in my life. Crazy was a lot more carefree. Dealing with the death of a parent when you're young makes you grow up fairly quickly. I was old before my time because of that. In my mind I always felt that I had a responsibility to home. There was no one putting that pressure on me, I was just programmed that way. Kathleen took on a lot after Mam died, and maybe I felt I had to take some of that pressure off her – even if that was by coming home at the weekends to clean the house or do the laundry and ironing.

As time went on I relaxed a little each year. Crazy's happy-go-lucky personality had a huge bearing on that, and we balanced each other out. I was a lot more sports-driven than she was back then, and I'd like to think I changed her outlook a little in that regard. She would suggest going to Charlie Brown's for a pint and I'd agree all right, but only on the condition that we went for a run first. It wasn't the guilt that got to me, I just didn't like the thought of knowing that there might be someone else out there working harder than me. I needed to put in the same effort. In fact, I needed to put in more. If that meant going for a twenty-minute run before one drink, then at least I covered my arse.

When we first started college, we were so naive. We hadn't had the cop-on to apply for a sports scholarship before we went to Athlone IT. However, we weren't even in the place a day when we got one. One of our first lectures was interrupted by some-body looking for 'Cora Staunton and Yvonne Byrne'. I turned and looked at Crazy. We were both thinking the same thing.

We're only in the place a few days – what have we done?

A rugby player was supposed to get the scholarship but he hadn't bothered turning up, so the institute offered to split it be-tween the two of us instead. A few weeks later they gave us two full scholarships. Financially, it was a huge help. Dad paid my rent for the first semester, but I used the scholarship money, as well as some money I had saved from my summer job working in the shop in Mayo General Hospital, to pay for the rest of the academic year.

Above: I loved being outdoors as a kid. Here I am on my new (second-hand) bike aged about eight or nine.

Above: Michelle McGing and I have been playing football together since we were seven. This was when we were still lining out with the boys in 1992.

Below: My brother David and I were in the same class together from senior infants. We are not too happy about having to share our Communion day! *Back, left to right*: Sheena, Collette, Mam, Dad, Granny Mary, Peter. *Front*: Michael, me, David, Brian, Kathleen.

Top: A rare family photo, minus Dad. *Back, left to right*: Sheena, Peter, Collette, Kathleen, Mum. *Front*: Uncle Martin, Michael, Brian, me, David.

Above: The Carra Community Games team in 1993. I loved participating every summer.

Left: Delighted after beating Kerry in the final of the U14 All-Ireland Championship in 1994.

Above: Celebrating our first national school win at an indoor soccer tournament in Castlebar. *Back, left to right*: Cormac Hayes, Darren Hughes, Paul McGuinness, Noel Gibbons, David Gill, David Staunton. *Front*: Declan Hughes, me, James Corbett, Brian Staunton.

Right: I made my Confirmation with my two brothers, David and Brian. David and I were in sixth class and Brian was in fifth. I was a pure tomboy, so I wouldn't wear a dress and went for a trouser suit. They were all the rage then, I swear.

Below: Our Burriscarra National School Gaelic football team. As usual I played alongside my brothers, Brian (*top left*) and David beside me on the left.

Above: The All-Ireland U14 Blitz winners with Mayo in 1994.

Left: With clubmate Michelle McGing after beating Sligo in the U16 Connacht final in 1995.

Below: Having fun with my two sisters, Collette and Sheena, during Mum's last Christmas dinner in 1997.

Above: We beat Meath in 1999 to reach the All-Ireland final for the first time. It was a great feeling.

Below: My first All-Ireland final, though I only lasted less than a minute due to my broken collarbone. I was heartbroken not to play, but a super performance by the girls saw Mayo win their first ever All-Ireland senior title.

Above: Meeting the President before the All-Ireland senior final in October 2000. God, I loved Croke Park on All-Ireland final day.

Left: Celebrating my second goal on our way to winning the 2000 final. These are moments I will never forget.

Below: Celebrating our 2000 win with Claire Egan. It was particularly special having missed out on the '99 final because of injury.

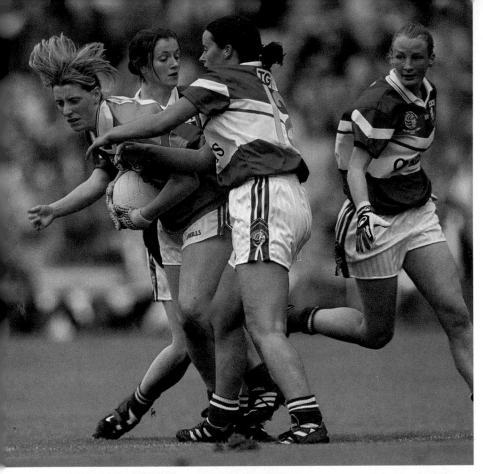

Above: Going for three-in-a-row against Laois in the 2001 All-Ireland final.

Above: Seconds after the hooter goes in the 2001 All-Ireland final; a moment I'll never forget. I collected a short kick-out from Denise Horan inside the 21-yard line which lost us the game. I'd spend the next few months blaming myself.

Right: Back to better times in November 2002 when I captained Carnacon to our first Senior Club All-Ireland title. This followed an All-Ireland win with Mayo in October.

Above: Coaching the Mayo minors with Crazy in 2003. It was a tough time as we lost Aisling McGing that July. Crazy's mum, Margaret, is also pictured.

Left: We were pushed every step of the way by a tough Galway team in the 2003 All-Ireland semi-final.

Below: My sporting idol Sonia O'Sullivan coming back to accompany myself, Fiona McHale and Marie Corbett across the finish line of the West of Ireland Women's Marathon.

In terms of football, things were different in college, in the sense that the calibre of talent wasn't as high as Mayo or Carnacon. I enjoyed that first year because it was a change, and regardless of the standard we still took training very seriously. In 2002, in my third year of college, we won a Division 2 League title against the Garda College – the national police force in Ireland – and in 2004 we got to the final of the Lynch Cup, only to lose to Dublin City University (DCU). That was the extent of our success when it came to our college football careers, but I'd like to think that despite not winning any silverware we helped to raise the standard of football in Athlone IT because we demanded so much more of the institute.

At the start of second year, myself, Crazy and her cousin Avril Robinson, who also played on the college team, asked the head of sport, Richie O'Hora, and sports officer, Ger Heavin, if they would meet us for a chat. Compared to the men's football teams, we didn't think we were being treated equally. We didn't have enough footballs for a start. We didn't have enough training aids or support either, and overall we needed better standards.

They listened, and they delivered. Maybe they thought we were little upstarts, but if we hadn't asked, or cared enough to bring it to their attention, then the standard of football wouldn't have gone up. You can moan all you like, but if you want change you must push for change, and between ourselves, Ger and Richie we figured it out.

In 2002, when we won the Division 2 League title against the Garda College (6–13 to 0–10), Crazy was in fact our manager. She did a good job too. A few weeks beforehand she had her knee cruciate operated on, so she filled in as manager for a brief spell while she was recovering. She didn't overlook a thing. We were ahead of ourselves now in terms of preparation, given everything we were learning in health and fitness lectures, and in the team meeting the day before the game, Crazy made sure we were all clued in to what we had to do for the next twenty-four hours.

'Hydrate,' she told us. 'Drink plenty of water and look after yourselves.' One of the girls went above and beyond, taking Crazy's advice to a whole other level. On the morning of the game she called to say she wasn't feeling the best. It turned out that the poor thing had drunk twenty-four bottles of water. How she didn't explode is still beyond us!

It was Freshers' Week in Athlone IT when we won our second senior All-Ireland final with Mayo in 2000. We were the reigning champions yet the punters still tipped Waterford. They had Catriona Casey back, who missed the 1999 final with a broken leg, while sixteen-year-old Mary O'Rourke was the next up-and-coming star in ladies football.

Finbar trained us harder in 2000 than he had the year before. What really egged us on, however, was people's lack of belief in us. Finbar realized that too, and to our itinerary for the All-Ireland final weekend he attached photocopies of two separate articles. The first was a senior final preview in the *Gaelic Women* magazine that read 'The Experts' View – Waterford 5 Mayo 0'. The second article was from the newspaper *Ireland on Sunday*, whose headline had nothing but disrespect for us: WATERFORD LOOK A BANKER IN FINAL FLING. Had no one realized how hard we had worked, or even that being the reigning All-Ireland champions meant something? I'm not saying we had any right to win back the Brendan Martin Cup, but we certainly knew how hard it was to win the damn thing and that had to count for something.

This time round I played the entire game. However, I was lucky to be handed the number 14 jersey in the first place because a few weeks earlier I had called it quits. During a training session in MacHale Park, I walked. I had a bust-up with Finbar. Someone made a mistake, and I had a go at them. Finbar wasn't in the mood for a tantrum.

'Cora, who put you in charge?' he roared. 'That's the last time I want to hear you criticize someone like that!'

I continued to protest my point.

'If you keep it going, you can get off the pitch now. There's a gate down there, and it isn't locked if you want to go.'

'Right, I'll fuck off then!' – and off I marched into the dressing room.

My directness and stubbornness landed me in it again. I had no car to take off in so I had to wait until the end of training to make my escape with someone else. Margaret Byrne tried to calm me down, but I wasn't having any of it. Finbar wasn't having any of it either, and the word was that I had to apologize to him if I was to be allowed back. I was completely in the wrong. I realized that when I calmed down, and I apologized. But Finbar didn't make it easy for me. He said he needed to think about it and he would come back to me.

I waited for the house phone to ring. Sunday went by. Monday and Tuesday did too, and I was starting to sweat. It meant so much to me to play for Mayo, and I was worried that I had blown that honour. Eventually, word got to me – probably through Margaret

Byrne – that I could return to training on the Wednesday night. Did it teach me a lesson? It did. Never tell Finbar where to go again!

It also taught me something about criticizing my teammates. I know that's how some people will remember me, and I know over the years I've upset a few people. I've worked on it, absolutely, but that's always going to be a part of who I am as a footballer. My standards were high, and if you couldn't face criticism then it didn't take me long to figure that out. If I thought your run could have been timed better, I told you. If I thought you should have passed the ball into space, I told you. And I told you because I cared. Maybe my demeanour wasn't to everyone's taste, but that's who I am. Teammates who knew me best realized that it came from a place of pure desire to win. Nowhere else.

It was easier to prepare mentally for our second All-Ireland final in Croke Park. We knew what to expect, and that softened the nerves somewhat. This time out, conditions were greasy, so there was still an air of concern. Unlike the year before, it was Waterford who led by a point at half-time (0–5 to 1–3). Mary O'Donnell, Anna Lisa Crotty and substitute Aoife Murphy caused us problems, but Christina Heffernan, Helena Lohan and Rachel Barrett started carving out plays for us. Midway through the second half we were two points adrift before Crazy netted us a penalty after my cousin, Maria Staunton, was hauled down inside the small square.

Waterford kept coming back to go ahead of us, and it wasn't until five minutes to go that I snuck over a point and a late goal to put us one point in front (3–6 to 0–14). With ten seconds left on the clock, it still wasn't over. Waterford had a chance to tie the game when Marion Troy was fouled after an exhausting run. The free was taken short, and kicked narrowly wide. I watched the referee, Christy Haughney, like a hawk. I kept another eye on the clock, waiting for the countdown to the hooter. When it blew, I had won my second senior All-Ireland medal.

For the next six days we celebrated across the county. We went to Ballyhaunis, Claremorris, Westport, Ballinrobe, Belmullet, and even did a brief stint across in Sligo. On Friday we hit Louisburgh on the west coast, and by that point I was in no way prepared for the Connacht Club Championship semi-final with Carnacon that Sunday.

I was celebrating as if it was my first win, which in a way it was, and I became oblivious to the responsibility I had to the club. Word got back to Beatrice and Jimmy that the celebrations were still going strong, and by day six they had lost faith that I would cop myself on. They drove to Louisburgh and attempted to haul me out of Durkin's pub. Jimmy came in and tried. But I wasn't budging. The craic was far too good. At that point I wasn't even thinking about my teammates. It was incredibly selfish of me, and looking back, I shouldn't have been so stubborn. It took over an hour, but they eventually convinced me to leave. That was one of the few times I have ever fallen out with Beatrice.

I turned up late to the game in Ballygar. I was still dying, and I struggled even to do a lap in the warm-up. Out of the corner of my eye I could see that Beatrice was raging. She had a right to be cross. It wasn't how Carnacon did things, and it wasn't how I did things. For the first forty minutes I was atrocious, the remnants of a week's alcohol consumption swirling around inside me. My marker, Emma O'Malley, saw that I was struggling too, and I took a shove from her out near the sideline. Well, that did it. I turned and punched her full-on, into the stomach. It was the only time in my entire career that I got that physical in a game. But my hangover couldn't hack it, and luckily, the referee didn't see my thump.

O'Malley's thump got me going, and I scored 2–10 in the next twenty minutes. We won the game, and things eventually softened between myself and Beatrice and Jimmy. As they always had done, they had looked out for me even when I was behaving like a dope. Being at the top had briefly blinded me to that fact. I disrespected them, and I shouldn't have. I had no reason to. I was an All-Ireland champion, fair enough, but for a week I forgot what side my bread was buttered on.

Now, I can appreciate that at that time I had no idea of how hard it was to achieve the level of success we had. We had won the National League and the All-Ireland with Mayo, and I figured it was just a case of turning up for club games and winning would be easy. I regret that. I regret ever thinking like that, and for acting the way I did, because Beatrice and Jimmy had put their lives and souls into Carnacon. It's not something I'm embarrassed about, but it does make me cringe. It's so far removed from the person I am now, but you live and learn.

I learned that winning never comes easy, and never have I forgotten since what matters most.

Two weeks after the All-Ireland final I was back to college, playing in a Freshers' Blitz with Athlone IT in Trinity College, Dublin. In the first game I broke my nose and played on. I had been here before. And, if it didn't hinder me, then I wasn't coming off. But worse was to come. In the last game against Maynooth, the shoulder of Claire Mortimer – who played her club football with

Louisburgh in Mayo – connected with my jaw. I knew straight away by the crunch of bone that there was no playing on this time. I hit the deck, and vaguely remember drifting in and out with the pain.

My jaw was broken in three places, and my teeth were pushed back into my gums. As I sat on the damp grass waiting for an ambulance, the game continued. I don't remember the result, but the girls said it turned into one of the dirtiest games they'd ever played. Mary Beades of Roscommon was one of the tournament organizers, and she offered to come in the ambulance with me to the Mater Hospital in Phibsborough. Lying there in the back, my first question to the paramedics was, 'How long will I be out?' They just laughed, thinking it was the gas talking. But I was totally serious. I had just won my first All-Star award and was due to play in the All-Star game in Claremorris the following weekend. Now the All-Stars are announced at the LGFA's annual black-tie awards ceremony in the Citywest Hotel in Dublin, but back then they were announced earlier and a match was played in the All-Ireland winning county. I didn't want to miss my first outing.

I sat on a wheelchair in the emergency room with my boots clanking off the plastic-coated flooring. The blood had long deepened the blue of my jersey, and the pain was now bordering on a nine. All they could do was give me an injection to numb the pain, so I stayed the night with my sister Collette before checking into the Dublin Dental Hospital the next morning. En route to the hospital, we caught a glimpse of the *Star* newspaper, and there it was: ALL-STAR CORA SUFFERS OP BLOW. The article stated that I had broken my jaw in a soccer game. They also quoted Dad as 'demanding answers as to how a belt of an elbow could result in his 19-year-old daughter having to get her wisdom teeth removed and her jaw wired'. Dad hadn't known about the incident when the *Star* rang him the previous evening, and he certainly never demanded any answers. It was sport, and he knew how many injuries I'd suffered, played on with, and had come back from.

Over the next few days in hospital, my sisters Collette and Sheena visited, and Crazy did her best too to keep me entertained. She'd bring in a stupid present on each visit, like a rubber plant. It almost killed me to crack a smile for her each time. But I appreciated it. I went into surgery on a Friday night at 10 p.m., and they wired my jaw. By Sunday I had convinced them to let me home early so that I could go to the All-Star game in Claremorris. I was never going to play, but I wanted to show face at the banquet and be there to collect my first All-Star. When I stood up to collect the bronze statuette, the crowd gave me a standing ovation. I'm guessing it was more out of sympathy for yet another injury, but it was a lovely gesture.

At home, I was unable to go the few metres up to bed with the pain, so I slept on the couch. Kathleen was due to head out on her first date with her husband-to-be, Mike Conroy. Instead she had to send our brother Michael to Warde's Pub in Ballyglass while she kept an eye on me. I had an awful fear of puking. I think that's what worried Kathleen too. I hadn't eaten in days and was weak with the hunger as much as I was with the pain. I couldn't even manage a swallow. I could only get down crushed-up morphine tablets.

For the next nine weeks I was in and out of college, and up and down to Athlone. I didn't miss many classes, given the mid-term and Christmas breaks, but I made sure to attend as many training sessions as I could, even if I was in pain. And, all the while, Margaret Byrne's milkshake dinners were keeping me alive.

It was tough, but it's how you deal with injuries and setbacks that makes you mentally tougher. You build up resilience; and, to some extent, a front. You let on that you're tougher than you really are, and that's what got me through. You lie to yourself as much as you do to others, just to trick your mind into thinking that it's better. I had already been through much worse, and this was just another layer on what was already a tough exterior.

5

Teamwork

I CAN PINPOINT THE NIGHT WHEN THINGS CHANGED FOR ME AND I became a little more introverted and aware that I was a public figure, open to criticism. Since then I've become more wary of people and selective in whom I trust. It was in the autumn of 2000 when we were celebrating our second All-Ireland win. On the fifth day of the session, we went to stay in the Teach Iorrais Hotel in Geesala near Belmullet. It was just the team in the middle of nowhere and I loved that. After a mad week we were united again, back inside our own bubble, reminiscing, and not an Up and Down in sight.

As the evening went on, I was at the bar, chatting to a friend, when some fella with a few jars in him came towards us.

'Hey, Cora!'

I half turned and gave him a small wave, knowing that he was too full to the gills to be entertained.

He persisted. 'Hey, Cora! Hey, Cora!'

I turned around again, and this time I gave him a nod and a wave. This guy took umbrage and started to lay into me. Initially I ignored it, but he suddenly turned aggressive.

'Ah, you're only a selfish auld bitch anyways!' he spat. 'You're too big for your boots now, aren't ya? Who the fuck do you think you are?'

And on and on it went. Insult after insult. You have to remember, I was just eighteen years of age at the time and I was being verbally abused in public, across a bar in a busy hotel. For what? Just sitting and not entertaining some fella who wouldn't even remember me the next day? Finbar and Jonathan were quick to read the situation and ushered him into the foyer.

That moment stuck with me. I know he had drink taken, but it wouldn't be the last time something like that happened during my career. And God forbid I stood up to someone who spoke to me like that and told them what I really thought, because then they would be justified in thinking I was a bitch.

After that I distanced myself in social gatherings. That's not to say I sat in the corner on my own, not having the craic. I'd have been in the middle of it, but with my own gang. When it's not your own gang, all people see is Cora the footballer. They don't see an individual, and that's hard to deal with.

To add to that, there were also rumours about my sexuality. I'm not gay, but it was easier for people to just make the assumption. I learned quickly that I couldn't control what they thought or said about me. It was wasted energy. Once my family and friends knew the real me, that's all that mattered. That said, there were times when those rumours got into my psyche.

I have really good friends who are gay, and looking back, my actions were unfair to them because of their sexuality. I was afraid to socialize with them in a gay pub or a nightclub for fear that someone would automatically make an assumption about me. It was selfish, I know, but it's the truth. If I'm being completely honest, homosexuality was something I found hard to understand when I was younger. I came from a small rural community and I didn't know anyone who was gay. But then, you grow up, you evolve, and your ignorance goes away. I'm no longer worried about what people might assume.

I'd like to meet a fella some day, get married and have children. I'd love that, but it's not the end of the world if I don't. I have a great life as it is. I'm blessed with an incredible family and unbelievably supportive friends, and that to me equals any match made in heaven. The truth is, though, it's hard for me to meet people. I know I'm no superstar, but I can tell when people are intimidated by me because of how they see me on the pitch. They think I'm the same person on a night out, and that's hard. I don't know if they're talking to me because of my profile as a Mayo footballer or because they really do want to get to know me. The fact that I'm quiet and awkward off the field doesn't help. I don't do emotions or physical contact either and that only compounds the problem. It makes me uncomfortable. Mam and Dad loved us all very, very much, but hugs just weren't something that were dished out at home. My sisters even know not to hug me. The only exception, pretty much, are my nieces and nephews.

I don't trust many people. Loyalty means a lot to me. Maybe that came from growing up with just fourteen pupils in my class in primary school. It was so tight-knit; you only had each other so you stood by one another no matter what. Football, and sport in general, is very dependent on loyalty and trust, and it's a character trait that I pride myself on.

Then again, maybe I've been burned in the past. Maybe that's where it all comes from. There's been so much crap said and written about me. If I didn't speak to someone in the right tone, they'd be giving out about me. If I looked sideways, they'd be giving out about me. There was no winning, and it all goes back to the Cora people see on the pitch. Maybe it's different for GAA lads. Maybe they enjoy the attention, but I don't. Whether it's good or bad, I will always feel very awkward about it. I'll say hello, absolutely, and entertain a bit of chit-chat. As the years went by I got better at dealing with this and I became much more outgoing. At some point, however, I need to go back to where I'm comfortable, and that's with those I trust.

As a team in 2001, our own trust issues saw us fall from grace. With two All-Ireland medals in our back pockets, egos expanded overnight. We had something we never had before: attention. It felt good to be acknowledged for what we had achieved. However, collectively, the status that went with that is what caused our downfall.

Finbar never took nonsense from anyone, yet he had no control over what went on in the real world. And in the real world, egos were being massaged. As I see it now, a few of us were competing against each other subconsciously. Typically, the likes of myself, Diane O'Hora and Christina and Marcella Heffernan took the headlines, depending on who was flavour of the month. And, although there was never any vindictiveness in it, relationships became strained as the year went on because of that.

Our bid for three-in-a-row had started on a good note with a team holiday to Fuerteventura. In the depths of winter we fund-raised, soloing and walking across the county. We raised £28,000 by ourselves, while Seamus Murray, the financial director of our sponsors CBE – an international point-of-sale technology firm – managed to convince the famous Irish band the Saw Doctors to hold a fundraising gig for us in the Travellers Friend Hotel. That brought in between £2,000 and £3,000 and it meant we could enjoy a pre-season training camp in the Canary Islands. At the time it was very unusual for ladies footballers to go on a training holiday, but that's the level we were operating at. If the men's teams were doing it, then we were too. Finbar had the foresight, and get-go, to make it happen, and we were lucky to have sponsors who also saw the benefit of it.

The last time I had been on a team holiday was in 1995, when Beatrice and Jimmy took a Mayo team out to New York. At the time they were involved in the underage county set-up as well as with Carnacon, so a few of us in the club were lucky enough to get to go. I was thirteen at the time, and it was my first time on an airplane. Mam was apprehensive about letting me go, and I didn't understand her reasoning. She would have known she was sick, yet she made sure I got to go and enjoy the trip. Beatrice promised Mam that she'd mind me, which she did, but I still managed to run wild. It was a trip of a lifetime, costing £22,000 for the party of forty-one, and over ten days we met every Mayo man, woman and child living in New York. We stayed in the Royal Regency Hotel in Yonkers and played two games in Gaelic Park. We ice-skated, we bowled, and the experience was unbelievable.

The same went for the Mayo team holiday to Fuerteventura in the spring of 2001. We were constantly up to devilment and pulling pranks. We'd go from one apartment to the other turning everything upside down, or putting everything from the kitchen into someone's bedroom, or vice versa. Crazy would lead and a cohort of messers would follow her. We never sat still. We were always up to something or annoying someone. Three mornings Finbar had us up at 7 a.m. to run on the beach. He was trying to keep us level-headed, but we were having none of it. We'd go out for a drink the night before a training session. Then on the nights we didn't have training the following morning we'd stay in just to see if we could annoy him a little bit! He always had the last laugh, though, because we'd always suffer the consequences.

The day we came home, we had a National League game against Longford in Crossmolina. That wasn't the best idea in the world, and naturally they beat us. We were the reigning All-Ireland and National League champions losing to a side we should have beaten. Worse still, we were losing to ourselves. Maybe living in close quarters for a week made us get on each other's nerves, because we did nothing that day but fight among ourselves. Of course, we used the holiday as an excuse, when in truth we were starting to grate on each other.

There had always been divides. For example, between Carnacon and Hollymount, or Carnacon and The Neale. Winning had masked a lot of cracks, not least our underlying hatred for each other's clubs. When we wore the Mayo jersey and stood side by side, we had respect for one another. However, sometimes we didn't fully click. You can pretend all day, but when you peel back the layers, you see what's been hiding underneath all along. And anyway, you can't have thirty determined women – or men for that matter – and not have an argument.

71

In 1999, the media had Diane O'Hora as their star. In 2000, it was me, and Christina Heffernan was always in the mix. We all had strong personalities, and there was no question that we were all striving for greatness. The other girls might have a different take on it now, but I think that's what it boiled down to – status. We all wanted to be the best player.

Finbar wasn't around to rein us in much that year, or to tell us a few truths about ourselves. His father was battling illness, and his priorities lay elsewhere. After training us on a Sunday, he'd fly to London to sit with his dad who was being treated in hospital there. Then he'd fly back on Wednesday to train us again that evening. His focus, understandably, wasn't there. He'd tell you that himself. And without him, we were all too stubborn to try to find a solution to our tetchiness with each other. Our performances were poor that season, and our consistency wasn't what it usually was. In the league we had lost to Longford, Clare and Monaghan, and but for wins over Meath, Dublin and Waterford we wouldn't have made it to the semi-final. There, Tyrone beat us.

Come championship, our first game wasn't until the All-Ireland semi-final against Clare in September, as all the other counties in Connacht were competing in the junior championship that year. Finbar's father passed away in August, and he missed a number of weeks with us in the midst of the summer. By the time he returned, it had got to the stage where we were on the verge of not talking to one another. He did his best to kill it. He was used to dealing with us, but this was up a level.

One night, he huddled us all in at training.

'We win together, or we lose together,' he said.

It was simple, and there was no other way to look at it. Finbar had been through a lot, and we didn't need to add to his stresses. So we put our differences aside in the lead-up to the semi. Then three days before the game we had another reality check. One of our forwards, Denise McDonagh, was nearly killed in a motorcycle accident. Denise was a soldier based in the Curragh in Kildare, and when she was returning to base she somehow came off the army mountain motorcycle she was riding. Her helmet cracked on impact when she hit the road, then the car behind her went over her leg as the driver tried to swerve around her.

Denise was still determined to play against Clare come hell or high water. For three years she had burrowed her way on to the starting fifteen, and only days before the accident Finbar had told her she would be wearing the number 14 jersey. Her face and forehead were in shreds and her entire thigh looked like a giant blackberry, yet she powered through the pain for the opening twenty-five minutes.

I scored a goal close on the fifteen-minute mark to give us a 1–4 to 0–5 lead at half-time. Marcella Heffernan, Edel Biggins, Claire Egan and sixteen-year-old Emma Mullin played well also, and we went on to win 1–11 to 0–9 to reach our third successive senior All-Ireland final.

We were quietly confident going into the final against Laois, despite them having the advantage of having played six games to our one. They had lost the last seven finals they'd appeared in, so mentally we thought we were tougher. But the biggest error of my career so far was about to cost us three-in-a-row in Croke Park.

The win over Clare in the semi had eased tensions within the team. Winning does that, and we were more than comfortable now with the runnings of All-Ireland final day. The crowd was the biggest of our three appearances to date, with 20,207 people filing into the stadium. Laois went three points clear early on, but we came to life three minutes before half-time, scoring 1–3 – the goal by Claire Egan – to lead by two points at the break (1–10 to 1–8). The lead changed regularly, and Mary Kirwan was on fire for them, scoring 1–7, as was Sue Ramsbottom. With fifteen minutes left, Laois were in front by two points.

Emma Mullin pointed, and we were now within a point. We hunted for the equalizer, and with seventy seconds left, we got it. Forty metres out from the Laois goal I planted myself over the ball, with the mid-tier of the Davin Stand in my eyeline. I had already kicked ten points – eight from frees – so I knew I had it in me to nail the equalizer. Nail it I did, and like a mad woman I rushed back down the pitch to defend against a late Laois winner.

They got a shot off, which floated wide, and somehow with fifty-nine minutes and forty-five seconds played, the dream was still alive. For a draw, at least. I came inside our 20-metre line to collect the short kick-out from Denise Horan to make sure we won possession.

Just win the kick-out, hold it, and we'll escape.

But, just as the ball floated into my hands, the referee Marty Duffy blew his whistle. I remember it as clear as day, as he came alongside my right shoulder and pointed towards the posts. It was a free in for Laois!

What the ... ?!

I didn't know what Duffy had blown for, but I had the instinct to casually kick the ball away a few yards to try to kill the clock. The rule I broke was this one: 'The ball, from a kick-out, must cross the 20-metre line before being played by another player.' Everyone in Mayo of a certain generation now knows that rule. For me, those words are forever branded on to my brain.

Mary Kirwan now had a chance to kick the winning point, and with it blast Laois' seven All-Ireland defeats into oblivion. The clock counted down. Three, two ... Before she ever struck the ball, I knew she had it. I could tell by the movement of her hips. I stood between Kirwan and the posts, my hands on my head. Behind me, on the Hill 16 end, our goalkeeper Denise Horan watched the ball float over her head. In an instant, Mayo's dreams of three-in-a-row were dismantled.

For minutes afterwards, I was dismantled myself. I lay flat on the pitch, broken, crying into the blades of grass. Back then I felt freer to show that type of emotion. In the years since I learned to stifle such open displays of devastation. They were few and far between because when my profile grew, I didn't want to show any weakness, not even a hint of it. I had to hold it together. Not just for me, but for the players coming up behind me.

For Denise Horan, the feeling was ten times worse. She was our captain and had readied herself all year to climb the steps of the Hogan Stand and lift the Brendan Martin Cup. In just a few seconds, what should have been the best day of her life turned into the worst. She knew the rule when she kicked the ball. I didn't. But, regardless, the blame lay with both of us. Denise gave nine years of her life to Mayo football, and for that one blip she came in for an awful lot of flak. For months after there were throwaway comments made about that kick-out. But no one saw what that woman did for her county when things weren't under the microscope. For days after the game she cried. I cried too.

The night of the game, at the banquet in the Citywest Hotel, I couldn't cope at all. The All-Stars were due to be awarded. I was in a bad way. The thought of having to potentially make my way on to the stage to collect a bronze statuette in front of a couple of hundred people when all I wanted was an All-Ireland medal saw me bolt for the door half an hour before the announcement.

I escaped to the bar and ordered baby Guinnesses for everyone at our table. The plan was to numb the pain, and the embarrassment of it all. But as I watched the barman pour the Baileys, I decided I wasn't going to return to the banquet. One by one I emptied the shot glasses down the hatch, and with each trickle of warmth, I floated away. An hour later, a few of the girls found me in the bathroom. Together, they carried me across the foyer and lugged me into my bedroom on the far side of the hotel – which in itself was worthy of an All-Star of their own.

I missed the presentation, but it didn't bother me one bit. It wouldn't be the last All-Star presentation I'd miss either.

6

A Year to Remember

It was like monsoon season in November 2002 in Mayo; even the birds were afraid to move, the raindrops were so big. It was the morning of the 2002 senior All-Ireland club quarter-final, and Ballyboden St Enda's were doing their own manoeuvres around storm-felled trees on the N5 from Dublin. No one knew if the game would go ahead. One thing was certain, not a bucket was safe in the parish.

They weren't safe either in Ballintubber or Killawalla, as Paddy Reilly, the groundsman of Clogher pitch, went door to door for a bucket collection of a different kind. While doing the rounds, he rallied a small army. The enemy was coming, and if the pitch was deemed unplayable then Carnacon would have to relinquish home advantage. And, come hell or high water (quite literally!), we weren't going to let it happen.

The community scattered themselves across the pitch. Armed with wellies, wheelbarrows, buckets and pitchforks, they bailed water from the pitch for close to two hours, sacrificing Sunday Mass as they went. All the way through they watched the clock, as news had filtered through that the referee, Johnny Hayes, would inspect the pitch at 1.45 p.m. The gates were locked on his arrival, by someone cute enough to buy us some time. But it was obvious from the first few metres of Hayes stepping out on to the field that the chances of having the game played were slim. Back on solid ground, he declared the pitch unplayable, and Ballyboden were delighted as the battle would now shift to the capital the following weekend.

Paddy Reilly's army pleaded with Hayes to give them one more hour of mercy. He granted them their wish, not believing for a second it was possible. But Hayes didn't know much about the folks of Carnacon. We're a driven bunch. On the field it's us versus the world. That was always the Carnacon mentality, our stubbornness. And off the field we're exactly the same. How many buckets of water the lads loaded up that day I'll never know, but it meant everything to the twenty-seven of us shivering inside the dressing room waiting to go out.

Hundreds had abandoned their cars on the ditches in and around Clogher, and they too huddled outside the gate waiting for news of Hayes' second pitch inspection. Watching over them, from the plaque on the clubhouse wall, was David McGuinness – my neighbour who tragically drowned when we were in primary school. The clubhouse was dedicated to him, and two other lads who had passed away in the parish, Joseph Walsh and Seamus Hession. Even though they were long gone, they were still part of who we were in Carnacon.

As the afternoon began its descent, and patience wore thin, Hayes announced at 3 p.m. that the pitch was playable. Nowadays, the likelihood is that the game would be called off the night before, but there wasn't a hope we were giving up the chance of a home game.

After the shift the lads put in bucketing the place dry, we had no choice but to win. The fact that we had only ever been beaten once in Clogher in the All-Ireland series – in 1998, by Ballymacarbry of Waterford – was also a motivating factor. They were unreal that day, and bate us out the gate, and back in again. But in the four years since, things had changed. We were more experienced, and we were much hungrier to succeed as a club. A few months earlier, Mayo had won back the Brendan Martin Cup. We redeemed our-selves from the hurt and shame of 2001, defeating Monaghan by a point (0–12 to 1–8) to claim our third All-Ireland title in four years. As a group, we'd reverted to the all-in attitude of 1999, and Christina Heffernan captained us brilliantly.

There was a new togetherness, and a new happiness. That win ignited something in the Carnacon gang. We wanted an All-Ireland title of our own. None of us had ever won the Dolores Tyrrell Memorial Cup, and it was no longer a dream, it was some-thing we yearned to have now. I had changed too. For a start, I had matured.

Beatrice and Jimmy had made me captain, and I felt a huge sense of responsibility to bring the cup back to the people of Car-nacon. I'd been captain before, but this felt different. There was never any doubt that I would put in the work and push others to do the same. And when I saw everyone pulling together that day in Clogher with the buckets, it gave me an overwhelming feeling of pride, and of community.

The win over Ballyboden in the senior All-Ireland club quarter-final was really a win for all of us. We were football addicts all over again, craving another victory. In the semi-final we beat the reigning All-Ireland champions, Donoughmore, a side that boasted the likes of Cork stalwarts Juliet Murphy, Rena Buckley and Mary O'Connor. We didn't care who they were. We were fearless, and floating. Everyone was in the form of their lives, and Claire Egan was making a name for herself as one of the best midfielders ever to play the game. Her power and ferocious ball-winning skills set her apart. And I know, because I was naive enough to think I could take her on.

For all 5ft 5in of her, she made plucking the ball down from the sky look easy. If you were lining up against her there was something intimidating, even stern, about her. I'm not sure which one of us nicknamed her 'Smiley', but the irony of it stuck. There was a time when Smiley would drift in and out of games. A mistake would pick away at her subconsciously, and she'd lose focus. She'd tell you that herself. In the early noughties, after our successes with Mayo, she adapted, and was less hard on herself. That's not an easy thing to do, but for Carnacon it meant we were now getting the best she had to offer. The funny thing is, Smiley's a blow-in. But she thought like us. She was as driven as us, and that's all that mattered.

When Claire was growing up there was no club in Louisburgh, so every Sunday morning her father Jim would raid the local shop of the weekend newspapers and drive his daughter fifty minutes to training in Clogher. More often than not, her mother, Mary, and younger brother, Fintan, went for the spin too – and, sure enough, they morphed into Carnaconians.

Beatrice and Jimmy saw the talent in Claire early on. They saw her raw passion, the fire, and that was more than enough.

A few years ago, Smiley floated the idea of transferring to a club in Dublin where she had lived and worked for a number of years.

It made sense, but she was nearly burned at the stake by the rest of us for even thinking it. It was emotional blackmail on our part, but Carnacon is as close to a football cult as you can get. It's a way of life, and we didn't want her to leave our compound in the west.

If anyone was motoring well in 2002 ahead of our first senior All-Ireland club final, it was Smiley. But seventeen-year-old Aisling McGing was also making a name for herself, which wasn't easy given that her elder sisters were Michelle (an All-Star winner) and Sharon (a former corner-back for Mayo). Their uncle, Johnny – their cousin, Caroline's father – was a beast of a player for Ballintubber, and that's probably where the McGings all got their footballing brains. Michelle and myself had played together since our early days playing with the Carra boys, and Aisling was now following in her sisters' footsteps, carving out a niche of her own as a gutsy wing-back.

Then we had fifteen-year-old Fiona McHale at corner-forward. She had yet to sit her Junior Cert, but even then you could tell she had it. Her movement was exceptional. More than anything, her desire to win flowed out of every pore. We were lucky to have the two of them, Aisling and Fiona. They were impressionable, and automatically immersed themselves in the club's culture – a culture of dedication and togetherness created by the likes of Michelle Corbett, Maria Staunton, Imelda Jordan, Catherine Larkin, Mary Heneghan, Margaret Horan, Maria Casey, Niamh Lally, Michelle McGing, myself and, of course, Jimmy and Beatrice. It set the tone for the next generation, and the club's future depended on that. We didn't have huge numbers. We didn't have a nursery. Essentially we were a family, so skipping training wasn't an option. We depended on each other, and we delivered. And that's Carnacon in a nutshell.

In the build-up to the final against Carrickmore of Tyrone, the place went mental. Bunting, flags, cars, tyres, tractors – you name it, it was covered in red and green. Our old rivals, Hollymount, had been the only other Mayo club to reach a senior All-Ireland club final, first in 1987 and again in 1999, though they lost both times. They had beaten us in the 1999 county final, so, I won't lie, the thought of getting one over on them got us going.

Surprisingly, the captaincy didn't weigh on me. I knew the prestige that went with it. I knew what it felt like because when I was sixteen years old, Jimmy and Beatrice made me captain the year we won our first senior county title. So now, coming on twenty-one, I was more than ready to lead the club to its first national final. Things had come full circle, but it meant nothing unless we buried the Ulster champions.

On the day of the final in St Loman's Park in Mullingar there wasn't a soul left in Carnacon. The only thing left standing was the statue of the Virgin Mary outside the church. Neither was there a drop of milk left in Mike Willie's shop on the corner, with everyone emigrating to Mullingar for the day with their flasks.

We started well, and I kicked the first five points into the wind and added a goal from a free to give Carnacon a 1–6 to 0–3 lead at the turnaround. Carrickmore weren't done, and with eighteen minutes remaining, scores from Eilish Gormley, Lynette Hughes and Patricia McGurk brought them back within two points. It's funny, because in the end the win came down to a short kick-out. After all we had been through the year before with Mayo, Denise Horan and myself, everyone in the county had a new pastime of watching goalkeepers' kick-outs. And that's what Joyce O'Hara did with ten minutes left on the clock. She read the ball as it skewed short off the Carrickmore keeper's boot, pounced on it and passed it off to Fiona McHale, who belted it into the net. In that moment I knew we had it, and that it would be our greatest ever win as a club.

When the whistle blew, we were mobbed. We barely had a second to ourselves to find one another in the madness, and it was the best feeling in the world. Over the years, every win was as great at the particular moment in time, but that win will always have a special place in my heart. I can still see the tears streaming down Jimmy's face an hour after the game, and Beatrice with a smile that couldn't be wiped away for months after. Between the two of them, they put our anonymous little village on the map.

In 1986, when Ballina Ladies Football Club disbanded, Jimmy had headed off down to the postbox in the village with a cheque for the County Board to register Carnacon Ladies Football Club. Back then we weren't even winning coin tosses, yet they were committed to building the club from the ground up. They nurtured our skills, and we always had a ball in our hands. To them, the most crucial element of the game was ball skill. It was never about the physical element of the game, it was always about getting the basics right. It was that, married with our work ethic and loyalty to one another, that saw the club begin to flourish.

It wasn't easy, though. For years we only had one set of jerseys for every team from the U12s up to the seniors. Granted, there weren't that many of us, so we shared and made do.

Jimmy would crank up his Ford Capri and collect everyone and anyone who was remotely interested in kicking a ball. Once he even managed to fit nine of the minor team into his car for a game in Kiltimagh. Another time he borrowed a trailer to ferry another lot of us to a game against Hollymount.

His vast knowledge of the game was incredible. More than anything, he cared. He cared about giving us an outlet for our talent, regardless of age or standard. In 1987, alongside Paddy Sheridan, he coached Mayo to a junior All-Ireland title against Wexford, and he was involved in the U14 team that won the All-Ireland in 1994 with Mattie Casey. He also served as a development officer with the County Board that same year and trebled the numbers of teams taking part in Féile.

You see, Jimmy didn't just care about us, he cared about ladies football. Beatrice was the same. Whether as a player, an administrator or coach, she only ever wanted to help us be the best we could be. Her mindset was our barometer, and between Jimmy and herself, they made us into the people we are today. On a personal level, the most important thing they did for me was they never differentiated me. I was the same as everyone else, and that kept me grounded. I never had any privileges. I was just Cora, the little girl they knew, sipping on Coca-Cola, talking football before everything else took off.

That day in Mullingar they brought me and the rest of the team to the top of the world, and the view was magical. There was one special person missing, however. Willie 'The Shoe' McNeely had passed away that June of cancer, aged forty-seven. He had followed us from the beginning of time, and I thought of him as I carried the Dolores Tyrrell Memorial Cup into the dressing room in St Loman's Park. He would have loved it, the happiness and the craic. Above all else, Willie would have loved the sight of an All-Ireland title coming back to his beloved west.

The homecoming in Carnacon was something else. Hundreds gathered inside and outside the community centre where it all began – where I banged footballs off the freshly painted walls and weighed blackberries with my friends before class. It was special too because Art Ó Súilleabháin, my old principal, was the MC welcoming us home. He had encouraged me to try every sport under the sun, and listening to him speak took me back to many a PE lesson we had in the same hall with Art teaching us the rules and skills of yet another sport. My first coach, Seán Hallinan, also said a few words on behalf of the Ballintubber Bord na nOg, and I remembered how he made myself and Michelle McGing mark the best boys. That brought out the best in us because we believed in ourselves and in our talents.

Things had come full circle, and I was grateful to them, and to everyone in Carnacon.

The studio lighting dimmed, and Eamon Dunphy swivelled himself around in my direction.

'Start the clock.'

I was only twenty-one, but here I was facing Eamon on *The Weakest Link*, alongside jockey Johnny Murtagh and retired Irish rugby player Neil Francis, trying to raise funds for charity. Dunphy wasn't as scary as the BBC's Anne Robinson, but he still had me on edge. I managed to get to the third round, when I couldn't think of the name of the world's first cloned sheep. I was slagged about Dolly for years after, but I was just delighted I wasn't the first to go. The shame of that went to Murtagh.

It was a time in my career when offers and expressions of interest started flooding in. I don't have an agent; I never have, and probably never will. I never really saw the point of investing in one. I generally make up my own mind about what to do, my sister Collette looks over the contracts, and that's it. The fewer people in the equation, I find, the smoother the process. In 2016, someone in RTE asked me to take part in the new show *Dancing with the Stars*. I refused point blank. It's the only offer that genuinely terrified me and made me laugh at the same time. Don't get me wrong, I like a challenge, but don't take me too far out of my comfort zone.

Since that first appearance on *The Weakest Link* I've been on *Know Your Sport, The Den, The Late Late GAA Special, Up for the Match* and a few other bits and pieces of television. But it all really kicked off in 2002/03.

By that stage Mayo were very much in the spotlight, and invitations to every kind of function under the sun were coming through the door at home. Half the time, however, I was none the wiser as to what I was going to until I got there. One year, the former Taoiseach, Bertie Ahern, invited me to the annual Taoiseach's Dinner in the Citywest Hotel. Crazy was mad for road to see what the shenanigans would be like, and I was equally delighted that she would be there to protect me. That was run-of-the-mill for any event I went to. If Crazy was up for going, or even if she wasn't, she'd be there for me, defusing my shyness and awkwardness.

If I had a function in Dublin, I would call in to my sister Collette and she'd always do our hair and make-up, and make sure we were presentable for whatever event we were going to. We were like two country buffs going up to the big smoke. No matter where the event was, in the Shelbourne or in the Four Seasons, Collette would always make us look somewhat respectable. I hate dressing up to the nines, I always have. I cursed Collette a few times but thank God we had her in our corner because it could have been very embarrassing without her.

That particular night at the Taoiseach's Dinner we spent a good half-hour trying to find our table. What we didn't realize was that I was actually Bertie's guest, sitting beside him and his daughters Cecelia and Georgina. I was too young to take it all in, or to put myself out there and network in those circles, but those were the types of opportunities coming my way.

In 2003, Lucozade got in touch, and I became the first Irish female athlete to sign with them for a television advertising campaign. Collette looked over the paperwork and I signed it, not realizing the significance of what it meant for women in sport at the time. The first advert I did was filmed in the Wicklow Mountains at 6 a.m. Myself, Irish soccer star Damien Duff, Munster rugby players Ronan O'Gara and Peter Stringer, and Tipperary hurler Eoin Kelly were put up in Clontarf Castle the night before, then ferried into the mountains the following morning.

To be honest, I was in awe of the lads. At the same time I was slightly embarrassed by it all. I didn't see myself on the same level as them. They were all professional sportsmen, bar Eoin Kelly, but he was still the closest thing you could get to it. I didn't really understand why I was there. It was the first time I could recall an amateur female athlete in a national television campaign. Sonia O'Sullivan might have been in some things over the years, but she was an Olympian and a global superstar. I was just Cora from Carnacon, yet here I was with all these fellas who were at the pinnacle of their careers.

The week before, Duff had signed for Chelsea for £17 million, but there were no airs and graces about him or any of them. They welcomed me for who I was and what I had done, and I appreciated that. As we waited for hours in our tent to be called to set, O'Gara would be up to antics any chance he got, having the craic and entertaining us all. It was great fun, and it was also nice to hear about the normality of all their lives too.

That's why I like speaking to other sportspeople. They get you, and you get them. We all know what we've put in – the hours of training and travelling, the career moves, the sacrificing of relationships and family occasions. There's a mutual understanding and respect because of that.

We later did another shoot in Dalymount Park in Dublin. At the end of the day, O'Gara turned and handed me his rugby boots.

'There you go, girl. Best of luck with everything.'

I thought I was made. Ronan O'Gara was one of rugby's greatest number 10s to have played the game, and someone whose kicking technique I had watched time and time again. And here I was holding his football boots in my hands.

'They're a size nine and probably way too big for you like, but sure they might come in handy anyways. I'm actually a size ten, but I wear my boots a size too small because I find it helps with my kicking.'

I loved hearing all those little nuggets. I'm sure that was common knowledge, but at the time I felt like he'd let me in on a big secret.

Stringer gave me a signed rugby ball, and Damien Duff a soccer ball, and I smiled the whole way home to Mayo.

Lucozade, and John Givens of JGA Sports Management in particular, were very good to me. I'd call to a warehouse in Dublin and they'd give me crates of the stuff to take home. They have also looked after me with match tickets for various events, such as the 2006 Heineken Cup semi-final between Munster and Leinster in Lansdowne Road, and Ireland and France in the 2006 World Cup qualifier with Thierry Henry, Zinedine Zidane and Patrick Vieira, and he and his good ole pal Roy Keane tearing shreds off each other. Every Christmas they'd send a gift, such as an iPod or a Nintendo DS. They were lovely gestures and ones I appreciated, given that as an amateur sports person you rarely got such expensive gifts. The deal naturally came to an end when Olympic boxer Katie Taylor came along. I was never going to win that one.

I signed with Puma too and worked with Conor Ridge of Horizon Sports Management, alongside Tyrone footballer Seán Kavanagh and Laois' Ross Munnelly. Again I was the only female athlete signed, and again I didn't realize at the time the importance of it. I don't even think I told my family about those Lucozade adverts. If I did it was probably in passing after I magically appeared on the television in the sitting room.

I let things like that fly over my head. Looking back, I now realize what that visibility might have meant to aspiring female athletes. I couldn't stand the sight of myself on television, or the sound of my voice, so I didn't use the status I had to push the promotion of women's sport. At the time, winning All-Irelands was all that was on my mind. I do now think I could have done things differently. Maybe I could have embraced the national media a bit more to promote ladies football. Then again, I don't think the media was ready to embrace female athletes, or our stories.

I didn't, and still don't, like putting myself out there. Some people do it to have a profile, but I do it to increase the visibility of women in sport, and to be a role model for younger girls coming through. In recent years I've got more comfortable with the idea that I am a role model. There was a time when that label made me shudder. I didn't want it. I didn't understand it. I just wanted to be Cora. Now I see the bigger picture, and I'm lucky enough through my work as a Sky Sports Mentor to have the opportunity to go into schools and tell boys and girls my story, and to promote my sport.

That said, there is a limit to what I'll do and dancing in public is a step too far!

7

Number 5

THERE'S ONE PATCH OF TURF IN BALLINROBE GAA PITCH that's cursed. It's on the dugout side about 65 metres from the town end. It's where I snapped my collarbone when I wasn't cute enough to get out of Claire 'Smiley' Egan's way in 1999. Four years later, that exact patch of grass got the better of me again.

It was during the 2003 Division 1 National League semi-final against Laois in early April, and the ground was still pretty sticky. I went to tackle a defender, but when I planted my right leg to push off, it didn't budge. At the same time, the momentum of my upper body took me in the other direction. Pop! I heard it as clear as day, and the pain was at least an eight out of ten.

It was our first meeting with Laois since losing to them in the 2001 All-Ireland final when Mary Kirwan burst our bubble for the three-in-a-row. We wanted revenge, and I was enjoying my football. Finbar had moved me to midfield, and it was refreshing. I was fitter, my vision was improving, and I was learning off one of the best in Smiley. As half-time closed in we were six points up, but then my boot stuck in the mud. I was able to walk off, but immediately pockets of fluid surrounded my knee. I prayed it wasn't

91

anything major. After breaking my collarbone, my jaw, and now this, I didn't think I could handle anything too drastic.

The following day I went to see Anne Egan in Athlone – Finbar's sister. She could see it was serious and referred me to Dr Ray Moran at the Sports Surgery Clinic in Santry. I had to wait two weeks for my appointment, so Anne looked after me with regular sessions as she would continue to do throughout the year. Then, Ray told me that I had torn my anterior cruciate ligament, but all I could think about was when I might be back. Ray said I'd be out for a few weeks, and that I'd have to build the strength back up in my knee. Surgery was an option, but there wasn't a hope in hell I would go for that. I didn't have time for surgery. Championship was just six weeks away, so all I could do was manage the pain and hammer into my rehab.

Most days after college I bummed a lift to Finbar's sister's house. Anne was a physio in Athlone, and she'd iron out the scar tissue in my knee. For the first few weeks I was in pain, but when you're so focused on getting yourself right again, you overlook it. I knew too that if there was any chance that I could be ready for Roscommon in the opening round of the Connacht SFC, then I had to go at it hard. Pain, or no pain.

I needed a lot more support around my knee if I was going to be able to play. A member of the backroom team mentioned an American website that sold knee supports, and the order went in. One. Right. Medium. Knee. Brace. I couldn't believe the size of it when it arrived. It was huge. We forgot to factor in American sizes, so the thing was nearly halfway up my quad. There were bars on either side that gave the support I needed, but I hadn't anticipated the downsides. I became too reliant on it. It was a catch-22:

I needed it for support, but over the course of six weeks my quad and hamstring muscles wasted within its grip. The bars ate away at my skin too. And, if that wasn't bad enough, there was also the embarrassment at the size of it.

During my recovery I was lucky to have something else in my life to distract me. One night at training, Finbar called myself and Crazy to have a chat. He asked us if we could take the Mayo minors job, and coach the team between the two of us. We both just looked at him. We didn't know if he was being serious or having us on. But he was serious, and he was persuasive.

It was mid-May and Crazy was returning from a cruciate injury that had gotten infected after the operation, and I was in the middle of mending my own knee. We were both going to be standing on the sidelines for a few weeks anyway, so it made sense to take it on. By helping to distract us, Finbar also gave us a life lesson. We needed to see how tough the role of manager was, and we did. In hindsight, if I had known the effort that went into it, I would have said no. Between training three or four nights a week with the Mayo seniors, two nights with the minors, and then club training, it was a lot of football, and organizing.

I was a player first and foremost, but we also wanted to prove that we could rise to a different challenge. I knew that Crazy and I would work well together. Our respect and trust for each other had always been the key to our friendship. So, as joint managers, we already had key ingredients to make it work. With both of us coming back from injury, it also gave us a focus. It kept my footballing brain ticking over. If I couldn't be on the pitch, then this was the next best thing. But I found it hard, and frustrating. Once the whistle went, that was it. I couldn't score. I couldn't influence the game. I couldn't enjoy it. If we needed a goal, I just wanted to run out and swing my leg at the ball. In that split second, however, you realize you can't. That feeling is as frustrating as hell.

We had some skilful players to work with. There was my own lot from Carnacon – Aisling McGing, her cousin Caroline, Noelle Tierney and Fiona McHale – and the likes of Annette Gallagher (Belmullet), Emma Mullin (The Neale) and Triona McNicholas (Moy Davitts). They were a lively gang, and Crazy and I had a good rapport with them. If someone had to be dropped or taken aside, Crazy was the one to do it. You might think that I'd just come straight out with it, but it won't surprise you when I say that Crazy just had a better way of delivering bad news.

The minor championship didn't start until later in the summer, so initially we just enjoyed imparting our knowledge. It felt good to give back and to watch players grow in confidence. I got a kick out of that, and when I returned to action myself at the start of the summer, I was re-energized.

Off the field, the County Board were also doing great work with Margaret Byrne in as treasurer alongside P. J. Loftus as chairman, and they restructured how things were done. With Mayo's first All-Ireland final win in 1999 there had been a surge in clubs springing up across the county. The previous board had struggled with that influx, but now structures and supports were being put in place to support that growth. Finance was a major part of that, and in the spring of 2003 they struck a three-year sponsorship deal with the sportswear brand Azzurri worth €30,000 a year – the biggest sponsorship deal in the history of ladies football at that time. It was Finbar who had initiated talks with Azzurri, and it was great to see a company invest so much in us, and in the sport.

I was fit and ready to play against Roscommon in the opening round of the Connacht Championship – which we won 3–13 to 0–6 – and we were delighted too to have the likes of Crazy, Diane O'Hora and Sinéad Costello back from injury. It was also the year that our rivalry with Galway kicked off. It was their first season playing senior football having won the 2002 junior All-Ireland final, and we went on to beat them three times in the championship that year alone.

The first time we met Galway was in the second round of the Connacht Senior Championship on Saturday, 19 July 2003. It was the reigning junior All-Ireland champions against the senior, but that day was remembered for other reasons. It wasn't a vintage Mayo performance, but our experience and fitness were definitely superior and we outran them on a scoreline of 3–16 to 1–12. After the celebrations, someone tapped me on the shoulder as I walked down the old tunnel in MacHale Park. To this day I can't remember who it was, but they told me that someone needed to find Sharon and Michelle McGing. I didn't know what they meant, but quickly discovered that their younger sister, Aisling, had been involved in a car accident. She was in hospital, and someone had to tell the girls the news.

I went straight to the dressing room to tell them. Aisling wasn't part of the squad that day because she didn't make the cut for championship. She was a quality defender, just eighteen years of age, but the depth of the squad meant management had the luxury to drop good players. The year before we had won a senior All-Ireland and a senior All-Ireland club together, and that September Aisling was going to live with myself and Crazy in Athlone. We would be in our final year of college, and she was due to start a hairdressing course. But it wasn't to be.

That July day there was a two-car collision between Ballintubber and Ballyheane – just 6 miles from MacHale Park. Aisling had been en route to support her sisters, wearing her Mayo jersey, and was a passenger in one of the cars involved in the collision. The drivers of both cars, and Aisling, were taken to hospital, and later the drivers were released with minor injuries.

Myself and Crazy quickly changed out of our gear and drove to Mayo General Hospital in Castlebar, where we sat in the corridor with Aisling's cousin, Caroline, and waited. Aisling's parents, Teresa and Jimmy, were already there, as were Sharon and Michelle. They told us that Aisling was conscious and had spoken to them, and it gave us a glimmer of hope. Later that night, however, hope turned to horror when Aisling passed away from her injuries, which included damage to an artery in her heart. We could hear the wailing, and that sound still haunts me. The emotion and the rawness of the heartache stay with you.

In the midst of their grief, the McGings allowed myself and Crazy to see Aisling, and I'm forever grateful that they did that. She looked so peaceful lying there, and on either side of her we whispered our goodbyes.

Aisling was a star on our Mayo minors team. More than that, she was a friend – someone I could imagine myself still being good friends with today. She had a great sense of devilment in her. She was witty and beautiful, and just like that, she was gone.

Time stops in moments like those; the shock numbs you. It's hard to know what to do with yourself. Even though it was late when Crazy and myself left the hospital, we had to do something. So we went across the road to the TF Royal Hotel for a drink. We didn't say much. There was nothing we could say. It was like we were just floating, staring into space for an hour or two.

At 11 p.m., Crazy dropped me home. Dad and the lads weren't there, and my sisters had flown to Greece that morning for a holiday, so I was home alone. There was a peacefulness to the place, yet a loneliness too. I managed to find the kitchen table in the darkness, and sitting there I bawled my eyes out.

The following morning I went to the McGings' house in Killawalla. Aisling's parents, her sisters Fiona, Michelle and Sharon, brothers James and Tom, and extended family members were all there. I just wanted to do something to help, though there's nothing you really can do bar butter bread, make sandwiches, ferry cups of tea, and just be there. During the day, Crazy, myself and a few of the girls took Tom for a spin to Castlebar. It was to help him escape from it all, if just for a few hours. It was something small, but I know that's what I would have wanted around the time of Mam's passing, for someone just to take me out of the house.

From a club point of view, Aisling's death knocked us. Like any GAA club, Carnacon is like a family. We were Aisling's second family, so it hurt. For the removal, the Mayo flag flew at half-mast over Killawalla Community Centre. The red and green flags taped to the railings outside the centre fluttered in the summer sun, and inside, Aisling's number 5 jersey hung proudly. Her debs dress was there too, and her most prized possession – her red Adidas football boots.

Her removal and funeral were the biggest I've ever seen. People queued for up to two hours, and as the line of sympathizers crawled along, it never seemed to shorten. We knew it would be big but no one had envisioned the numbers that turned up. The removal to St Patrick's Church was due to start at 8 p.m. but there were still people there three hours later at 11 p.m. The outpouring was incredible, and it showed exactly how highly regarded the McGings are – and you'd like to think that support helped them through.

As Aisling was carried into the church, the Mayo and Carnacon girls formed a guard of honour. We stood side by side, wiping away tears and handing tissues down the line as the coffin passed us by. The funeral was tough because it was our final goodbye. I was asked to read a Prayer of the Faithful. That meant a lot, and the Mass was a lovely tribute to Aisling. For the offertory procession, Michelle carried Aisling's football boots and her five All-Ireland medals to the altar, and Sharon carried her letter of acceptance into the hairdressing course in Athlone. Afterwards they joined their sister Fiona, and together they sang Garth Brooks' song 'Unanswered Prayers'. It was gorgeous, and their collective strength blew us all away. As Aisling's coffin was carried out of the church, 'Everything I Do' by Bryan Adams played through the speakers. Every time I hear that song now, I think of Aisling, and smile.

That night, a few of the Mayo players went back to Ballinrobe for a drink in Inches Bar. We were subdued, but it was good to be together. We were on a drinking ban with Mayo but we figured two or three bottles of Budweiser was nothing in the grander scheme of things. We didn't go mad. We just sat there, supped on our drinks and recounted stories. The following night at training, Finbar lost the plot with us. I don't know how he found out, or what he was told, but he laid into us for having a drink. The

Connacht final was eighteen days away and we were supposed to be on a drinking ban, he bellowed at us. He was sympathetic to what was going on, but he still didn't believe it was acceptable for us to be breaking the rules during the championship. There were no other consequences, but that was enough. I know we were to give our all to the cause, but sometimes life gets in the way of that. I thought to myself, *What a fucking prick!* We had lost a friend and a teammate. What else were we going to do? It's not like we went on a three-day bender. We needed one another for moral support. Going for a drink was just an excuse. What we really wanted, and needed, was each other.

There's no question that Aisling's death galvanized us. It's hard to describe exactly how. I think we minded each other a bit more. We became much more conscious as a group of just how short life was, and subconsciously we reminded ourselves to be there for one another.

It was harder to take for the Mayo minors because Aisling was their teammate. Yet they showed such maturity, and, looking back, it was they who helped me through. Because she hadn't made the senior squad, I knew how much playing with the minor team meant to Aisling. So my motivation to get that bunch of girls to a minor All-Ireland final multiplied. Aisling's cousins, Caroline and Marie, were also on the team, so we had to stay strong for them too. And, just like when I lost Mam, football became an outlet, a support. That's what really kept us all going in the weeks that followed.

When it came to the senior set-up, we also had to be strong for Michelle and Sharon. Our first game back was that Connacht final. It was just twenty-two days after the accident, and it was against Galway again, in MacHale Park again. They had beaten Roscommon to get there.

Driving to the game that day felt strange, knowing what happened the last time we were there. I can't even imagine how it must have felt for the McGings, or even how they got through the day, but they did. Before the game, referee Marty Duffy blew his whistle for a minute's silence. For those sixty seconds, rivalry didn't matter.

When the game started, we were slow off the mark. I guess the emotion of the day had weighed on us. Michelle and Sharon both came off the bench, and I think when we saw them running on we picked it up, winning by eleven points in the end (4–9 to 0–10). But we were never in any doubt that we were going to win that game given the circumstances. We had to.

The following few weeks were obviously difficult. We missed Aisling, but we had to get on with it. We beat Waterford in the senior All-Ireland quarter-final in Cusack Park, and Michelle was inspirational, winning Player of the Match. Gone were the days of Waterford dominating us. By now we had not only learned how to play the game, we had learned how to read the game too, and we were thinking for ourselves.

Off the field, however, a huge storm was about to hit. Prior to the All-Ireland semi-final against Galway – our third meeting in the championship – Central Council informed the Mayo County Board that we weren't allowed to wear our Azzurri jerseys. If we did, we'd be breaking the rules, which stated that all jerseys worn in televised games had to be supplied by O'Neills because of a deal the LGFA had done with them. It was complete bull.

That May, delegates at a Central Council meeting were informed of the LGFA's deal with O'Neills – a deal that had yet to be signed, they were told, but it was considered to be a gentlemen's agreement. Mayo and Finbar had been in talks with Azzurri as early as February, and following discussions a three-year deal was signed, well before the O'Neills deal came to light. The Mayo County Board had an agreement to uphold. We couldn't just go against that and wear O'Neills.

We knew that the LGFA would give us O'Neills jerseys to wear for the semi-final, and we told them we'd wear them. Some genius came up with the idea of covering the O'Neills logo; at least then we wouldn't be breaking our own contract with Azzurri. Finbar loved to go against the grain, so he drove it. Other managers wouldn't want their players getting distracted by something like that, but he was a man of principle, and not exactly a fan of the LGFA either. He believed that the Association didn't like him. He spoke his mind and, if I'd to guess, he was probably right.

In my opinion, Finbar did the right thing. Azzurri had invested €30,000 to kit us out for an entire season, with tracksuits, T-shirts, shorts, socks, gear bags and windcheaters given to each player. All we were getting from O'Neills was a jersey for the semi-final and, if we made it, a jersey for the final. It didn't make sense. Why would we dismiss the company that believed in us, and had invested in us? So, before the game, each one of us cut off a two-inch strip of green electrical tape and patted it down over the O'Neills logo. It was like putting on camouflage before going into battle.

Needless to say, the LGFA weren't impressed.

Maybe it did distract us because Galway pushed us all the way. We only managed to register one score in the first half, a goal, and we trailed 1–0 to 1–4 at the turnaround. With fifteen minutes to go we trailed by six points, and it was Galway's for the taking. But then Christina Heffernan fired over a mighty point, I converted a few frees, and we were level and deadlocked with five minutes of added time.

We knew we were lucky to be getting a shot at extra-time. With everything that had gone on in recent weeks, we dug our heels in. We wanted to get back to Croke Park for Aisling so we weren't going to let this second chance go to waste. With three minutes left in extra-time, Martha Carter trundled off in an ambulance with suspected concussion, but we didn't let it throw us. Diane O'Hora, myself and Annette Gallagher all raised white flags and, in the end, we clawed past Galway by two points, 1–11 to 1–9.

In between the jersey row drama and preparations for our fifth All-Ireland final in Croke Park, myself and Crazy had to prepare the Mayo minors for their own All-Ireland. The last time the county contested it was in 1999, when we were both playing, and we lost, so we wanted to make amends this time around. However, we were up against a serious Cork outfit. They had won their fourth U14 All-Ireland in a row that year, and the conveyor belt was starting to kick in.

At half-time we led by a goal, with Emma Mullin and Maeve Ann O'Reilly netting a goal each. But then the likes of Geraldine O'Flynn, Rena Buckley and Norita Kelly took over for Cork, and they ended up winning 1–15 to 3–5. Bríd Stack lifted the trophy, while yet another future All-Star winner, Angela Walsh, was named Player of the Match.

Our gang gave it everything, and now I realize it was an achievement to come so close to a team that boasted many players who would go on to win multiple All-Ireland titles. I was proud of the girls that day. They had been beaten by the better team, but personally it was a pity that we didn't win it for Aisling. It might have brought about a little bit of closure for that side. Aisling was one of them, and I think if we had won it would have been the ultimate way for her teammates to have honoured her. At least we still had the Brendan Martin Cup to try to win with her sisters Michelle and Sharon.

My knee was holding up, but I couldn't handle the support any more. It was starting to cause me some discomfort, and I felt that it was limiting the range of motion in my kicking. So, a few days out from the final against Dublin, I made the decision to play without it. I knew it was a big risk, but I convinced myself that strapping it would free up my movement. Plus, I wouldn't have the pain of the support bars digging into me.

I didn't seek any medical advice, which in hindsight was madness. I shouldn't have even played. But, you do what you have to do. Aside from the injury, I wasn't fit enough either. Granted, I had played in all the championship games, but I was dragging myself around the place rather than going full tilt, so I was only operating at 70 per cent or so.

But, I had the chance to play in another All-Ireland final, so one leg or no leg, I wasn't missing it.

I struggled for the entire game, but we all did. We only managed to score four points between us in fifty-eight minutes. It was awful stuff. We couldn't pass. We couldn't shoot. We couldn't do anything. Nerves didn't come into it, but for some reason things just weren't clicking. The LGFA, I'm sure, were hopeful that Dublin's first appearance in a senior All-Ireland final would put ladies football on the map, but all the punters got was a dismal game.

The Dubs weren't much better than us, and at half-time we led by two points (0–4 to 0–2). It was they who chipped away at the scoreboard in the second half, however, and when Gemma Fay gave them the lead with two minutes to go, we had yet to register a score in the entire half. From the kick-out, Claire O'Hara carried the ball 20 metres out of the back line. She drew the foul and won a free about 40 metres out on the Hogan Stand side. I stepped up to take it. There were a hundred or so seconds left on the clock. I thought about going for a point. It was just inside my range, but I knew my knee wouldn't have the strength behind it. We needed a goal, so I figured if I aimed for the back post and landed it in, anything could happen.

I hoofed it as high as I could, making sure to gauge the distance so that it wouldn't go over the end-line. I needed the Dublin defence to panic, and as the ball dropped, someone in a blue jersey did just that. They half caught the ball, and it spilled in front of Diane O'Hora. She picked it up, swivelled, lashed her left leg at it, and the ball hit the roof of the net. The angle was so tight that had it fallen to a right-legged player, we might not have won.

The place went nuts! It was the first time ever in my intercounty career that I didn't register a single score in a game, but I didn't care. Sure I was disappointed in my own performance, but you'll take that kind of win any day. As a group, we dedicated the win to Aisling. We knew what it meant to the McGing family, and that was the important thing, that we did it for them. It was the greatest escape we ever had, and sometimes you make your own luck too.

What I couldn't have known then is that that's where Mayo's luck ran out. The next few years would be blotted with dramas and disappointments. Worse still, I'd never win another All-Ireland with Mayo.

8

End of an Era

THE DECISION WAS EASY: I WASN'T GOING TO HAVE THE OPERATION. If there was the slightest chance that I could work through the pain, then that was what I would do. I'd managed to pull through most of 2003 with a dodgy ACL anyway, so I figured I would rehab over the winter and see where it got me. My knee didn't bother me in a major way. By the autumn of 2003 I'd learned to live with it. If I gave it a chance, and worked on rebuilding my hamstrings and quads, I would regain the natural support I needed. And besides, lots of people played on with torn ligaments, depending on the grade of tear.

So through the winter of 2003/04, if I wasn't in the gym in Athlone IT, I was in the pay-as-you-go gym at the Westport Leisure Park Centre. I looked up programmes on the internet and did curls, squats, lunges, leg presses and step-ups. It was a release, too, from everything else that was going on that winter.

Two months after the All-Ireland victory, everything turned upside down in just a matter of days. Carnacon were knocked out of the Senior All-Ireland Club Championship, beaten by Donoughmore of Cork in the semi-final (0–4 to 0–7) – a game in which I only managed to score a single point. For the first time we felt what it was like to lose as a club on the national stage. To make matters worse, Mayo were issued a €20,000 fine by the Ladies Gaelic Football Association for wearing Azzurri jerseys in the All-Ireland final. The fine was unprecedented in the GAA, never mind the LGFA. It was complete madness.

The news broke on the wet November evening when delegates gathered for a Central Council meeting in a Tullamore hotel. The then president of the LGFA, Geraldine Giles, stood up to put the Central Council's proposal of a fine to the floor; prior to that, they had fined Mayo €2,000 for using green electrical tape to blot out the O'Neills logo in the semi-final, and also for not wearing O'Neills jerseys in the minor All-Ireland final. When Giles finished reading out the reasons for the fine, the delegates voted and the proposal was passed. The two Mayo delegates at the meeting that night didn't vote because they were advised not to, given that the County Board's legal team was looking into matters at a higher level.

For me, as a player, all I saw was the gear, and the investment Azzurri had made in us. They were genuine about women in sport, and it felt like we were making progress. It was the direct result of what we, as a team, had achieved on the field over the previous five years. We were simply being rewarded for our hard work, and rightly so. In some quarters of the national media we were accused of being 'elitist', or there was an angle about 'player power'; there was an element of 'Who do they think they are?' Female athletes didn't get that kind of money back then, so of course we must have had notions. We didn't. All we were trying to do was be better players. Financial backing isn't the be-all-and-end-all: if you can't put the ball over the bar, you won't be successful. That said, the support from our sponsors, CBE, and Azzurri was key to us raising our own standards. We also set a precedent for other female county teams to believe in their own worth and value when it came to sponsorship deals.

We thought things would be rectified come the start of the 2004 National League in February, but they weren't. We still hadn't paid the €20,000 fine as we were contesting it, but the LGFA thankfully still allowed us to compete in the league. We just wanted to play, and to be fair to Finbar and the management team, they protected us from what was happening off the pitch as much as possible. All the same, you'd want to be living under a rock not to be aware of what was going on.

Come April, the jersey row completely blew up, just before we were due to play Cork in the Division 1 National League final. We thought things were looking up when John Prenty, the secretary of the Connacht Council, was appointed to mediate between the LGFA and the County Board. On 24 March he'd met both the LGFA and the Board in Athlone, and after several hours a number of recommendations were drawn up. Each party was to bring them back to their respective delegates to approve, or reject. Nine recommendations were made, the principal one being that the overall €22,000 fine be reduced to €2,200. The understanding at that point was that if the recommendations were deemed unacceptable by either side, a vote would be taken by the Central Council on whether to remove Mayo from all activities of the Association for breach of Rule 15.

Finally, a proposal was made that the €2,200 fine be paid to charity rather than to the LGFA, removing the issue of rules, as technically it would not be a fine if it were not paid to the LGFA.

The majority of the Mayo delegates backed the recommendations but it was requested that the Mayo County Board be given leave to seek a two-year derogation on their contract with Azzurri, rather than the one-year derogation recommended by the mediator. A call was made to John Prenty to check if this would have an impact. In his opinion, if the Mayo delegates voted to accept, subject to two amendments, then they would not be banned at the following night's Central Council meeting. We thought that would be the end of it.

A fax was drafted outlining the specifics of the County Board meeting that took place the previous night. It was read over the phone to the mediator, who said it would be acceptable. However, after consultation with the chairman, the secretary was told not to send the letter. John Prenty communicated the decision of the Mayo County Board to Central Council in a fax which stated that given the rejection of the full recommendations, the mediation had failed, and a vote should be taken at the Central Council meeting. It was now the Thursday of the week before the Division 1 National League final against Cork, and at the Central Council meeting, the vote on whether Mayo should be removed from the competition carried, forty-six votes to one. Just like that, we were out.

Our captain, Nuala O'Shea, was woken by a phone call at 1.30 a.m. to tell her the news, and the following morning it was confirmed in writing to the Board. Just like that, the hours I'd spent rehabbing my knee were all for nothing. Our Up and Downs that spring in Balla and Ballyhaunis were all for nothing too. What the hell were we even playing ladies football for? I know things are not always black and white – they never are with ladies football – but it was a complete mess. It shouldn't have got to that stage, yet it was allowed to.

An emergency meeting of the Board was called that night at 7 p.m. and a vote was passed to appeal the decision under Rule 260 on the basis of new evidence coming to light. That is, that the 'full and proper representation' of the decision at the Tuesday night County Board meeting was not communicated to the mediator, or to Central Council.

So now, with an appeal in place, there was still some hope that we would be allowed back into the competition. But there was more drama to come. At the same meeting, our former teammate Denise Horan, also a club delegate for Tourmakeady, called for a vote of no confidence in the County Board.

Denise had her reasons to call for such a vote, and I know she meant well, but I don't think it helped matters. The way I saw it, the appeal was our priority now. Also, the County Board at that time had worked extremely hard to reorganize themselves. They were trying to put better structures in place, they were promoting the game, and they were getting businesses to believe and invest in us. They had a great relationship with our sponsors, CBE and Azzurri, and maybe in the heat of the moment people forgot all the good things that they had done.

It was agreed that the vote of no confidence in the County Board be delayed until we heard if the appeal was successful or not. Thankfully, the following evening, at an emergency meeting held by the management committee of the LGFA, the appeal was upheld. We were back in, and had a National League final to prepare for in eight days' time.

At a subsequent meeting after the National League final, Denise submitted a letter in which she asked for her motion of a vote of no confidence to be withdrawn. I was in the room the night her letter was read out, and we thought that particular drama was over. That's until two other delegates from separate clubs re-proposed Denise's vote. A counter-proposal was put in, and then another vote was declared. It was like a civil war had erupted. It was ridiculous. The whole thing was falling to pieces, and I just couldn't sit there and take it any more. As a player, I spoke up. I said that the present County Board had done nothing but their best for the players over the past few years. They had made sure that we were looked after, and the fact that they secured the Azzurri and CBE sponsorships meant that financially we were able to pre-pare as professionally as we possibly could. I called on people to think about that before they voted again, so they realized that it would be the players who would suffer the most out of anyone in that room. In the end, there was an open vote on both motions, and it was a massive yes in favour of the County Board. I'm not saying I changed things by speaking up, but I do think people's eyes were opened as to how this business was affecting the players. We weren't in ladies football for the boardroom politics, we were there to compete on the field of play. At the end of the day we just wanted to win, and do our families proud.

Having been reinstated after months of turmoil, we faced a new force in ladies football. Cork had got their act together under their new coach Eamonn Ryan, and when we played them in the National League final in May 2004, I sensed they had what it took to be winners. The game was a triple-header in Pearse

111

Stadium: Galway were taking on Limerick in the hurling league, and in the football, the senior Galway men's team faced Tyrone in the National League semi-final replay. Extra-time in the football caused our own game to be delayed by an hour, and waiting around was torture.

For weeks you psyche yourself up for a specific time of day, and just like that, it's out of your control. Then it's a balancing act to keep your concentration, and conserve your energy. When we eventually did get out on to the pitch, the place was mobbed with kids. Galway had beaten Mickey Harte's Tyrone, and it was mayhem outside. Our first-half performance was just as manic. We weren't with it at all. The drama of the last few weeks had taken its toll.

Cork were fearless. They came out of the traps at a rate we hadn't anticipated and at half-time they were beating us by six points. In the dressing room, Finbar had a go at us. We had lost our focus. We were lethargic, and we weren't as hungry as Cork. We needed to get our act together. We had won four All-Ireland titles in five years, yet we had just one league title to our name. It's not that we were ever dismissive of the league, it just hadn't happened for us. So, there and then, we decided we weren't leaving another opportunity behind us.

In the second half we took over. Jackie Moran came on and shook us all up while Claire O'Hara, Nuala O'Shea and Helena Lohan shut down Cork. I fired over 1–9 myself and in the end we won by three points (1–14 to 1–11). Cork suddenly stopped playing for some reason, and we were allowed to redeem ourselves. They have since admitted that they froze that day in Pearse Stadium. They couldn't believe they were up six points against the reigning All-Ireland champions. And, to their detriment, they also didn't believe they could finish us off. After the game I remember thinking to myself that they were a serious outfit. So much so that when I got home, I pulled the match programme straight out of my gear bag and calculated their average age – twenty. I knew then they'd be coming for us.

It's no secret the respect I have for Cork, and how they carried themselves during the decade they dominated ladies football. There wasn't an ounce of arrogance or cockiness in them and that, to me, said a lot about them as individuals. You could see where it all came from – Eamonn Ryan. His modesty made them the team they were, and I hugely admired him, and them, for that. Over the years on various All-Star trips, I loved the way the Cork girls looked after him and respected him. I was almost envious of that relationship, and the bond they had. We had a similar type of bond with Finbar, but in subsequent seasons we never found that depth of collective respect with another coach again. It was lovely to see the Cork players interacting with Eamonn; the Mayo gang massively admired it. So much so that other counties almost hated us for it. They might go for dinner and invite us to go along, and the other county players would make a comment about it somewhere along the lines of, 'Sure, ye'll only socialize with the Cork ones ...' But we respected Cork, and there was definitely a mutual feeling between us.

During the 2010 All-Star trip to San Francisco, I finally built up the courage to speak to Eamonn Ryan for the first time. We were in a bar on a night out, and a few things struck me. The first was, we didn't instantly connect. It was like we both needed a bit of drink on board to have the courage to talk to each other. He's quite shy, as am I, so the two of us were initially cagey. I remember, however, that there were a couple of times over the course of the week when he was very complimentary to me, and that was massive. It was almost like I had made it. Getting a compliment off someone with Eamonn's knowledge and approach to coaching was huge for me.

This might surprise people, but it was rare enough that I got praise from a coach. They presumed I didn't need it, but I did. They presumed my confidence was constantly sky high, but it wasn't. And there were times when a word or two in my ear would have made an enormous difference. 'Do you know what, Cora, you did that well there', or 'Your runs took defenders away'. If I got head-lines in the newspaper, it wouldn't make a blind bit of difference to me. Yet if a coach genuinely praised me, I grew a mile. Saying a brief 'well done' as I walked off the field didn't cut it, but I think coaches were afraid to go beneath the surface with me. They might have been anxious as to how I would react, but deep down I was the same as any other player.

Finbar was good at that. He could tell when I needed picking up and when to leave me alone. In the years after his departure, I pretty much went seasons on end without an ounce of praise. It wasn't the chopping and changing in coaches that caused that, I just think some coaches genuinely didn't know what to say to me at times. That, and they presumed I was confident, when at times I wasn't. I'm not saying I needed attention – far from it – but every now and then a quiet word of encouragement would have gone a long way. Because, no matter how experienced you are, everyone needs a little encouragement. It's human nature.

I'm sure I'm not the only one to feel like that. I bet there are lots of experienced players who can relate to that. You're expected to be confident for the younger ones coming through, but during my career there were times when I drove to training knowing damn well I was putting on a front. I pretended I was confident because I wanted the team to feel confident. Inside, however, I could have been having a crisis.

I became an expert at playing the part. I never doubted my ability because I knew I had put in the hard work. None the less, there were times when my confidence took a hit. I felt I could never show that side of me. That's why encouragement is something I'd certainly be very conscious of now as a coach, regardless of a player's experience or ability.

Finbar's time was coming to an end. And, to an extent, so was ours. Winning the 2004 Division 1 National League lured us into a false sense of security, because when the championship came around we weren't at the races. We lost to Galway twice in the Connacht Championship, the first time in the round robin series, and later by a massive fourteen points in the provincial final. To lose by that much was sickening. It was infuriating too, given that we were the reigning All-Ireland champions and now National League champions, yet we let ourselves be beaten by that much. We should have been better than that, but we weren't.

Looking back, the carry-on over the jerseys had distracted us; some players even got disenchanted by the whole thing and jetted off to the US on J1 visas. To be fair to Galway, they had come a long way in the last twelve months, and now it was they who were hurting us. That year we played them four times in the senior championship and lost all but one. We were getting wins, but we were only spluttering along. We managed to beat Cork in the All-Ireland quarter-final, only to set up yet another tie with P. J. Fahy's Galway side in the semi-final that September. There was just no getting away from them!

It was like a war that day in O'Moore Park, and the officials' calls didn't help. In total, there were four players sin-binned – three for Mayo and one for Galway – while Diane O'Hora was red-carded for an accidental elbow to the face of Marie O'Connell. There was no malicious intent, but Diane's dismissal meant she'd miss the All-Ireland final, if we got there. She couldn't believe it when Tony Clarke took the red rectangle from his pocket. I can still see her walking off the field in tears, and seventeen-year-old Fiona McHale, ten years her junior, comforting her as she went. It was the first time in six years that any of us had been red-carded, and the incident angered us so much that it gave us the adrenalin rush to produce a draw in the last minute.

The replay was a week later in Hyde Park, Roscommon, and again we were level at the end of the sixty minutes. In added time we kept going, but Galway did everything right. They won by a point (3–9 to 3–10) and reached their first senior All-Ireland final. When the whistle went, I felt empty. That single point brought the curtain down on the best era in Mayo football. We were in shock. We should have seen it coming, because Galway had been improving during the previous seasons.

We dragged ourselves off that pitch towards the changing room. Family and friends stood at the gate, patting us on the back as we went, while deep down we were all wondering if the greatest times of our lives had just passed us by. Finbar had told us at the start of the year that 2004 would be his last. So we knew when the whistle blew that it was the end of our time with Finbar Egan, a man who had moulded us into machines and, on reflection, had changed the landscape of ladies football. Waterford had been there before us, but Finbar completely professionalized the approach to the game – how we trained, how we looked, how we were perceived, and how we perceived ourselves.

I was very upset when he left. He had guided us to four senior All-Ireland titles and two Division 1 National League titles, but Finbar did so much more than that. He was the first coach to make me think deeply about the game; about every move, and every counter-move. I learned so much from Beatrice Casey and Jimmy Corbett as a young girl but, with Finbar, it went under my skin. For six years we lived in his bubble of obsession. We hung on his every word, and fixated on his standards. And then, the bubble burst.

When I heard who'd got the senior job, I couldn't believe it. Finbar was always going to be a hard act to follow but, at the very least, I thought the County Board would appoint someone on the same level. There was a new board in place but I assumed they had the same ambition as the previous one. I was wrong. As a team we had committed six years of our lives to getting ourselves to the highest level, often living like hermits so obsessed were we with keeping our standards high. We were all willing to make sacrifices if it meant succeeding. That took effort, a lot of effort, and I wanted desperately to keep it that way. Some might think I was hanging on to the past, but our successes had laid a solid foundation for a bright future for Mayo football. To me it felt that this one wrong decision caused the whole thing to unravel.

Con Moynihan got the Mayo job, and he was someone I would never have given it to. He'd coached Galway to the 2002 junior

All-Ireland final, fair enough, but I felt we deserved better. For-mer players Denise Horan and Sinéad Costello agreed to go in as selectors to make the transition smooth, and to help maintain the winning culture. But after just a few weeks their patience thinned, and they called it quits.

It was just us now, and Con, and with every training session my frustration grew. I wasn't the only one getting annoyed either. Con had his ways, and my idea of a professional set-up was very differ-ent to his. One night in March 2005 on the back pitch in MacHale Park, we ran around a square of cones for twenty minutes. I couldn't see the reason behind it. I couldn't see how this was going to make any of us better footballers. With Finbar, every drill had a purpose. Every second of a training session was tailored to a match situation, and you knew damn well why you were doing what you were doing. We had gone from training like dogs and vomiting on the sideline to running around cones, the only varia-tion a change in direction.

After one of our first National League games under Con that year, we were taken to a local chipper in Ballinasloe. I was fuming. We had gone from healthy sandwiches to greasy chips; it was like watching what we had created dissolve before our very eyes. When it came to game plans and knowing our opponents' strengths and weaknesses, that too dropped down the priority list. Before going out to play Waterford in the 2005 Division 1 National League, our goalkeeper, Linda Connolly, spoke up as we were getting ready to go out on to the field.

'Con, can you tell us anything about Waterford?'

The reply was short and lacked the detail we would normally have got from Finbar.

The funny thing was, the question backfired on Linda when a few goals went past her in the first half. Back in the dressing room, Con turned to her and said, 'Well now, Linda, can you tell me anything about Waterford?'

He had a point, but the one we were trying to make was that we were used to so much more in terms of preparation and professionalism. This wasn't about comparing Con to Finbar, it was about what we had come to expect, from management and from ourselves.

Claire Egan was captain that day, but she refused to play. She was recovering from an ankle injury, and with a shove she could have played, but the truth was she couldn't handle the situation any more, and neither could I. We went from dealing with a shrewd character to shouting and the banging of fists. We also went from speaking individually to a coach three times a week to barely being able to approach Con.

I'm not saying everyone felt like that, but the majority of us did, and it all came to a head at a team meeting in the dressing rooms in MacHale Park. The players organized it to voice a few concerns, but soon it turned into a deeper discussion.

'Do ye want me to go?' Con asked us straight out.

A few mumbled 'yes', but I stood up and emphasized the point: 'Yes, we do want you to go.'

At the same time, twenty-two-year-old Claire O'Hara of Castlebar Mitchels barricaded herself across the door. She didn't want another change.

'No, we don't want you to go!' she said.

Our opinions were divided. We were sending mixed messages, but that night Con walked anyway. The incident strained the team dynamic, and it was something that lingered. Finbar had kept us united, even though there were always different groups and disagreements. He had a way of bringing the team together. It was us versus the rest of the world, and no matter what, we had each other's backs. Con wasn't strong enough to do that.

In hindsight, we weren't strong enough to pull ourselves together either, and that was a pity. With Con gone, the County Board appointed the junior Mayo management team until a replacement was found. Stephen Bourke, Danny Fahey, Noel Kearney and Tommy Walsh were all in their twenties, and we jokingly nicknamed them Westlife. They did well to get us to an All-Ireland semi-final against Cork, but Eamonn Ryan's players wanted to redeem themselves for the 2004 National League final defeat we had inflicted on them. In O'Moore Park in Portlaoise our captain Claire Egan played a mighty game in the middle of the field, and we were two points up with three minutes to go (1–9 to 0–10). Yet somehow Cork chipped away at us, and with twenty-nine seconds on the clock, Juliet Murphy found herself in a position to kick the winning point, and she wasn't going to miss: 0–13 to 1–9, game over.

They went nuts. It was their first time beating us, and reaching a senior All-Ireland final. They deserved to win it, but I still believe that if Finbar had been over us that year we would never have allowed Cork to get into a position to stage a comeback in the first place. Professionally Finbar was a loss, but personally I missed him too. I was trying to adjust to life without him, and my performance dropped off a little during the year because of it.

All things considered, as a team we did well to reach that All-Ireland semi-final in 2005. It was our competitive nature as individuals, and the work we had done in the previous years, that carried us up to that point. After that, we never had a hope.

Over the next few years we were wrongfully labelled as a team that was never happy with whoever coached us. That was a totally unfair assessment. It was a yarn spun to cover up mistakes made at administrative level when it came to appointing the right person for the job. The County Board had settled. They didn't take the time to really look for the right person for the job, and it backfired. Also, in our defence, we never, ever went behind a manager or coach's back. If there was an issue, we approached them about it. As players, however, we shouldn't have been put in that position in the first place, and we wouldn't have been if expectations had been met.

You give up everything. You throw your life into football. But you're also relying on someone else to deliver on their end of things. What do you do when it's not good enough and they're not delivering? It's like they're taking your chance away. It's not intentional, but as players, we had intent. We wanted to get back to being the best, but the thread just kept on unravelling.

9

Trouble Ahead

I KNOW EXACTLY WHERE I WAS ON 6 JUNE 2006, WHEN THE CALL came through. I was on my way home from doing a coaching session in a local primary school when our goalkeeper Linda Connolly phoned to tell me that Claire Egan's mother had passed away suddenly.

Mary Egan was a nurse and one of the most caring people I had ever met. She looked after everyone in the community. She was an absolute lady, and for years she was every part of the Carnacon and Mayo story, alongside her husband Jim. They were at every game, club and county, and were, without doubt, Claire's biggest supporters, and ours. They were there in the good days and in the bad. They had mingled and made friends with every other parent on the sidelines and in the stands across the country, so when Mary passed away, there was no question that we'd miss her.

Claire returned to training a week or two later. The strength she showed at that time was unbelievable, and it was she who pulled us together. In the years since my mam died, people who have lost a parent have often come to me for advice, and it's nice to be able to help. I was sixteen when I lost Mam, so it's something I've had time to deal with. But there's not much advice you can give. Everyone deals with death differently, so all you can do is answer their questions as best you know how, and be there for them. That's it.

The passing of Claire's mam aside, 2006 in general wasn't a good year. We were now on to our third manager in twelve months, and we were understandably unsettled. A lot of players decided to call it a day when they should have been playing in their prime – the likes of Mary T. Garvey, Sarah Tyrell, Edel Biggins and Lisa Cafferkey. They were done with the turmoil and baggage that had come with playing for Mayo.

This third manager of ours was Charlie Lambert from Westport who was working for the Mayo Sports Partnership at the time. He came on board in February 2006, and all things considered, he did quite well. I knew Charlie through my work coaching around the county, and he was a passionate Mayo man who wanted to return us to the good old days. We reached the All-Ireland quarter-final, only to be beaten by the reigning champions Cork, and when the season finished Charlie too called it a day. The time commitment had taken its toll, and he had other priorities now.

Eight weeks later, in November, Carnacon lost the senior All-Ireland club final to Donaghmoyne of Monaghan by a point. Over the past three years it had just seemed to be one bad thing after the other. I needed a change of scenery. Crazy did too. So when she asked me to join the Mayo League soccer team I jumped at it. When I was fifteen, I had been invited to trials for the Irish U16 soccer team. Mam was very ill at the time so I never made it to the sessions but I'd always enjoyed playing.

The Mayo League soccer team had become the first Mayo team to qualify for a senior FAI Cup final that December, and the buzz about the place was great. The coach, Aidan Flatley, didn't mind that I joined the squad late in the season, and thankfully the girls were happy to have me. The majority of us had all played football together at some point. Emma Mullin and Aoife Herbert were our star forwards, Crazy was in goal and Martha Carter and Triona McNicholas were midfielders, like myself.

The final was due to be played on 1 December in Lansdowne Road as a double-header with the men's showdown between St Patrick's Athletic and Derry City, but for some reason our game against University College Dublin was moved to Richmond Park. UCD were favourites, having won the cup three times, not to mention having dominated the Dublin League for a number of years. And us? We were just a bunch of GAA heads looking for a release, and craving another win.

But we surprised them. Eleven minutes in, Aoife Herbert scored a cracker of a goal, and for the next seventy-nine minutes we parked the bus. I was lucky enough to come on midway through the second half, and at the final whistle the high from winning was just what I needed. It re-energized me. It re-energized all of us, and when it came to going back to Mayo football in 2007, we were ready.

On 12 January 2007, we sat in the dressing rooms in MacHale Park and waited to meet our new manager. He would be our fourth in two years. Frank Browne was a Wexford man who moved to Ballyhaunis in 1993 to work as an air traffic controller in Knock Airport, before meeting his lovely wife Deirdre and settling down. He had recently finished up with the Mayo hurlers and was looking for a new challenge. We were it.

To the left of the dressing-room door stood a flipchart. Frank introduced himself with a smile. 'The plan on how to win the All-Ireland will be written on this,' he said, folding over the cover of the chart.

The page was blank.

'So, let's start filling it in ...'

Frank had never even seen a ladies football game, never mind coached a ladies team. He was a hurling man, and I had my doubts. But, as he started to talk, I came around. He saw a positive in everything. He was passionate, and more importantly he was straight up. I could tell he was a stickler for preparation, and that caught my attention. Granted, he may never have coached a ladies football team, but he knew how to build the right foundations. That's key for any good coach. From what we ate to what we wore to how we played, they were all inches Frank had wanted us to regain if we were to win back the Brendan Martin Cup.

Before that initial meeting in MacHale Park, Frank's perception of us was that we were a cocky and arrogant group – or at least that's what other people told him before he took the job. The talk about us being difficult to deal with had stuck. But as the weeks went by, all he saw were genuine, honest, hard-working people who just wanted to win another All-Ireland. Nothing more. Yes, I'm sure we were awkward at times, but I think most people who came in to work with us would now realize that we were a determined group of women desperate to restore our pride. We were prepared to do anything to win another All-Ireland title.

Frank's game plan was simple. The backs defended, the forwards scored, and the midfielders channelled the ball between the two. If those basic jobs were done we would be OK. He set the bar that first night, and we trained harder than we had done for some years. Frank's only error was that he appointed the secretary of the County Board, Mary Malone, as a selector, and another woman called Caroline Brogan as a liaison officer.

Mary had played football with Mayo at junior level back in the day and was involved with Swinford, while Caroline had been involved in ladies football through her club, Claremorris. Maybe there wasn't anyone else willing to put their hands up, but bringing them in was a move that would prove to be Frank's undoing.

To be honest, I wasn't a fan of either. And they didn't like me. They thought I was full of it, but they didn't know me. I got the impression that they thought a few of us had nothing better to do than sit around thinking up ways to 'get rid' of managers.

'Could we not just get along and have fun?' one of them asked us one day.

Are you serious? I thought to myself. I wasn't there for the fun of it, I was there to get another All-Ireland medal.

None the less there was a good atmosphere at training. Frank's views were refreshing, and when we got to the Division 1 National League semi-final against Cork in April, it was the first time in a long time that we believed in ourselves.

In Banagher, County Offaly, we ended the Rebels' thirty-one-game winning streak which had spanned twenty-six months. They were on a steam train, going for three All-Irelands in a row, and finally we caught a break. It felt good to see things coming together, and as we sat on the bus on the way home I really believed that things were turning around. We'd gone through two bad years but we were now back to beating the All-Ireland champions and I couldn't help but be encouraged by that.

The next month we followed this with victory in the 2007 Division 1 National League final against Galway (1–13 to 0–6), and two months after that, in July, we reached the Connacht SFC final, against Galway again. With twenty minutes left they were walking all over us. We were nine points down, and our league win counted for nothing. Our heads hadn't been in the game for some reason. We shouldn't have let that gap widen the way it did. But, just like in the old days, we dug in and clawed our way back. That feeling of *yes, we've got this* returned, and that was purely because our self-belief had shot up after the National League win.

With sixty seconds left on the clock the game was level at 3–15 apiece. I won a free 40 metres out. Prior to that I'd missed three frees on the trot. But this time I obliged and put the ball between the posts to secure a one-point win and a showdown with Monaghan in the All-Ireland quarter-final.

We had a slight logistical problem, however: four of us were due in Austria the same week to play UEFA Champions League soccer! Myself, Crazy, Aoife Herbert and Michelle Ruane were all members of the Mayo League team being shipped to the continent to represent Ireland after our win in the senior FAI Cup the previous December. It was a once-in-a-lifetime opportunity. The soccer gang wanted us to go to Austria, and the Mayo gang wanted us to stay. So we came up with a plan and negotiated a compromise for both management teams.

We were in Group A, up against Neulengbach of Austria, Klub Sportowy of Poland and Hibernian of Scotland, and we were out of our depth. I think we lost one game 9–0. The other teams were made up of semi-professionals who had won multiple domestic leagues and cups, while some of us were GAA players who had only signed up for a bit of craic the previous winter. We played the first game against Neulengbach, then myself, Crazy and Aoife flew home on the Friday and trained. On the Saturday we beat Monaghan in the All-Ireland quarter-final, and the following morning we hopped back on a plane to Austria.

Our final group game wasn't until the Tuesday, so myself, Crazy, Aoife and our kit man, Jeremy Dee, decided to go for a drink or two to celebrate. We didn't think it would do any harm, but I felt guilty afterwards. It wouldn't have happened on a football trip, we just got carried away with the euphoria of getting to an All-Ireland semi-final. We knew we didn't have a hope in the soccer, and if a member of management was happy to go with us, then what was the harm? But it was out of character for us: 99 per cent of the time we had tunnel vision when it came to winning, to training, to putting the team first. Football was our life, and that's what we demanded of each other, and our coaches.

In that All-Ireland semi-final we defeated Tyrone, 2–13 to 2–8. I slotted home a penalty in the first half, but Tyrone managed to stay level with us at half-time. Gemma Begley was doing well for them, but we pulled away in the final few minutes and secured a place in our first All-Ireland final since 2003.

Two weeks before the game against Cork, members of the management team informed us that they had arranged free tanning and hair appointments at a beautician's in Claremorris in the week leading up to the final. They should have been focusing on football. I was hopping over it. They had also organized for two hairdressers to be in the Citywest Hotel the night of the All-Ireland final banquet, and we hadn't even won anything yet. Maybe they thought they were being helpful. Some appreciated it, but I wasn't one of them. That said, at the end of the day it wasn't fake tan that caused us to play poorly.

There were seven in the team – Helena Lohan, Christina Heffernan, Nuala O'Shea, Marcella Heffernan, Claire Egan, Crazy and myself – bidding for a fifth All-Ireland title. We were all up for it, especially the seven of us, who just wanted to feel that sense of euphoria from winning in Croker one more time. Our self-belief had also been awakened by the addition of solid young players – the likes of Aoife Herbert, Lisa Cafferkey and Fiona McHale – and we felt more secure with the depth of the squad.

The reality was that we were up against a Cork side looking to become just the second team ever to win a three-in-a-row. They controlled the entire game and led by six points at half-time, 0–3 to 1–6. Our captain, Christina Heffernan, spoke in the dressing room, as did Diane O'Hora and myself. We all said the same thing: we hadn't yet played and were only six points down. We got a big match-up wrong, though. No matter who we put on Valerie Mulcahy, she found a gap. Her second goal widened Cork's advantage to twelve points in the final quarter, and defensively they had been all over us too. Every time I got the ball there were four or five around me. Up until the last minute, all I had managed to score was a point. I did register a late goal, but it was far too late, and Cork won by five points to complete their three-in-a-row – something we had never managed to achieve ourselves.

We were gutted. We knew we hadn't performed, and that's the hardest thing to get over. We also knew that we'd been outclassed, which made it a little easier to accept.

Looking back, there had been a divide in the camp for most of the season. Frank never addressed it, and he was right not to. It had to work itself out. We all got on with it, but the split existed. Christina and Marcella Heffernan and a few of the younger players were closer to Mary Malone and Caroline Brogan, while me, Crazy, Martha Carter and Smiley backed Frank. He had stood his ground on several things that year. For example, he didn't let the chairman of the County Board, Bernard Commiskey, on to the team bus for the journey into Croke Park. Bernard hadn't been on the bus for a game before that, and he wasn't going to be let on now. We had a routine and we were sticking to it, and because of that Mary and Caroline weren't fans of some of Frank's decisions. Maybe they were afraid that he was getting too much power, or that theirs was diminishing. The fact that Frank was mobilizing a new backroom team for 2008 and they weren't in his plans probably didn't help.

At the December 2007 County Board meeting, a motion was passed to set up a panel to formally interview all those nominated for the senior job for next season. We were led to believe that Frank had been signed up for a three-year term, but guiding us to a league title, a Connacht title and an All-Ireland final didn't appear to count for anything. The man had restored our pride by getting us back to Croke Park. In my eyes, that was progress.

As all this was unfolding over the winter, I had worries of my own. During the year my knee had begun to cause me problems. Despite this I didn't stop until after the senior All-Ireland club final that December. We beat Inch Rovers of Cork to lift the Dolores Tyrrell Memorial Cup for the second time in Carnacon's history, and in the days after that game I stopped pretending to myself that my knee would be OK. For five years I had told myself I could live with it, but it had finally become too much.

I'd first realized I needed to get it seen to in August when I was playing with Kiltimagh Knock Utd in an FAI Intermediate Cup final against Annacrotty of Limerick in Cork. I'm not the most skilful centre-mid, but I scored a goal to put us 1–0 up and, stupidly, did a cartwheel (of sorts) to celebrate. I landed badly, and my leg jolted. Immediately I knew something was wrong. I couldn't bend my leg. It was like my knee had locked itself. For the next few minutes I hobbled around the centre circle before making my way to the sideline. I sat down on the grass and, as the game continued, tried to unjam my knee by slowly manoeuvring it up and down. After about four minutes it cracked itself open. It wasn't overly painful, but I sensed it wasn't right. I got up and went again. I scored two more goals and we won the cup (4–0), but I didn't bother trying any fancier cartwheels.

After the All-Ireland I was certain I couldn't fool myself any more. Psychologically I had always battled through pain. I'd almost enjoyed the challenge of it, but now I needed to get real.

I booked an appointment to see Dr Ray Moran at the Sports Surgery Clinic in Santry, and as he looked at the results of the scan I asked him if I could last another couple of years without an operation. He looked at me as if I had completely lost my mind. On my way to the clinic I had convinced myself that Ray would tell me that I didn't need an operation, but it turned out I needed two.

The wear and tear on my knee was so bad they had to split it into two procedures: first they had to repair extensive cartilage damage, and then they had to repair my ACL. Normally those two procedures are done in one go but my cartilage damage was so bad he had to tackle each injury separately. I was taken aback. There and then I had to make a call on whether or not I would go on the 2008 All-Star trip to Dubai. Without thinking twice, Ray told me that I'd have plenty of All-Star trips in the future, that the operations couldn't wait. And he was right.

In the middle of December I headed to Dublin for the first operation. I told only a few close friends about it, and even then I played it down. Only one or two people knew about the second operation five weeks later on 26 January 2008. I remember the date because I was due to head off on the All-Star trip the same day, and a text came through from a member of the travelling group: 'I can't believe you're not here!' Outside of those I told, I didn't want anyone knowing. I didn't want a big hullabaloo made about it, or for people to start retiring me. After my first consultation with Ray, I'd informed the LGFA that I couldn't travel to the UAE due to work commitments. In fact I'd be sitting in a hospital bed in Santry waiting to undergo surgery, for the second time in just over a month.

A few days after I got out of hospital, myself, Crazy and Claire Egan headed to the Welcome Inn in Castlebar to attend the January meeting of the Mayo County Board. The saga with Frank still wasn't sorted out. I had publicly stated that my future with Mayo would be in doubt if Frank wasn't given the job, so we went to the meeting to give him our backing. He was our fourth manager in three seasons, and we didn't want a fifth. Most of us felt that way because we were craving consistency.

I managed to make it up the stairs, my crutches hitting off every step as I went. When we got to the door of the meeting room we were stopped by Caroline Brogan, the newly appointed County Board chairperson. 'Officers and delegates only – no players or media' read the message on the door behind her. Delegates are limited to three representatives per meeting, and Beatrice, Jimmy and selector Michael McHale had all just gone in the door before me. Crazy's dual status as player and delegate meant she was allowed to enter after the intervention of her Hollymount clubmate Paddy Sheridan. Smiley and I, however, had to wait outside because we weren't delegates.

I couldn't believe it. We had served the county longer than everyone on the County Board put together, and now it was restricted access. I had just spent €7,500 on getting my knee fixed so I could put a Mayo jersey back on. The LGFA paid €5,000 of it from their Injury Fund but I was still €2,500 out of pocket, and now I was being kicked out of a County Board meeting. I should have just walked away from Mayo football right there and then, but I couldn't. I couldn't give them the satisfaction of it. So for the next three hours, Smiley and I stood in the corridor with the four journalists who had also been banned from the meeting.

Inside, Hollymount's proposal that Frank stay on as manager was seconded by Castlebar Mitchels, but it was defeated 15–8. How delegates saw the logic in that I do not know. To this day I don't know how they made a sensible case for Frank not to be reappointed. It was insane. The County Board had also stated that four candidates were interviewed for the job. Yet they were not in a position to reveal the identity of any of them, apart from Frank. At 10.48 p.m., the media was called in and told that the County Board would take charge of the senior team until a manager was in place.

As well as being selectors, Caroline Brogan was the chairperson of the Board and Mary Malone the secretary. It was hard not to feel that they didn't really respect the players all that much when our preferred manager was pushed out and there was no urgency in finding a replacement. A week before the Division 1 National League opener against Kerry in February 2008, we were still without a manager. Numbers were limited and most players who wanted Frank back had refused to travel under the circumstances. Somehow, Mary and Caroline rallied enough bodies together to make up a team to head to Annascaul on the Dingle Peninsula. That team lost by twenty-two points.

I was injured at the time with my knee, but if I had been fit I wouldn't have gotten on that bus. I admired those that didn't because they were protesting on principle. All my career I played for Mayo, not the County Board. And I wouldn't have been able to bring myself to get on that bus given how we'd been refused entry into the meeting, when all we wanted to do was keep the man who got us back to Croke Park. Then again, what would we know? We were just troublemakers.

10

Breaking Barriers

SOME FRIENDS ARE MORE SPECIAL THAN OTHERS, AND CAROLINE Brennan is one of those friends. She's the reason I've been able to do what I've loved doing for so long, and no amount of thanks will ever cover it. For as long as I can remember I have been welcome in Caroline's home in Ballyglass. It could be 7 a.m. or midnight but she wouldn't think twice about getting out of bed and setting up a fold-up physio table in her hallway for me. She understood me. She understood my agitation and frustration when it came to injury, and she also understood my drive to play at all costs.

That's the tough balancing act physios have to handle. Caroline gets that balance right better than most because we're cut from the same cloth. She used to play in goal for Carnacon and won two All-Irelands with Mayo. She could relate to my stubbornness because she had the same mentality as a player. So, when it came to rehabbing my knee at the start of 2008, it was Caroline who walked me through the entire process.

When I discussed my recovery with Dr Ray Moran I'd told him in no uncertain terms that I needed the quickest programme there was at the time.

'I'll give you the advanced recovery programme, which is four to six months.'

I planned on being back before then.

It was daft, but I wanted to prove to Ray, and everyone else, that I could get back on the pitch much sooner than they had anticipated. Setting myself a challenge helped me cope with long rehab. Once I had a goal I was able to be more positive about how I approached it. I spent countless hours in Westport Leisure Park, jumping and bending to reinforce the fibres in my ACL. And if I wasn't there, I was in my sitting room, balancing on a wobble board.

No question, it was difficult. It was baby step after baby step, and for anyone who plays sport at a high level, that's the hard part. The monotony. The repetition. Over, and over. You want to go from nought to a hundred miles an hour in the space of a few weeks, but it doesn't work like that. It was incredibly frustrating, but Caroline made it so much more bearable.

Every free minute I had was spent rebuilding my knee and almost always Caroline was there by my side checking on me yet never taking a penny for it. She also knew when to push me and when to rein me in. I was eleven weeks into the programme when I wanted to try to run. She agreed to meet me at the soccer pitch the next evening. I was so excited. To be so close to running again was such a big deal for me, and I was so happy to be putting my football boots back on that night. We warmed up for what seemed like a lifetime, squatting and lunging. But when it came to running, I couldn't go more than a hundred metres.

When I pulled up, I turned around to Caroline. The look on her face said it all. It was exactly the outcome she had expected. She had known all along that it was too soon. She knew too that it was better to let me find that out for myself. I was so disappointed, but I insisted that we'd be back in two weeks to try again. And we were, slowly but surely upping the distance, adding cones and diagonal runs and turns.

After that first attempt to run I realized just how much more I still had to do, and it made me even more determined to push myself. It also reminded me of a player who had played with Mayo in my early years. She had injured her knee in 1997 or so, and to this day she runs with a limp. I realized that the same thing could happen to me. So, as much as I wanted to prove Ray and everyone else wrong, I also knew I had to mind myself.

It was a tedious process. One step forward, two steps back. But, with Caroline's support, I got there.

My first game back with Mayo was a twenty-minute stint in a league game against Laois in May 2008. And, to tell you the truth, I was a little bit freaked out. I was nervous at the thought of something popping again, and afraid too that I would have to go through the hell of it all, all over again. I was also uncomfortable with the fact that I wasn't as sharp as I would normally have been at that time of the year. I felt unprepared, and that had me on edge. The girls too had initially been cautious around me at training, with no one wanting to take me out a second time. However, once I got the first belt, and had my first fall, I knew I'd be OK.

Although I was back on the field, there was still a lot more work that I needed to do. People think that when the rehab is done you're good to go. But really you're only halfway there. I didn't want to be one of those players whose injury was the main topic of conversation.

'Oh, she's not the same player she used to be ...'

So, for my own peace of mind I worked extra hard to try to come back as a better version of myself.

Off the field, the County Board remained intact. I didn't want to tolerate them, but I had to. My focus was on football, so I just got on with it. At least things had been ironed out with the appointment of Michael Ryder as the Mayo coach at the end of February. He'd previously been the chairman of Corofin GAA Club in Galway, and he was a lovely man. He probably wasn't the most technical coach I ever had but we all had a goal to get back to Croke Park and win this time out.

In the middle of July, seven months after the first operation, I played my first full championship game for Mayo. It was against Sligo in the Connacht final, and it was nice to blow off the cobwebs. I felt fresh. The lay-off made me hungry again, and every time I got on the ball I did well. We finished up winning our fourth Connacht SFC title in seven years 3–15 to 0–9, and I was relieved to have bagged 2–8. It felt good, not only to be playing in MacHale Park again, but it was a relief to know my rhythm had come back.

In the All-Ireland semi-final we faced a resurgent Monaghan side. They hadn't been in a final for six years and they were doing well under John McAleer. Two weeks out from the game we suffered a blow when our captain Claire O'Hara tore her hamstring. It was the fourth time she'd torn it over the years, and each time she persisted in coming back. That mustn't have been easy. The easy option would have been to walk away, but Claire cared too much about Mayo to do that. Martha Carter started in midfield that day, and we shuffled a few people around, but we missed Claire in defence. The Ulster champions had a few up-and-coming players like the McAnespie twins, Ciara and Aoife, who were play-ing alongside veterans like Niamh Kindlon.

Again, we fell a fraction short of what was required. We led by a point at half-time in Páirc Tailteann in Navan, and I scored eight of our ten first-half points. They did a better job of smothering us in the second half and in fact dominated us completely, beating us by seven points in the end.

That was the story more often than not during the years when managers were rolling over every few months. We were always only a handful of points away from an All-Ireland or National League final. Once again we'd been in front at half-time and not been able to deliver. It was so frustrating. We had the players and the talent but, somehow, it failed to click when we needed it to. Mentally, I think the majority of us were strong. We had been there before; we knew what it took. But somehow, on the field, our game plan would fall apart. Back when we were winning we could make our own decisions and deliver, so maybe it just boiled down to poor decision-making on any given day. There's no one reason I can give you to explain it. Every year was different, but there's no denying that the turnover in managers and the politics off the field didn't do Mayo ladies football any favours.

At the beginning of the 2009 season we lost another manager. Michael Ryder was gone, though he was never officially informed of that fact. His departure had nothing to do with us, the players, but you'd think the decent thing for the County Board to have done would be to inform the manager of the senior county team that his services were no longer required. Michael had wanted to stay but the powers-that-be once again sabotaged it all. He rang several County Board officials to see where he stood at the start of

2009 but apparently none of his phone calls were returned. He had no choice then but to ring some of the players to see if we knew anything. Could you imagine that? We didn't know anything about it because our interactions with the Board were obviously limited, so we couldn't help him. He was treated disgracefully and you wouldn't blame him for walking off into the sunset. Why would he bother dealing with that kind of carry-on? So, just like that, Michael Ryder was another one struck off the list.

Once again, despite our not having had anything to do with the decision, the story doing the rounds was that the players had gotten rid of another manager. That perception hung over a certain group of players for years, if not decades.

In January 2009 Kevin Reidy from Galway replaced Michael. Kevin had worked with a number of men's clubs, and on a professional level we had a good working relationship. In fact I'd put him up there with Finbar and Frank when it came to player management. He was strict, but fair. He came in with no baggage or hidden agenda so he quickly settled. Kevin always wanted the best for us. In previous years the players had been the ones pushing for higher standards of professionalism, but he took that on when he arrived, which was a welcome change. This time we could just turn up and play, and enjoy knowing that we had prepared well. If you were one of the girls close to breaking on to the starting fifteen, Kevin gave you a chance to prove yourself too. That created a settled team, as everyone knew that they would get a fair chance. The team always came first for Kevin, and we respected him for that.

He reminded me a small bit of Cork's Eamonn Ryan, and that year they came up against each other on the sideline during the Division 1 National League final. As per the recent pattern, Cork once again got the better of us. Three months later we drew them again in the All-Ireland semi-final, and we felt we were in a much better place to have a second crack at them. Emma Mullin scored a point in the first minute, and we thought we were settled. But then Player of the Match Briege Corkery came from wing-back to bang over two excellent points and put the momentum back with Cork. We only managed to score one other point in the first half and trailed by six at the break. The sin-binning of Smiley didn't help, but we had a right go in the second half. Cork scored 1–3 on the trot, but I answered with 1–2 to keep in touch. Corkery popped up again in the last minute for a goal and with that they would go on to bid for their fifth successive All-Ireland title. It was the fourth time in five years that Cork had dumped us out of the championship. Once again we were so close, yet so far.

Off the field at this time, my experiences were, thankfully, more rewarding. I started working with the Mayo Travellers Support Group in April 2009. I had completed my Masters in Health Promotion in NUI Galway and this involved work experience with the health promotion unit in Castlebar. So when a health coordinator role opened up, I jumped at it. Apart from loving what I did, there was no mention of football, so I was able to get away from it all and just be myself. I could head into work on the week of a final and there wouldn't be a peep out of anyone about the match. It was bliss. Some of my teammates who worked in banks or in schools had to withstand the barrage of questions that go with the hype of a big game in Mayo, but thankfully I could escape all that. If we won a match they didn't talk about it, and if we lost a match they didn't talk about it. And that suited me perfectly.

My job involves promoting health and wellness among the Travelling community and I'd like to think that we make a real difference to people's lives. Traveller men live fourteen years less than settled men. Traveller women live eleven years less than settled women. It's my job to improve those stats through education and training. There are nearly 400 Traveller families in Mayo, and I've been lucky enough to work with a number of women who we've trained on subjects like cancer screening, breast checks, cervical checks, heart disease, diabetes, mental health issues, obesity and so on. The course was a part-time, four-year FETAC training course funded by the Health Service Executive and if the participants passed, they were employed as community health workers to educate their peers on those very health issues. For me, being a part of that process was hugely rewarding.

As in any community, there are a wide number of issues to be tackled and I count myself lucky to have been part of something that really made a difference to other people's lives. I can't speak highly enough of everyone I've worked with there in the last decade. I taught them but they also taught me. At times, the women amazed me. There could be so many things going on in other areas of their lives yet they kept it together so well. If it was me, I'd have unravelled a long time ago.

Over the years I've seen the discrimination these women and their families have had to put up with and it really makes me mad. I honestly don't know how they handle it. There've been numerous times when I've met some of the Traveller women from the course in town and stopped to have a quick chat. I would feel the eyes burning into the back of my head. I knew people were looking, and I knew what they were thinking. *What is she doing talking to them?* That type of discrimination is a daily occurrence.

As a society, we paint every Traveller with the same brush, and that's difficult for me to wrap my head around. If a member of their community is barred from a premises, they're all barred. That's unfair. In any community there's good and bad so there's no excuse for the everyday discrimination they experience. Since 2009 I have worked with some of the nicest and most caring people out there, but I consider myself lucky not to be in their shoes when I see what they have to endure. Every day they teach me something new about life, and while it took some time to trust each other, we got there. I hope that some day all of us will be able to do the same thing. At the very least, giving them some respect as fellow human beings who are part of our society would be a good place to start.

11

Rock Bottom

IT WAS THE COLDEST JANUARY IN TWENTY-FIVE YEARS. TEMPERATURES reached as low as minus 11°C across the border in Sligo, but we were still happy to wrap up and get back to pre-season training. We had kept ourselves in good nick over the winter, bar a few nights out in Rocky Moran's Bar in Castlebar, and we were ready to go again in 2010. Things had gone well in Kevin Reidy's first year. We'd reached a National League final and an All-Ireland semi-final, losing to the reigning champions both times, so we were getting there.

By this stage of my career I had won four All-Irelands with Mayo (1999, 2000, 2002, 2003) and lost two (2001, 2007). I had also won three Division 1 National League titles (2000, 2004, 2007) and lost two (2002, 2009). But the most exciting thing for me now was the fact that for the first time in five years we would have the same coach for two years running. If we could get things consistent again off the pitch then we'd surely become more consistent on it.

However, that's not how it worked out. Kevin returned, but he only stayed for two training sessions. Suddenly he did a U-turn and was gone. We still don't know why. We pleaded with him to stay for the sake of continuity, but his mind was firmly made up. He never told us his reasons for going, but we could only presume that something had happened between him and the County Board. He was so professional that he never once involved us in the politics.

We still talk today, and Kevin has the height of respect for us. He figured out early on how driven we were, and even though we suspected that he had been given a remit from the County Board to get rid of the so-called troublemakers, he saw that we were actually the most hard-working out of the lot. Our drive is what drove everyone else. We did anything that we were told would make us better players, and a better team. We were the first ones to arrive at training and the last ones out the gate, and coaches like Kevin and Michael Ryder saw that. Behind closed doors, the truth was that the 'troublemakers' were the ones setting the standards, and that made it difficult to chuck us on to the scrap heap.

His departure now meant that Mayo football was back to square one. Our relationship with the County Board remained tense, but we swallowed our pride. We were tired of all the arguing, animosity and drama. Every club in the county was sick too of the senior team topping every agenda. We wanted to move Mayo football forward, once and for all. So when Crazy, myself and Martha Carter were asked to be player representatives and to meet with three members of the Board in the McWilliam Park Hotel in Claremorris that January, we willingly did so.

It was awkward, but it was civil. Even after all that had gone on I just wanted to get back to the top, and to get a manager who would take hold of the reins and get us there. If that meant working with people who had previously put obstacles in our way, then so be it. We talked about how the County Board might go about finding a new manager and who would be the best fit. We wanted a bit of thought to go into it. In the past there had been instances when people were given the job just to tick a box, and that's really where the trouble began in the first place. We expected better. This time out we needed the right person to get the job. Frank Browne had been that person, but he wasn't given a second chance. Kevin Reidy had been that person too, only he left. So if it took an extra few weeks to speak to more candidates, then so be it. It had to be done the right way, and the wait would be worth it.

The meeting lasted two hours, and by the end of it we had agreed on roughly twenty names, including people like James Horan, Noel Connelly and Pat Holmes, all former managers of the Mayo men's football team. It was hard to believe that we'd ever be lucky enough to get someone of their calibre but we had to aim for the best if we wanted Mayo ladies football to get back to its winning ways.

When we left the McWilliam Park Hotel that night I felt we had made progress. We had cleaned the slate and moved on. But within a day we got word that the County Board had appointed their new man. It was unexpected to say the least. My first thought was, *That was pretty fast.* My second had me wondering who the hell on the list had said yes.

No one on that initial agreed list had said yes. Instead, Pat Costello, a former manager with the Galway ladies senior team, was appointed. At that time he was managing the Mayo ladies U14 team, and while the player representatives didn't expect to be consulted on the final decision, at the very least we expected the Board to pick someone from among the candidates we had compiled together. Costello's name was never mentioned during the two-hour meeting, by either side, only in a brief phone call afterwards from Caroline Brogan to Martha Carter. We were long gone from the room when the call came through, but it all made sense in the following days. They never intended to consult our list. I'm guessing that the Board knew they were going to appoint Costello before our meeting even took place. Again, the players' opinions seemed to count for nothing. Again, we were willing to work with the Board but all they were doing was taking the easy option.

Despite our disappointment at being overlooked once more, and despite the fact that Pat had previously had a poor stint with the Galway ladies, we were still willing to give him a chance. He could have been the right fit for all we knew, so at the very least we'd try to find out. Our first session took place in Mayo Abbey at the end of January 2010. Only six of us turned up – myself, Crazy, Martha Carter, Marie Corbett, Aine Clarke and Aileen Gilroy. It wasn't exactly a good sign of what was to come. The pitch was frozen, and when we got there Pat was putting cones out on the 45 wearing a short-sleeved Mayo jersey. How the man didn't get hypothermia that night I do not know. It was madness.

We got out of the car, did the session in sub-zero temperatures, and didn't complain once because we were so hell-bent on trying to make things work. Those of us who bothered to show up that night were then landed with the task of having to ring round and beg other players to come back. For some the years of inconsistency had taken its toll, and that summer a lot of the younger players decided to opt for a J1 instead of football.

To be fair to Pat, he was committed. On the downside, he didn't have much support. He had two selectors, Agnes McDonagh and

Therese Connolly, but it was Pat who set up all the sessions, took the training, the warm-up and the cool-down, and it very much slowed the whole process down. The experience and depth of the backroom team just wasn't there. Players want training to be snappy, but it was hard for Pat to deliver on that because of the lack of support. At that time, backroom teams in ladies football were beginning to evolve, and other counties had staff coming out their ears. We didn't have anything like the same level of resources.

We had a poor National League campaign, and in order for us to claim a play-off spot we had to beat Cork. Instead, they hammered us by nineteen points out in Ballinrobe, which made it even more embarrassing. For some reason Pat didn't play Claire Egan that day. I reckon it was a personality clash. That annoyed me. It annoyed a few of us. Claire was our most physical player, and it didn't make sense to have her sitting on the bench. In saying that, even if Smiley had had the game of her life that day, I don't think it would have made much of a difference. We were miles off the mark.

It was now March, and we were three months out from championship. There was no captain or vice-captain yet appointed for the season, so the previous year's captain, Martha Carter, and a few of the older players decided that there should be a players' meeting. We needed to see how we could improve the set-up because we knew we were on the road to nowhere. We told Pat, Agnes and Therese that the players had organized a meeting in Castlebar Rugby Club because we wanted to be as transparent as possible with them in order to come up with the right solution. We were conscious of wanting to do the right thing so we told them that we wanted to see how we could improve ourselves as a group, and then fill them in after on exactly what came out in the wash.

We still wanted Pat to coach us, and if we could tweak a few things among ourselves, and management, then we had a good chance of getting back on track.

We made our way to the dressing rooms and parked ourselves on the benches in a semi-circle. Someone borrowed a flipchart from work, and on its large sheets we started to brainstorm. We needed a list of things that we as players had to work on, as well as a list of things management could improve. For forty-five minutes we called each other out, and by the end of it we had twenty items listed on the page. Seventeen of them related to us, the players, the other three related to management. That wasn't easy, but we knew it had to be done. It was probably the frankest meeting we'd had with each other in years, and it felt good. There was no point in hiding and letting things fester any more. If we didn't do anything about it now, it would be too late.

On the management page, the three items had one common theme: Pat needed to get some help in. We could see he was doing the bulk of the work when it came to training, and we appreciated the effort, but in many ways it detracted from the quality of the sessions. If Pat could bring in one or two others to take care of the logistics of the set-up then he'd have more time to coach. After the meeting, Crazy, Fiona McHale and Lisa Cafferkey met with Pat to tell him what the girls had come up with. He seemed happy to take everything that was said on board. I didn't doubt for a second that we had done the right thing. We had approached it professionally, we were open and honest, and if each of us could improve by a fraction then we'd be in with a shout.

The following Sunday we trained on the small pitch at the back of Breaffy House Hotel, on the outskirts of Castlebar. The session went well, and afterwards Pat organized a team meeting in the warmth of the hotel. We presumed it was a follow-up to the players' meeting forty-eight hours earlier, and that management and players were going to discuss how we'd put things in place before championship.

We filed down the corridor and into a small conference room. Pat, Agnes and Therese were already seated on a podium of sorts when we arrived. Pat stood up to speak. For the next fifteen minutes he proceeded to defend himself and have a go at the team, especially the older players.

We were stunned. We had thought that the previous meeting with Pat had gone well but he'd obviously had a change of heart. At the end of the sermon he announced that he was stepping down. He felt he was being undermined by the players – and with that, he walked out the door. If he'd had a microphone, I'd say he'd have dropped it.

Agnes and Therese followed him, and we were left staring at each other in stunned silence. We couldn't believe what had just happened. We thought we were taking a positive step as a group – management included – but it turned out to be anything but.

We were about eight weeks out from championship, and we knew how we would be portrayed all over again. Troublemakers.

In Mayo it was mostly pinned on Crazy, because she had been one of the messengers. In the national media the 'older players' were blamed, with slogans of 'player power' filling the sports pages. In reality, nobody should have been singled out. What started out as a team meeting halfway through the season had turned into a total mess. We hadn't wanted to get rid of Pat, we had just wanted to improve things. He was our seventh manager in six years, and yet again everything was falling apart.

Over the next six weeks, tensions between the Board and the players worsened. The Board asked Pat to reconsider his decision, but on 16 May he confirmed he wouldn't be returning. What happened ten days later was the worst night in the history of Mayo ladies football. At a specially convened meeting of the County Board, club delegates voted to pull their own senior intercounty team out of the championship. The motion was passed.

I couldn't believe it. What did they think that would fix? There were other ways it could have been resolved, but this was now another controversy Mayo didn't need. I have a theory that the real reason they pulled us out was to get rid of the group of 'troublemakers' once and for all. We had genuinely tried to work with them, but it seemed now that the relationship was beyond repair. Two days later the Connacht Council received an email stating that Mayo would not be fielding a team in the 2010 championship, and the following Monday the County Board released this statement to the media:

The Mayo Ladies County Board wish to explain the circumstances which have led to our senior team being withdrawn from this year's championship.

At a meeting with the executive committee of the Mayo Ladies County Board on 19 April, Pat Costello tendered his resignation as manager of the Mayo ladies senior football team, stating that his position was no longer tenable due to him being constantly undermined by certain players within the panel.

He had explained his decision to the panel on the day before.

The matter was discussed at length at a full County Board meeting on 28 April. At this meeting, the club delegates voted

151

by forty-seven votes to two for Pat Costello to be asked to re-consider his position, and remove any players from the panel that he felt were undermining the progress of the team as a whole.

He replied on 16 May to inform us that he would not be returning to the post. This reply was read out at a specially convened meeting of the Mayo Ladies County Board on Thursday, 20 May.

The club delegates then proposed and passed a motion by twenty-six votes to five that we withdraw from this year's championship in order to deal with this problem properly in the long-term interest of ladies football.

Last year's captain and vice-captain were kept informed of progress at each stage of this whole procedure.

We hope that this statement clarifies the facts in connection with our withdrawal from championship. We are currently looking into the problems which have led to this unfortunate situation, along with other matters raised by delegates during these meetings.

In the long-term interest of ladies football? How the hell was it in the long-term interest of ladies football? What about all the people who were doing their best to get young girls in their area to take up the game? Or the parents who were driving their little ones to training every week? How was it in *their* interest?

There wasn't a chance in hell that I was going to quit. It was difficult to be slated like that, and there were tears. But I was never, ever going to let them get the better of me, or us. We were the people who cared about Mayo football the most. When this whole thing started, we just wanted a way forward, but it had turned into an absolute circus.

News filtered out across the country, and we knew it would be blamed on the players. Why wasn't anyone asking questions of the County Board? Where was their accountability in all of this? Why had Mayo football come to this? No one mentioned the poor job they had done since they came in and how this might have caused the problems in the first place. As well as the issues with senior management, they had no structures in place. There was no development plan, and they were more than content to have our underage teams compete in B championships when they should have been competing in the A2 championship which they were perfectly capable of doing. That's not Mayo football.

There was no foresight, and there was no strategy when it came to appointing managers. The same year, the minor manager was put in a week before championship. It wasn't remotely good enough. Players were always the scapegoats. Any time the Board let someone go, or someone walked, we were the ones who got the blame. It was so much easier for them to pin it on us rather than on themselves.

Three clubs knew otherwise. Club delegates from Castlebar and Knockmore joined Beatrice Casey of Carnacon and they spent hours tearing the rulebook apart to see if there was a solution to be found. And, there it was.

'County Boards must send forward a team for Inter-County Adult Championships. Failure to do so may result in the entire County being suspended for 12 months.'

The *entire county*. The 26–5 vote in the long-term interest of ladies football had now backfired. This would have a massive impact on club and county players of all ages and would undo all the good work that had gone into building up player numbers in their areas. Carnacon, Castlebar and Knockmore knew better than to let that happen. They came together and entered an appeal to Central Council based on the fact that every club would also be suspended for twelve months should Mayo be pulled out of the championship.

Delegates from the three clubs and the players' representatives – myself, Crazy and Triona McNicholas of Moy Davitts – travelled to a Central Council committee meeting in Tullamore that summer, and we all had our say. They listened. And finally, in the real long-term interest of ladies football, they voted overwhelmingly in favour of Mayo re-entering the championship. The situation didn't show ladies football in a good light, and the LGFA knew it. Theirs was now the fastest-growing sport in the country and they wanted things to stay that way.

The following night, the players trained without a coach in Foxford. For the next week we rang GAA, rugby and soccer clubs to find any sort of pitch to keep us ticking over. Attendance was sporadic but we kept going, even though realistically the year was a write-off. Kerry waited for us in the All-Ireland qualifier on the August bank holiday weekend and we were in no shape for it, but we gritted our teeth because we had to stick this thing out.

In the meantime, an official for the LGFA tasked to appoint a new manager rang Father Mike Murphy, a parish priest in Roundfort. They wanted to know if he'd take the job. They had deemed him 'acceptable', and Father Mike being the man that he is didn't want to let us down, so he said yes. I knew Father Mike well because I had worked with him before, coaching St Joseph's of Castlebar to a Senior B All-Ireland Schools title. He always had ladies football's best interests at heart, and for a few weeks he took the burden off us and just allowed us to play again.

We lost to Kerry by a point, and yet again another disappointing season was over. Another season wasted. Even after weeks of upheaval we were good enough to come within a point of Kerry. Those days were frustrating. Yet again I could have walked away, but didn't.

Over the next few months I became the subject of scrutiny. An independent committee made up of Central Council and LGFA officials rode into town to investigate exactly why the 2010 scenario had come about, and why there had been such a high turnover in management in recent years. The committee were put up in the McWilliam Park Hotel in Claremorris, and for two days they interviewed all kinds of people involved in Mayo football, including several players. The older players were brought in first, then the younger ones, of which there were twenty or so.

Marie Corbett was one of the younger players there that day. She was asked if she felt intimidated by the older players and she answered 'yes', in the sense that she was new to the panel and of course felt intimidated by the enormity of the situation. No young player wouldn't be intimidated on the first day they walk into a senior intercounty dressing room. She also told the committee how extremely helpful the older girls were to her – the likes of myself, Claire O'Hara, and many more. A lot of people don't realize that I am quite a compassionate person. All they see is my on-pitch persona – the images of me giving out to players and giving orders. They don't see me giving younger girls lifts to training, advice when they're struggling and all the small things that go on behind the scenes.

Around the same time, a member of the County Board approached Marie after a match in Ballyheane and gave her some advice.

'For your own good, stay away from Cora,' she was told.

One of my best friends. That wasn't easy. It stung. Why was my integrity being singled out and questioned in all of this? It was awful.

The worst of it was that some members of that committee who questioned the younger players that day had no problem texting me a few months later to ask me to attend a medal presentation in their home club in another county. That episode taught me a lot. For a start, some people will stab you in the back. I've been on All-Star trips with some of these people since and they've told me to my face what a 'wonderful ambassador' I am for ladies football. Yet, all the while, in the back of my mind, I know what was being insinuated about me and the older players in that room in the McWilliam Park Hotel in 2010.

Ultimately, I had to trust in myself. I knew I was a good person. I knew my friends were good people. And I knew we had it in us to achieve so much more together. That's what kept me going, my stubbornness and my friends.

It would take a number of months for the committee's report to come through. On 17 December 2010 it arrived into Fiona McHale's inbox, even though the report itself was dated 8 September 2010.

Conclusions

Having taken submissions from many clubs, players, former players, club officials, parents, former managers and County Board officials, we conclude that Ladies Gaelic Football is in a healthy state in Mayo. All contributors were loud in their praise of the current County Board for their running of the affairs in the county. Club competitions and fixtures have improved immensely under the present administration. Underage county teams are also thriving which is borne out by their achievements this year. The major area of concern is with the senior county team. In saying this, everyone to whom we spoke was of the opinion that the Mayo ladies senior team can be successful and bring more honours to the county.

A number of reasons were put forward for the failure to hold on to managers over the years but the majority by far felt that the problem lay with a few of the more senior players who constantly tried to exercise control over the team. It was said that this should have been tackled some years ago, when one manager left, but it was let carry on and managers preferred to leave rather than rock the boat. This situation was exasperated by the poor procedures adopted by the County Board in the appointment of managers. The clubs attending County Board in the current year were fed up with senior team problems at County Board meetings and decided to deal with the matter and bring the issue to a head. This led to the withdrawal of the team from the championship. Practically all said the issue won't be resolved until a manager is appointed who will deal with the players involved, if needed, and that such a manager must receive the full backing of County Board.

Recommendations

1. A manager needs to be put in place as soon as possible and that this manager is given at least a two years' contract, subject to review after year one. It is recommended that Central Council or another independent body should assist the County Board in appointing a manager.
2. An agreed liaison officer must be appointed to keep all sides informed of ongoing developments.
3. A full back-up team including physio, coach and selectors must also be appointed. It is recommended that a selector be appointed from each geographical region in the county, i.e., north, south, east and west.
4. Managers, selectors, liaison officers etc. must have their roles and duties clearly defined.
5. The incoming management team, including physio and liaison officer, must attend a county mentor workshop organized by Central Council.
6. All sides must buy into the philosophy that:

    (a) Players play
    (b) Managers manage
    (c) County Board administers football affairs in the county

7. The incoming team management should set up dialogue with players who have withdrawn from the panel or who do not wish to join the panel because of the intimidation factor. These fears must be allayed and they should be reassured about their welcome to the squad.

8. A code of conduct should be drawn up by Central Council for all persons involved in Ladies Gaelic Football. This should be along the lines of the codes contained in the Code of Ethics.
9. We recommend the holding of a Club Officer programme in the county.
10. A Volunteer recruitment programme should be run.

Finally we would like to restate our thanks to all contributors for their submissions to us and we hope that our suggestions which have been made in the spirit of reconciliation will assist Mayo LGFA to move forward with all footballing activity within the county and we wish all members of the LGFA in Mayo continued success in the future.

Gerry Doherty, Geraldine Giles, Peter Rice
08/09/10

The entire episode was the lowest point in my career. The clubs had turned against us, and some quarters had specifically turned against me. The report was commissioned and conducted by members of the organization it was investigating; how could it be anything but biased? I knew what was right, and what was wrong. My skin was thick enough to handle the back-stabbers, but still, that didn't make it any easier. It did, however, make me tougher.

12

Never Surrender

NEVER SURRENDER, EVER. SOMETIMES, THINGS WILL GO AGAINST you. That's just life, but you have to keep going no matter what. Those turbulent years with Mayo were bloody well tough going. There was a menace behind them. But, even if it was the last thing I did, I vowed to make my career last longer than those on the County Board who had dragged Mayo football down.

A few years later, Therese Connolly, who had been on Pat Costello's management team, approached myself and Crazy while we were having a drink in Rocky's Bar in Castlebar. She apologized for how we were treated at the time and acknowledged that it was wrong. I won't lie, that apology was difficult to accept. If truth be told, it never did take away the hurt and injustice of what we went through, but it was a nice gesture and I appreciate it now. Those days should have been some of the best football years of our lives. I try not to dwell on it any more, but every now and again I wonder, *What if?* The most important thing was that despite everything we had been through, the team didn't fall apart.

Different players had opportunities to get away from it all. Some had the option to play in the United States and make a bit of cash.

In the summer of 2001 I had been offered $6,000, a job and free accommodation from one particular club in the States, just to play for a few weeks in the summer sun. It was an offer most students would have jumped at. I'm not downplaying the standard of football there, and I'm not saying I wouldn't have enjoyed it. I'm sure I would have. But it wasn't the kind of challenge I wanted. I wanted to make Mayo and Carnacon the best they could be – that's the challenge I was after. That's how I feel about most opportunities that come my way. I'll ask two questions: will it challenge me, and will it make me a better player?

And 2011 was certainly a challenging year. Under our new manager Jason Taniane, we lost all six Division 1 National League games. I'm not sure if that had ever happened to Mayo before, but I didn't care about the stats. It happened to us. Taniane, another former Galway manager, was one of six candidates who were interviewed for the job, and he came in without an agenda. He saw us for who we were and what we were trying to achieve and did his best. Jason was dead-on, but he didn't have much of a base to work with as we had lost a few players because of the drama of the year before.

Ourselves and Tyrone were now in a relegation battle. Despite the dismal league campaign we still had some hope that we could pull it off. At half-time we led by four points (2–5 to 1–4) and that sliver of hope widened. In the second half, Clodagh Poyntz missed a penalty for Tyrone, before Triona McNicholas scored a goal for us. Things were going all right when Tyrone forward Gemma Begley was sent to the sin-bin and I pointed to put us five points in front. Then, everything crumbled. Laura McCreesh hit a second goal to bring Tyrone back into it. Then Begley returned and struck a late goal to put them one in front before Poyntz pointed to secure the win (3–8 to 3–10). And, just like that, we were banished to Division 2 football.

Crazy was working with the Camogie Association at the time and had left their annual congress in Belfast to drive to Tyrone for the game. She was as committed to Mayo football as anyone, and when we sat back in her car after the game, she started to cry.

'How have we reached rock bottom, Cora?'

I sat there and didn't say a word. What was there to say? We just had to keep going.

We continued to train for championship, and somehow we managed to win the Connacht title against Galway that summer (5–11 to 2–15). Crazy was captain, and in her acceptance speech she made it known to everyone in Tuam Stadium how much hurt we had gone through in the previous few years.

'Generally, when you are with a county team you have to battle against other counties,' she said. 'Unfortunately, the last few years we've had to battle in our own county to be our best, to be champions and to get back to the top. For those people who tried to keep us down, today is the day for these girls who kept on battling.

'This win is as sweet as any. This group of players has been damned and put down for wanting to be the best, for wanting to achieve and for being willing to work hard, but this year we've a management team that is willing to break down any barriers just to allow the players to express themselves and to let the team work hard. For us to come to Tuam Stadium, the home of Galway football, and to pull out a win is brilliant.'

We were happy with our lot. But we were brought back down to earth with a bang when Kerry beat us in the All-Ireland quarter-final by 3–11 to 0–10.

Thankfully, I've always had Carnacon to fall back on once the intercounty season has run its course. We won the county championship almost every year, and that made processing the losses with Mayo a little easier. This didn't help the girls from other clubs who didn't enjoy much success at club level. An injection of elation every now and then does wonders, so I realize how lucky I was to be part of such a successful club team. By 2011 it had been the best part of a decade since Mayo had won an All-Ireland title, yet every winter those players had started again, burying themselves in the mud and the cold. They kept the show on the road for Mayo during those barren years, and they never did get the credit they deserved.

In 2012, Jason Taniane moved on. He had been given a two-year term, but no one expected him to stay on once we had been relegated. Instead, Father Mike returned alongside Carnacon's Jimmy Corbett, and a new County Board was also appointed. And, even though we were down a division, things started to look up. For the first time in a long time everyone was rowing in the same direction. The new County Board began to focus on improving the underage structure. They put the right people in charge with the aim of re-suscitating Mayo, and it worked. We needed a revival of our own, and winning the Division 2 title would be a start.

From January to May, it was the only thing on all our minds. We were fixated on winning, and redemption. We knew we weren't playing the best senior teams out there, but that didn't bother us. We were just hell-bent on getting Mayo back to the top that we prepared for each game as if it was championship. We had new blood with the likes of seventeen-year-old Niamh Kelly, Aimee Bell and Deirdre Doherty, and when we reached the Division 2 final against our old rivals, Galway, it was an added incentive to get the win. We played out of our skins that day in Parnell Park, winning 4–17 to 2–7.

We were just so hungry to get back on top. Where we belonged.

I first met Peter Clarke in a coffee shop in Claremorris in January 2013. The Mayo County Board had contacted him to see if he was interested, and he'd wanted to get a sense of who he'd be working with. So, he drove two and a half hours from Dublin to meet me, and his willingness to understand what we were about impressed me. A good manager will do that. He'll take the time to get a sense of who he's got, and what it is that makes them tick. Coaching is a huge commitment. I've done it myself, so anyone with a bit of cop-on will do their homework. Otherwise, you won't get anywhere.

Father Mike and Jimmy stepped down at the start of 2013 because they had done what they had set out to do. So, when Clarke joined the transfer market that January, the Mayo County Board moved quickly. He stayed with us for two years, and having the same coach for two seasons was massive for us. In fact, it was the first time in almost a decade that we would have the same coach for back-to-back seasons. That stat is outrageous when you think about it, but at least from where we were things could only improve.

Peter came in with a full backroom team including a goalkeeping coach, a physio and a liaison officer, and with that came a lot of the basic standards that we had been asking for. We now had consistency in how we approached things; how we prepared, how we played, and how we strategized. It was so much easier for players to buy into the process. Everything was clear. There was a plan. And with every month that passed, that cohesion improved us. Consistency builds morale, and we were playing with confidence again.

In just twelve months we worked our way back into a Division 1 National League final. That's as good a measure as any of how much we had improved in a year. We beat Monaghan in the semi-final and I scored all of Mayo's tally in Ballinamore that day. But, it wasn't just me. Fiona McHale, Aileen Gilroy and Sarah Rowe had great games and they were all starting to make a name for themselves. In the end, Cork got the better of us in Parnell Park, beating us by seven points. It was their seventh National League title in nine years, and it would be the second such final we lost to Eamonn Ryan's side (2009, 2013).

That August we would suffer another disappointment, losing the 2013 All-Ireland quarter-final by a point to Kerry at St Brendan's Park in Birr. The pundits had us as outsiders, yet with ten minutes to go we were in front by two points. Then Louise Ni Mhuircheartaigh, substitute Margaret Fitzgerald and soon-to-be Irish rugby sevens star Louise Galvin all popped over points to snatch the win from us. I was so disappointed. We thought we had come much further, but obviously not. The only consolation was knowing that Peter Clarke would stay with us for 2014. We now had a stability that had been missing in recent years. Personally, that totally re-energized me. So, for the first time in a long time, I made sure to enjoy the off-season. I lived a little.

My cousin Caroline is the person who first got me into playing rugby. She lived across the field from us when I was growing up, but while I was busy soloing footballs up and down the garden,

Caroline never showed any interest. However, as she got older, she discovered rugby, and fell in love with that instead.

During the 2013 off-season Caroline asked me to play with Castlebar RFC. It only took me a few days to say yes. It was a new sport, a new challenge, and a new adrenalin hit. I managed to sweet-talk Crazy into playing too but we didn't tell a soul because we knew someone would try to put a stop to it somewhere. For a start, I was still playing with Carnacon in the Connacht Club Championship, and I didn't think it would go down well if Beatrice and Jimmy found out. To be fair, when they eventually did, they never pulled me on it. I'm sure they were annoyed, but they knew better than most that when my mind is made up, it's made up.

Our first rugby game was on the same weekend that about fifteen of us on the Mayo panel planned to go to Kilkenny for a weekend break. Road-tripping was something we did randomly. We'd pick a spot on the map, book a place to stay, and head away for a night or two. It was an escape, and a chance to enjoy each other's company outside the football bubble.

None of the football girls knew that on the Sunday myself and Crazy had to be in Longford at 12 noon for our rugby debuts. But we had to confide in Marie. She was travelling in the car with us so she would have to be an accomplice for our getaway. She promised to keep our secret but warned us not to get injured. Marie is Jimmy Corbett's daughter, so like her father, she's as loyal as they come. We first met through playing football together with Carnacon, and although there's a few years between us, it feels like we've been friends for ever. I'd trust her with my life, and if I asked her to take something to the grave with her, she would.

It wasn't the best idea to go on the lash, but we couldn't blow our cover. The following morning we were ropey enough, but I had promised Caroline we'd be there. At 9 a.m. we surfaced and pointed the car in the direction of Longford. It was a bitterly cold October afternoon, but that didn't bother me. I was intrigued. With twenty minutes to go, the coach called myself and Crazy. I didn't mind playing at 15, but if I had a choice, I'd play at number 10. It was a position I always took note of when watching Ronan O'Gara, and it's a pity that the big pair of football boots he gave me on the set of the Lucozade advert all those years earlier weren't put to better use.

I had played rugby only once before, when the women's rugby team in Athlone IT were stuck for numbers. This felt just as strange as it did back then. I had to adjust to the pace, the tactics and the angle of the runs, but after the initial shock I got used to it. It was easy enough to adapt. I didn't mind the physicality, and I enjoyed getting myself into gaps any chance I had. I got a thrill from avoiding defenders and getting into space. I got a kick out of the technical aspect too, but the training drove me batty. The coach was good, don't get me wrong, but you wouldn't exactly be getting fit from a training session. It was a different kind of fitness. Many a night, myself and Crazy would do a few Up and Downs after the session just to keep ourselves ticking over. I was lucky to be training away with Carnacon, but Crazy needed something extra, so that's what we did.

That winter we won the 2013 Connacht Rugby League, and I was delighted for Caroline and the girls. They put everything into it, and I enjoyed being part of the season. The following July I was invited to a training session with the provincial Connacht team. I didn't know anyone there, but something didn't sit right with me. I got the impression that the other players didn't want me there. Maybe I read too much into it and just felt isolated, but that was the feeling I had at the time. I felt that they were put off by me being there. This was their sport, and who was I coming in from nowhere, being asked to try out for Connacht? I threw myself into the session regardless. In fact I went at it harder than I normally would. I wanted to prove a point and justify why I deserved to be there. But my eagerness led to a collision with a winger and a broken nose. And, that was that. I figured it was a sign to give up rugby, so I did.

I was glad I took it up, and I enjoyed the experience while it lasted. I think breaking my nose was a reality check as I realized that I couldn't take any risks. Mayo football was making inroads again, so I made the call. Funnily enough, shortly after I packed it in, two members of the Irish rugby sevens management team asked to meet me in Castlebar. The Irish Rugby Football Union's sevens programme was only in its infancy, and I was told that if I was good enough, I'd make the team.

Deep down, I wasn't interested, but I went to a few sessions out of curiosity. I had just taken up the game so it was flattering to have been approached, but I was more intrigued to see how they did things, and if there was something we could implement in the Mayo set-up. These guys were setting the bar for women's sport in Ireland. But for one reason or another it didn't draw me in enough to want to make the swap. I also had a mortgage to pay, and the cost of living in Dublin wouldn't have allowed me to cover my repayments, so that reality put a halt to things fairly fast. Besides, I'd been involved in football for too long to just turn my back on it. So, I thanked them and walked away.

At the time, the IRFU's recruitment of ladies footballers ruffled a few feathers, but it made total sense to me. We had some of the required skill set already, and the opportunity to train like a professional and travel the world was a big selling point. Unfortunately, things haven't panned out so well for women's rugby in the last year or so. It appears that the sevens set-up was prioritized, and that might have been to the detriment of the fifteens. They too had their own struggles, fighting for higher standards during the 2017 Women's Rugby World Cup, and I can certainly empathize with that.

The GAA could probably learn a lot from the IRFU, if they ever went down the semi-professional route. But personally, I completely disagree with ever turning the GAA professional. There would only be a handful of elite players, and that would totally destroy the love of the GAA, which is what the amateur game is all about. It would become all about money and transfer markets. And, you have to ask yourself, why do we play Gaelic games in the first place? We play it because we love it. The GAA is all about passion. It's about where you come from. It's about representing your club and your family. It's about making your mark. 'I'm from Mayo,' and that's it. I couldn't play with another county.

But, let's assume the GAA did go professional. How would a county manager decide on his or her twenty-six players for match day? Who gets what financially? What about the players who are close to breaking into the thirty? What are they valued at? Do the likes of high-profile players such as Aidan O'Shea get more money than a less high-profile player like, let's say, Jason Doherty, who's a talented player in his own right? Is Aidan worth more than Brendan Harrison? And, would they still pick the likes of experienced veterans such as Alan Dillon and Andy Moran? I just don't know. You'd create so many divides and lose too many players. You'd also lose the connection we have with each other, and that connection is the very thing that's at the heart of the GAA.

Following my winter of rugby, in March 2014 I got to enjoy the LGFA All-Star Tour to Hong Kong. Walking through the doors of the Grand Hyatt Hotel where we were staying was like walking on to a movie set. From the décor to the two-storey wine cellar and skyscraper skyline overlooking Victoria Harbour, the luxury of it all was a whole other world, far removed from the muddy pitches we mangled over the winter months back in Ireland.

There were eighty of us in total on the tour – forty players, and forty of the LGFA's top officials and entourage – and I couldn't help but smell the money behind it all. Everything was the best. The fanciest. I couldn't shake off the feeling of guilt.

Who paid for all of this? Was it really all that necessary?

As All-Star winners, we were the ones in a privileged position. I appreciated that, I really did. But at the same time I wondered how much this nine-day tour had cost. Could the money have been spent in a better way? In a way that would have benefited the entire sport rather than just the select few? Could savings have been made and pumped into the LGFA's Injury Fund, a school's programme, or even a scheme to encourage retired intercounty players to give back to the sport?

I know that if it wasn't for ladies football I wouldn't have travelled to places like Singapore, Hong Kong, San Diego and San Francisco, and I did always appreciate it. That said, it was hard to wrap my head around the scale of sending eighty people across the globe to stay in a five-star hotel. I won't lie, though; the guilt subsided when we hit the hotel's champagne bar. Double standards, I know. But, while I was there, I was going to make the most of it. We all were.

After enjoying the first night out, a gang of us returned to the Hyatt at 7 a.m. and headed straight to breakfast. Then we grabbed an hour or two of sleep, because at 11 a.m. we were due back downstairs to catch the bus to Hong Kong Football Club for a training session. Unfortunately, a handful of players slept it in and delayed everything. The plan was to have training ahead of the All-Star Exhibition game on St Patrick's Day, but Paddy's Day had come early for the majority of us. We sensed we were in for a telling-off, and sure enough we got one. We were told that we couldn't be wandering around a five-star hotel at all hours of the morning; that we were there to represent our counties, and from then on they would be keeping a close eye on us.

The following night we were all at it again, but this time I had to be home early. I was due to be at a local television studio at 6 a.m. and I was under strict instructions to be in the lobby at 5.30 to be ready for the driver. It was a live broadcast, so under no circumstances could I be late. I partied later into the night than I had planned but I somehow still managed to get two hours' sleep before the alarm went off. Crazy was conked on the bed opposite me so I tiptoed my way into the bathroom to get myself looking somewhat respectable.

The second I opened the door, my feet felt suddenly cold, and wet. The floor was covered in water. I grabbed some towels and scattered them on to the marble slabs to soak up what they could.

Then I inspected the toilet. It didn't look like the water was coming from the base, so I removed the cistern cover to take a closer look. When I did, a jet of water shot across the room.

'Crazy!' I shouted. 'The place is flooding! Get up!'

I grabbed a second towel and quickly wrapped it around the pipe to stop the water spurting all over the place.

'Craaaaaaaaaaazy, the bathroom's flooding!'

Poor Crazy had only had half an hour's sleep, but as with any good goalkeeper, her reaction time was impressive.

'What the hell, Cora?' she gasped, standing in the doorway.

The water was starting to soak the carpet in the hallway. We were in a right state. If it kept going, it would flood Helen O'Rourke's room next door. O'Rourke was the CEO of the LGFA, and we were going to ruin this posh hotel on her. What terrified me just as much was the prospect of being late getting down to the lobby. I scrambled out the door, over the bed, and dialled reception to ask them to send help immediately. We were under serious pressure as the water was nearing the hallway, but I had to go.

'Crazy, I've to leave you. Sorry, but I'll be murdered if I'm not downstairs in the next two minutes!'

I knew she'd get the situation under control because that's what she does best, and in a flash I was gone. As I sprinted down the corridor there was a fella coming towards me at the same speed, carrying a mountain of towels.

'Room 514!' I shouted.

'Yes, yes! I help!'

Thankfully, they got it under control before it reached Helen's room.

My relationship with Helen and the LGFA is difficult to describe. To be honest, I never thought they liked me. Or at least that's what I presumed. I don't know if that stemmed from the jersey row, but we always appeared to be a thorn in their side. I knew at times it suited the LGFA to have me as one of their ambassadors, and then at other times not. So I suppose I was wary of the relationship because of that. There were always two sides to the LGFA: the side that needed you for something, and the side that did away with you if you didn't fit the bill at a given moment in time. The Association knew I could see through that, so my history with them is pretty chequered to say the least.

I spoke my mind too, and I didn't hide. I'm sure there were plenty of times over the years when officials cringed while listening to a radio or television interview with me, waiting to see if I toed the party line. But, what you see is what you get. I've always spoken my mind, and sometimes that didn't exactly make me flavour of the month.

In recent years we have seemed to find some common ground. Then again, maybe I just matured. I can't deny just how much ladies football has given me. It gave me an escape when Mam died. It gave me a way of life, a way of living. And it gave me brilliant friends. Since I learned how to solo an O'Neills football, the sport has come on leaps and bounds, but there's always more that can be done.

For one, I would love to see injured players being looked after better. The processes around the Injury Fund in terms of payment and public versus private treatment etc. could be a lot smoother for players. I've had first-hand experience of the LGFA process, and when I broke my nose playing rugby I discovered that the IRFU process is much more streamlined and player-friendly. That's my concern. If other sports are looking after their players better, then there's a good chance that ladies football could lose theirs. I really hope that doesn't become the case, but now is the time to really push for improved facilities for players and management as well as effective support structures across all levels of the sport. If we don't, then ladies football could very well be in trouble in years to come.

13

Doubt

AFTER TWO YEARS AT THE HELM, PETER CLARKE MOVED ON. HE had got us to the 2014 All-Ireland quarter-final, and just take a guess at who beat us. Cork. By nine points in Tullamore. It was the fourth successive quarter-final we had lost, and Peter probably felt he had taken us as far as we could go. So it was a brave move by Frank Browne to return to Mayo in 2015, given that the previous County Board had shafted him just a few years earlier.

Luckily, Frank isn't the type of man to hold grudges. He knew us as players, and as people, and that's all that mattered in his decision to come back. All he wanted was to help us win another All-Ireland title. But a lot had changed in seven years. Personnel had for a start. Nuala O'Shea, the Heffernans, Claire O'Hara and Diane O'Hora had all retired, and players like Fiona Doherty, Sarah Tierney, Rachel Kearns, Marie Corbett and sisters Grace and Niamh Kelly had all joined the panel. The game itself had changed too. Gym work, recovery, statisticians, dieticians, strength and conditioning etc. had all become key components of the game. But Frank had moved with the times.

Together, we spent the year re-laying foundations and nurturing new talent. I could tell that the likes of the players I've just mentioned had what it took. If we could get them to buy into everything then that would be half the battle. And they did. Not only did they listen, but they put in the effort, and you could see that.

In the Connacht SFC final against Galway I put over 1–15, but it was a point by Patricia Gleeson in the final two minutes that gave Galway their fourth successive provincial title with a final score of 0–21 to 1–17. It stung. After that I needed to get back on to the pitch as soon as possible, and the following week in a club league game I scored 9–12 in a 15–19 to 1–5 win over Westport. I needed to let off some steam after the Galway match and I suppose that was the best way to do it.

In the qualifiers in August we beat Tyrone to get us back into an All-Ireland quarter-final. It was our fifth in a row, but we fell at the same hurdle again. It was like Groundhog Day. It was the third time in five years that Kerry had beaten us, and I only managed two points from play. That August day in the Gaelic Grounds in Limerick was hard to stomach. We felt like we had made progress, but other teams had ramped up too. We had to find a way to bridge the gap.

In 2016, Frank added a few new faces to the backroom team, including an O'Connor Cup-winning coach in D. J. Collins of UL. DJ was tactically obsessed with every aspect of the game. He knew almost every opponent in the country too, their strengths and their weaknesses, and that really helped with our preparations. Frank also added a GAA-mad Galway woman called Aoife Lane, chairperson of the Women's Gaelic Players' Association (WGPA).

She was instrumental in setting up the Association in January 2015 and bringing equality for intercounty camogie players and ladies football.

It was a good backroom team, and we worked hard to get back to a Division 1 National League final in May. Only once again we faced the reigning league and All-Ireland champions Cork. They were bidding for a tenth league title in twelve years, and they did it too, beating us by a goal.

Three weeks later, management organized three days of training on Clare Island, at the entrance of Clew Bay. We were the first intercounty team to train on the island. There are only 145 inhabitants, so we made it home. If we weren't training then we were getting to know each other over cups of coffee, or relaxing on the beach watching the sun go down. That trip made us closer, and come the championship in July we were raring to go.

The new players had settled, and they were feeding off the older players' desire to get back to Croke Park. First, we won the Connacht SFC title against Galway in MacHale Park (3–20 to 0–14). Ten minutes into that game, Martha Carter broke her hand in three places. Yet she played on because she wanted to win so badly. It was madness, but that's character. I was happy with my own performance, scoring a total of 2–14, but what was more important was we were fine-tuning our rhythm.

The day after the Connacht final, we enjoyed ourselves. I always preferred the day after a big game over the night of one. I'd take a quiet pub over a nightclub any day of the week because you can really analyse the game together. At midday a text had come through on our Mayo WhatsApp group from Father Stephen Farragher.

Anyone going for a pint in Ballyhaunis this morning?

Frank had brought Father Stephen into the set-up and he was mainly there in the background, taking photographs and saying the odd prayer. He's a complete character, so we all pounced. Myself, Crazy, Marie Corbett, Doireann Hughes, Martha Carter, Aoife Lane, Frank and the local Guard all ended up in Gill's pub in Ballyhaunis. In the last few years I've made sure to savour moments like these. You know the end is coming, so you catch yourself every now and then and try to take it all in a bit more.

Come late afternoon we were all starved, so Father Stephen picked up the phone and called Parochial House.

'Mary, any chance you could put a fry on for us?' he asked his housekeeper.

And off we went, the gang of us, to munch on a fry courtesy of Mary, Father Farragher and the rest of the parish. You wouldn't make it up, but those days are among the best. That window of time when you're all there on the same wavelength, celebrating and enjoying each other's company – they're the moments I'm going to miss.

In the All-Ireland quarter-final in August we faced an up-and-coming Westmeath side who really tested us. We won thanks to a late point from Niamh Kelly. The new players were now really starting to step up. That victory meant we reached our first All-Ireland semi-final in seven years, and we would meet Dublin three weeks later.

At half-time in Breffni Park in Cavan we were down by six points. Dublin had raised two green flags and we were struggling. Yet, in the dressing room we knew we could come back. Right after the restart Dublin went eight points ahead, but we still didn't doubt ourselves. Suddenly we scored 1–5 without reply to draw level with minutes to go. It was back and forth with no one budging, and it looked to be heading for extra-time. But then, with forty-two seconds on the clock, Sinead Aherne broke down the left flank of the pitch. Sarah Tierney did well to shepherd her down the sideline, but for a split second she reached in and the referee blew for a foul. Sinead had been on fire all day, and she stepped over the ball as the clock was counting down. It was a pressure kick, but she got it over in time to send Dublin into their third successive All-Ireland final.

That defeat stung for several reasons. There was a possibility that it would be my last day wearing a Mayo jersey. I remember getting down on to my knees and crying, and Frank coming over to console me. More than anything, I think he was protecting me from the outside world. He knew I wouldn't want anyone to see me cry, and that gesture gave me a minute or two to compose myself for the group of journalists already heading my way.

It was my twenty-second season playing senior football, and at thirty-four years of age I wasn't getting any younger. I was beginning to realize it, and others were too. In the following weeks, Lidl visited my home in Castlecarra to do a video shoot for an advert. When they asked to see my medals, I read between the lines. They didn't tell me straight out that it was a retirement piece but I sensed that they were thinking ahead.

That winter, people expected me to call it a day, but I still hadn't given Frank an answer. I didn't want to be that player who took time off and came back in April or May either. That's not who I am. If I was back, I was back, and it would be all or nothing.

I played out in my head what retirement might look like. I thought about coaching at an elite level. I wondered if I'd even be able to coach a team outside Mayo. Probably not. I'd find that hard. I'm a one-club, one-county player.

The media continued to speculate. I talked everything through with one or two of the girls, but it wasn't until I met Andy Moran at a charity event in Breaffy House in mid-January 2017 that I made my decision. Andy was one of the best footballers in Mayo, and he was so matter-of-fact about it. What he said that day struck a chord.

'Are you still able to play, Cora?' he asked me quietly, out of earshot.

'I am.'

'So, why would you stop?'

It was the simplest question, and the simplest response. I had always said to myself that unless my body gave up, or I didn't enjoy it, I'd stick with it. Football was always a drug to me, and the reality was, I was still hooked.

In July 2017 we were two weeks out from the Connacht final against Galway and I was struggling with injury. The week before I'd had to stop myself from bursting into tears in front of the younger players at training. As usual I didn't want to show any weakness, but I felt it all right.

My back was locking, but I had to bear the pain because there wasn't a hope in hell I was missing a Connacht final against Galway. Even if I'd a leg hanging off me I would have played as it's no secret that I dislike Galway. I'm sure many of them haven't taken a liking to me either over the years. It's by far the thorniest rivalry in ladies football.

They've always been great to shout abuse. In the 2014 Connacht Club Championship final against Kilkerrin-Clonberne, one fella lost the plot all together. Towards the end of the game, one of our defenders, Doireann Hughes, got taken out of it, close to their dugout. Firstly, it was a dirty tackle. Then I saw the Kilkerrin-Clonberne manager, Willie Ward, bounding on to the pitch to stand over and roar at Doireann to get up. No matter what, you always stand up for your own, so I took off down the pitch and put myself between the two of them. Ward's face wasn't far off mine, and John Niland the referee was standing beside us.

'Ah, all you are is knacker!' he said to me, spit flying in all directions.

I stayed calm. 'You heard that, John,' I said, turning to Niland.

Not a single fan heard the abuse because they were all crammed into the stand on the far side. But John noted the incident and Ward was suspended for a few months as a result. That's the type of abuse ladies footballers can be subjected to, in some quarters at least. That might surprise a lot of people, it might not. Either way, that type of behaviour doesn't belong in the sport. But I won't lie, it hurt. Of course it did.

I grew a thick skin playing intercounty football for twenty-four years, but when there's a grown man – or anyone for that matter – calling you a 'knacker', it stings. There have been lots of incidents like that over the years and the verbal attacks are nearly always launched from the bank of some local pitch.

'Ah sure, she's just a selfish ole bitch!'

'She's just a glory hunter!'

'Ah, for feck sake, ref! She's playing ya again!'

In recent years my nieces have been up on those banks. They've had to listen to that shit talk and the booing, and try to wrap their little heads around it.

'Mommy, why's that man shouting at Aunty Cora?'

'Mommy, why is everyone booing Aunty Cora?'

'Mommy, why don't they like Aunty Cora?'

My niece, Aoife, is eight now, and she's at the age where she's beginning to comprehend things. I can see her trying to figure out the hatred, and that's hard to take. Half the time I don't hear it, so it's worse for my family because they have to stand there and listen to it. At least when I hear the abuse I've programmed myself to handle it, but to carry on like that in front of children, whether it's my niece or someone else's, just isn't on. And that's why I decided to play in the 2017 Connacht Championship final, back injury or no back injury.

Being restricted by injury was unfamiliar territory for me. Granted, I broke my jaw back in college, but that was in the off-season. And when I did my knee, I only missed the league. So this time around, the wondering and doubting about whether I would be mobile enough to play the game had me on the verge of a mini breakdown.

A week or so out from the final we had training in Claremorris. Next door to the pitch was our physio Brendan Fitzpatrick's clinic, and our strength and conditioning coach Ann Caffney had set up some ice baths. I knew I'd be safe there. Ann's very strait-laced, and that's the type of person I like. She's professional, but above all she treats me like any other player. Her ideas are progressive too. We were prowling, doing farmer split squats with weights, and she even had us hurdling to build up our power and burst of pace. Even at thirty-five years of age I was still craving to prove myself with any new exercises or drills she came up with. That year I'd won the jump test, hitting 42 inches, and I lifted 55 kilograms in the bench test. However, when it came to the sprint test,

Aileen Gilroy beat me every day, all day. I learned to live with that though. Just about.

Marie Corbett was in the ice bath by the time I got in. She was injured too, having got a bang on her shin from one of the hurdles. I was glad it was her. I was relieved really, because being a close friend, I knew I could cope talking to her about my back.

I had tried to train, but I was as stiff as a poker. My movement was extremely limited. Everyone was doing their best to try to pick me up, but it was bull. I could smell it a mile away. An MRI had shown up some scar tissue which the consultant, Dr Michael Moffatt, said was from overloading. But, maybe it was my body trying to tell me it was time to stop? So I thought to myself, *Is this the start of it? Is this the beginning of the end?*

I was worried because I wasn't at my sharpest going into a battle. The fact that I couldn't sleep with the pain didn't help. For the next week I took anti-inflammatories and Diazepam to help me sleep through it. The Friday before the game I forced myself to do sixty minutes in training, even though Dr Moffatt had strict orders for me to do only forty. I had to push beyond that limit. Despite the pain, it gave me a sense of comfort to know that I could go sixty minutes if I had to.

The morning of the game, I took more painkillers to tide me over. It wasn't enough. Galway buried us. Then they dug us up and buried us again. We were shocking! The whole lot of us. The final score said it all: they beat us 3–12 to 1–8. The warm-up in MacHale Park was intense, but when push came to shove we didn't turn up. At half-time we were already down by twelve points, and that lead demolished our confidence. I only managed to score a single point from play, and although I added six frees, my movement was incredibly limited.

'Were we too cocky?' I asked Crazy as we walked out.

Crazy had made a mess-up with a short kick-out that led to Galway's second goal, and that was all that was playing on her mind. I know I wasn't cocky. The injury aside, that's the Carnacon way of thinking. Despite having won numerous All-Ireland club titles, we're always on edge, no matter who we play. Here, though, I wasn't so sure. I had been trying to instil a confidence in the younger players, but you have to get the balance right. You try to give them a sense of self-belief, but at the same time, you can overdo it. And, I just wondered.

I think younger players struggle hugely under pressure nowadays. They're so used to having the older players stand up, and it was always the same eejits who talked at half-time – me, Crazy, Fiona McHale and Sarah Tierney. When I spoke, most of the time I felt like I was talking to the wall. The rest of the time I felt like they're thinking, *Will this one just ever shut up!* But it's all a learning curve for them, and I'd hope that in the future some young one will be up there doing the talking.

I also blamed myself in part for that loss against Galway. Normally, before any big match, I would have the opposition stalked and would have figured out the key players and their attributes. If Frank or any of the girls wanted my opinion on a player I could tell them. This time I didn't do that. I was so consumed with my back and worried about not being able to perform that it affected me. For the first time ever I had gone into a game doubting myself. Doubting my match fitness. Doubting my ability. Never had I doubted my ability. Now I was on the ropes, and it was eating away at me. That internal, grating feeling. I hated it.

Are you good enough any more? Are you past it?

It had affected my preparations. I didn't have a handle on things, and I blamed myself for that. I wasn't the general I needed to be because I didn't have the counter-attacks pre-mapped out in my mind.

Twenty-four hours after the game, John Gannon, our statistician, put footage of the game up on Dropbox. Four days later I knew everything there was to know about Kildare. The match was a month away but I wasn't going to be unprepared. This kind of preparation was something I needed to do in order to feel calm before any big game. I needed to feel like I knew what was happening all over the pitch, not just in my corner. I did it for myself, not for Frank or the other players, but if they wanted to ask about match-ups or game plans, I'd always be ready to offer an opinion. I didn't make any decisions, Frank was his own man, but he'd always listen. Sometimes we agreed, other times we didn't, but I think we always got something out of those conversations.

In the aftermath of getting hammered in that 2017 Connacht SFC final, we needed a change. We needed to get our hands on the ball more. We were too busy moving and grooving, stretching and doing plyometrics. When push came to shove, we weren't doing as much ball work as we should have been. Sarah Tierney mentioned it to Frank, and he took it on board. The next evening, he tasked his daughter to time how long we were working on the ball. She clocked twenty-eight minutes. Football is football. You can be as prepared as you like, but sometimes you just need to go out and play the damn thing.

Frank had a lot to be putting up with, with us. At the same time, he knew our hearts were in the right place. He was generous enough to listen to people's opinions, whether he was going to act on them or not. That's good management.

At the start of the year, Crazy and I had suggested to Frank that we should get Peter Leahy to come on board with us. Peter worked as a strength and conditioning coach and had previously coached the Westmeath ladies team. When he came in for a few sessions before the Connacht final, he introduced a new energy to our training sessions. Peter wasn't afraid to roar at us, but the next minute he was scraping you off the floor and dusting you off. The new pace came at the right time and made a key difference.

He took a few more sessions before the qualifier against Kildare, and we felt we were starting to get there. We were so engrossed in training that the Galway defeat was soon long forgotten. If we weren't going to beat Kildare, then we were in trouble. No disrespect to them, but they'd just come up from intermediate and had had a change in management, and the pressure of senior football is a lot tougher to handle. You never think you're going to beat a team, but you must believe you are. Thinking and believing are two different things.

I was working off the belief that we'd beat them, so when no word came through about arrangements for a recovery session after the game, I picked up the phone to find out what was happening. Management had decided not to have one. They thought that some food after the game and going home to bed would be better for us. I lost the plot. For the next four hours I argued with Frank over the need for a recovery session. After every big match we had a recovery session. Being immersed in water really gets the blood flow pumping again and that helps reduce any swelling on the legs. The games were coming thick and fast, so we needed every recovery session we could get. Eventually I gave up on Frank. I had a match in less than twenty-four hours to worry about.

Two hours later, a text came through on the team WhatsApp group. 'Recovery session in the Sheraton Hotel in Ballinasloe tomorrow after the game.'

They were the few things that myself and some others were fighting for all the time. Someone didn't see the benefit of having that session, or they didn't want to make the time to go through the process because they had something else on. A lot of the time there were things I didn't want to do but I knew they were the best thing for the team.

It was always me, Crazy, Claire, Martha or Fiona putting our heads out there to be shot at. Very few would fight for it. If you want to win, you have to fight for it, and you can't take any short cuts.

14

Home and Away

IN OCTOBER 2015 I FOUND MYSELF IN THE BACK OF A TAXI somewhere in downtown Shanghai, squeezed between the president of the GAA, Nickey Brennan, and his wife Máiréad. We were in China as guests of the 2015 Fexco Asian GAA Games. My first Asian Games was the year before in Kuala Lumpur.

That year my father had had a visit from P. J. McGrath, former chairman of the men's Mayo County Board. His son Páraic was a Mayo man living in Singapore, hanging on to his roots in a new world as vice-chairperson of the Asian County Board. Páraic wanted to invite me over as a guest ambassador, given my profile as a ladies footballer.

I went back to China again in 2016 and I can't recommend it enough. It's a brilliant tournament. What hits you is the number of Irish, and non-Irish, all mixed in together. The place is always bursting with pride. Every colour and creed descends on a place and they play our national games in the baking sun. Until you're out there in the thick of it, you don't comprehend just how big the GAA is beyond our back door.

So there I was, taking in the sights of Shanghai as the Irish consulate directed the taxi to Pudong. Brennan and myself chatted for the entire journey. He was incredibly laid-back and a lovely man. His take on the GAA and ladies football was refreshing. He reckoned we should be all under the one umbrella – the GAA, the Camogie Association and the Ladies Football Association – and I sensed that he was throwing the feelers out too.

He asked if I thought we should join the associations. I didn't hesitate to reply with a firm yes.

The conversation continued in the VIP area, where the aircon made it bearable for us to watch the games. I told him I thought that the top officials in ladies football and camogie were wary of losing their power should the associations merge. Brennan was diplomatic about it, as he had to be, but that was my stance on things, and it still is.

The LGFA and the Camogie Association should join with the GAA. It's a huge leap to make, I understand that. Maybe I'm not au fait with the logistics of it, but the reality is that ladies football should be much further down the road than it is. Since I started playing more than twenty years ago, the promotion of and media interest in the game have gone to another level. For me, the players deserve the bulk of the credit for getting their stories out there. In recent years the LGFA has also upped its game. The multi-million sponsorship deal in 2016 with Lidl played a huge part in that. It was a game changer in women's sport because Lidl's national advertising campaign portrayed players for what we were – serious athletes. That said, ladies football can always be taken to the next level, and amalgamation is the only way we're going to get there.

I've met all sorts of legends at the Asian Games over the years – the likes of Kerry's Eoin 'The Bomber' Liston, Dublin's Bernard Brogan, Down's James McCartan and Tipperary's Nicky English – and I always enjoyed their company. I liked picking their brains and seeing what made them tick. How did they train? How did they prepare? How did they recover? If anything, a lot of us are on the same wavelength, so it's nice to be able to have those conversations. I also had the pleasure of getting to know Mícheál Ó Muircheartaigh, his wife Helena and their daughter Doireann on the trip, and it's a friendship I cherish.

At a function during the 2016 Asian Games in Shanghai, the former Cavan player Nicholas Walsh wandered over and introduced himself. He needn't have because I knew only too well who he was. Nicholas had played a little bit of Aussie Rules with Melbourne before coming home to work for the Cavan GAA Board as a development officer. However, he became so immersed in how AFL players prepared themselves that he paid for himself to go back to Australia a few times to stay in touch with the game. And it paid off when he was offered a job with the Greater Western Sydney Giants in October 2011.

He wondered if I had any interest in playing Aussie Rules. I didn't have an answer for him because it was something I had literally never thought about. Just a few weeks earlier the AFL Women's League (AFLW) had been established, and Walsh's Giants were looking to put a team forward. He told me the league wouldn't officially start until 2017, but that it was something I should think about. I nodded out of politeness and we left it at that.

I didn't know much about Aussie Rules bar what I had watched on Saturday mornings when I was in college. I used to flick on

TG4 to watch Kerry's Tadgh Kennelly togged out for the Sydney Swans, or Mayo's Pearce Hanley playing with the Brisbane Lions. I knew Pearce, and if he had stayed around I think he would have gone on to be the best footballer in Mayo. However, the opportunity of playing in the AFL was always going to win out. The lifestyle of training as a professional in the sunshine for a start is a huge draw for any young fella, and they're absolutely right to grab that chance to develop and grow as athletes.

Just over six months later, in late June 2017, an email arrived from Alan McConnell, Director of Coaching at the Greater Western Sydney Giants. I presumed Nicholas had made Alan aware that I might be at a loose end but I had just decided that I was going back to play for Mayo for another year. I still found myself re-reading Alan's email, again and again. The fact that the Director of Coaching at a huge club had bothered to write to me made me sit up, and I realized they were serious. I started to think things over. I could make a few bob. I could see my brother, Brian, who had been living in Sydney since 2008. I could even take a career break and do a bit of travelling.

I replied to Alan's email. I said I'd think about it, but added that I was in the middle of the 2017 Mayo season and couldn't really focus on much else at that time. I didn't say a word to anyone. Not even to Crazy. It was just a seed, and while it was exciting, I was also afraid. I was afraid of leaving my nieces and nephews for four months. I saw them every day, and they were a huge part of my life – just as much as football, if not more. I wondered if my sister Kathleen and her husband Mike would be able to cope without the extra pair of hands around the place. That said, the Giants had certainly caught my interest.

191

Two weeks later, my phone beeped again. Galway had just crushed us in the Connacht final so I wasn't in the best of form. The last thing I wanted to think about was a foreign sport in a foreign country. We needed to get our own shit together. We were due to play Kildare next in the All-Ireland qualifier and my focus was on keeping my back injury at bay and getting a tighter ship run when it came to training. But Alan McConnell was eager. Very eager.

A week out from the Kildare game, at the start of August, a new WhatsApp group surfaced on my phone. It included me, Alan and Alan's son Ben, who lived in London. Alan wanted to send Ben over to Mayo to film me doing a few skills. He already had the whole thing planned out. Ben was going to fly into Knock Airport, come to the Kildare game and then do a skills session afterwards before flying back out. It was madness as I would somehow need to do all of this without anyone finding out.

I had to tell Crazy. I had to come up with a plan. I needed someone who was anonymous to the inner Mayo set-up to help us. Someone I could trust. Someone who wouldn't draw attention. If I asked a family member of a player to bring Ben to the game, there'd be all sorts of questions.

Then I had an idea. Jen Murphy was the woman. She's a gifted cartoonist and a huge Mayo fan, and even though we'd only met briefly on a few nights out, I sensed she was the type of person to be discreet. She was a friend of a few of the girls on the team so it made sense. She was going to the match anyway, so she happily agreed to collect Ben in Castlebar to bring him to and from the game. She knew that he wanted to film me, but she didn't know any more than that.

It was the first time we'd played Kildare in a senior champion-ship qualifier, and it told. The first half was very tight but we pulled away in the second half to win by twenty-one points in the end. I bagged 1–11 and I was relieved that the gym work I did on my back muscles carried me through. I was happy too that I had per-formed well with Ben there watching on the sidelines. His presence hadn't fazed me or put any extra pressure on me, but at the same time I was conscious that he was there; I knew I had to go out and play like I did in every game. After the game we exchanged a few messages and agreed to do a kick-around the following morning.

At 11 a.m., I walked into the Harlequin Hotel in Castlebar to discuss things in more detail. Ben broke it down. The Greater Western Sydney Giants didn't want me if I was no good. And I didn't want to go all that way if there was any doubt in my head that I wasn't up to it. They wanted me to go over to Australia in the next few weeks so they could see me play in person. They wanted to be sure I could pick up the skills quickly enough ahead of the pre-season.

The 2018 season would run for sixteen weeks, from January to March, with the season opener on 26 January. And so the permutations began. We calculated that I would have to fly to Australia in the next few weeks so that the coaches could make a call. If contracts needed to be discussed then there would have to be time for that too. This meant sneaking out of the country mid-championship without Frank or the team knowing. Plus I'd also have to prove myself worthy of playing in a professional league on the other side of the world.

It takes a lot to overwhelm me, but that conversation in the Har-lequin Hotel was reality hitting me in the face. Once I'd stepped out on to the pitch in MacHale Park for the kicking session, however, I instantly felt calmer inside. It's where I'm most at ease. On the turf, kicking. The Sherrin ball felt different. The cow hide leather felt rougher in my hands, but for forty minutes I made it work. Ben altered the camera angles on his GoPro as I went.

The only glitch was the bounce. It didn't feel natural, but I could work on that. Again, the draw of a new challenge had me hooked. I wanted to prove that I could master the unpredictable hop of the ball. As I lined up the stitching to knock the ball between the posts, the prospect of playing in the AFLW suddenly became more real with each kick of the ball.

The minute I stopped kicking, the pressure returned. My head was filled with doubts. I would be coming off the back of an eleven-month season, and a twenty-three-year career. I was thirty-five and struggling with a back injury. Could I really do it?

On the car ride back to Knock Airport, Ben talked contracts, working visas and marketing campaigns going big on me being the first international signing to the AFLW. It all went in one ear and out the other. I was too concerned with figuring out how I'd manage to disappear to Australia for a week in the middle of the season. As a parting gift, Ben handed me one deflated Sherrin ball. Then I headed home for my godchild Aoife's birthday party. Normality resumed. I was two hours late but I spun a yarn about being delayed at training and no one batted an eyelid.

That night, Alan McConnell rang me and told me they wanted me to visit the club. I didn't know what to think, but I knew I was thrilled that he was keen. My family still didn't know anything, but for the next few weeks I worked on that bounce any chance I got. The summer evenings were beginning to fade so I timed it exactly for when the sun dipped in the west, heading for the pitch in Clogher when I knew the chances of someone being down there were slim. From the boot of my car I'd yank out a bag full of O'Neills balls with the Sherrin buried inside. I had to be careful about it so I'd scatter the footballs to disguise what was really going on. I practised the kicking so much that I felt confident I could get it, but the bounce needed honing. According to the rules, I could possibly get away with not bouncing the ball. I could take fifteen steps, or even solo in between. As long as I played the ball it wouldn't be a foul. I did a bit of research into the game, and it wasn't all that far removed from what I already knew.

It was a massive thing to have going on in my life, but Mayo still came first. Mayo always did. Alan rang two to three times a week but other than that I tried not to think about the AFLW. It hadn't properly hit me, this new life that might be coming down the line. So I put it to the back of my head because if I thought about it, it would stress me out. And I couldn't afford to be stressed out because Donegal were waiting in the All-Ireland quarter-final on 19 August.

We were ready for them, and we were also motivated by Aoife McDonnell's video for the WGPA's #Behindtheplayer campaign, which explored the stories behind a cross-section of intercounty ladies footballers. McDonnell was the Donegal captain and a love-ly person no doubt, but we took umbrage to what she said in the last four seconds. She stated that if Donegal played to their full potential then they were probably the best team in the country. We couldn't stop playing it over and over.

We thought it was very disrespectful, not just to Mayo but to every other county. It was a very bold statement to make. Cork had won eleven of the last twelve All-Irelands, and all joking aside, Donegal had never even got to a senior All-Ireland semi-final in their history. They were cocky. They weren't worried about what we'd bring to the table, and we fed off that.

Training was going a hundred miles an hour in the first week of August, and the stronger you were, the better chance you had of surviving. For the first time since probably the Finbar days, I was completely wrecked after training. At the same time I was leaving with a smile on my face because I was learning something new. I was changing my game. I was making decoy runs in a way I'd never done before, and as a group, it was working.

Peter Leahy had only been with us a few weeks but he had us attacking the ball carriers and the runners with new intensity. He was letting us bash it out. Our aggression and intensity barometers were rising with every session. I was running around thinking, *I want to nail someone!* I was so pumped.

In the end, it was me who got nailed. We were down in Brickens GAA pitch and the twenty-seven of us were divided into four teams. The aim of the drill was to make a tackle, win the ball, and move on to the next grid, where the next lot of players waited to take your head off. The ball squirted out of a ruck and as I went down to get it, Martha Carter blew me out of it and I ended up on my arse.

'What the fuck was that about?' I roared, mid-jump, pushing her into the chest.

Then she went for me, and I went for her. It came to near blows, and it could have been worse only for Crazy and Marie Corbett quickly coming between us. We ungrappled ourselves and turned away. I was fuming, and so was she.

That's how intense those sessions had become. Fiona and Martha had also gone at it in a previous session, and although we'd be the best of friends, that's how fired up we all were about winning even a pass. Martha and I had both gone for the same ball. Fair was fair, but we were so cranky with each other that we avoided each other where we could all week. We were civil, but we needed our space.

A week on, and just three days out from the quarter-final against Donegal, we still hadn't had a full conversation. Then Martha sent a text message that broke the ice. I was too stubborn to make the first move, but I was glad Martha did, and we moved on. We've been around long enough to know that there comes a time to cop on. We're very alike, all the Carnacon ones, too alike. Yet, if I was going into battle in the morning, Martha Carter is one woman I'd be packing into my gear bag.

There's no question that Peter Leahy helped our season at a crucial moment. He brought something fresh to the set-up that helped to kick-start both players and management. In the previous few months, our attitude had stunk. As a group we had lost a little respect when it came to listening to management. We had heard it all before so I'd question the lads during a session, and my timing didn't help. That's who I am. If I didn't see the benefit of what we were doing in a particular drill, or I was frustrated by it, I wouldn't hide it. A few of the other older players were a little frustrated too. Peter's arrival helped both parties to refocus, and soon things felt like they were once again falling into place.

To add to the full schedule of training, kicking practice and phone calls with Alan, I was in Westport the Thursday before the Donegal game for a gig with AIB and the sports news website

Joe.ie. Myself, Mickey Conroy, James Horan, John Maughan and Kerry's Declan O'Sullivan and Aidan O'Mahony were all there to discuss the upcoming Mayo–Kerry men's game. That Friday I was in Dublin for work, and as I drove back on the M4 it felt like things were particularly mental. The distractions were good though as they took my mind off our own game.

That night, I headed for the clubhouse in Claremorris. Crazy and myself had been worried that the three-day break between training and the game could unravel the younger ones, so in between pots of tea and sandwiches we chatted and played charades and joked about the Copper Face Jacks-branded gloves I had been sent by Murphy's. It probably looked like a scene out of a nursing home, but we needed to decompress.

At the start of the game, Donegal put Ciara Hegarty in front of me as a sweeper. She's a great attacking player, but straight away they had negated their own threat. For a long time our game plan had been 'get the ball to Cora'. That year we threw a spanner in the works. Decoy here, decoy there. It was great because others were getting into the game, but I also still wanted to get on the ball.

As a forward, it's natural that you want to get into the game. You want to be a benefit to the team, and it was all I'd known. But I was slowly learning to adjust. Peter was key to that. He made me see scores I had set up, runs I made, the contributions that mattered even if I wasn't scoring myself. It was a new challenge, and at the age of thirty-five I was learning not to be the go-to woman.

Grace Kelly's goal against Donegal was when it became obvious to everyone else that we weren't the one- or two-dimensional team we had been in the past. I faked a run. A defender came with me.

Grace had a free run through to bury the ball in the net, and she made no mistake.

We were massive underdogs at 4/1, but we dug it out. We were level at half-time, and despite playing against the wind, we scored three second-half goals to run out six-point winners. Sisters Niamh and Grace Kelly played brilliantly, as did Orla Conlon and substitute Amy Dowling, and we were delighted to be back into an All-Ireland semi-final.

You enjoy those moments, but I wasn't long bursting the younger ones' bubbles. In recent years the more experienced crew would make sure that no one ran away with themselves. We hadn't won anything yet, and being a champion is all about consistency. It went back to my point about Donegal. One game doesn't make you the player, and one game doesn't make you the team. You have to prove yourself over and over again to be the best. It was that simple.

After the game, on my way home to Mayo, I felt sick on the bus. That was common enough for me after a big game. I don't know if it was mental exhaustion or what, but I plonked myself on the couch the minute I got in the door. For two hours I just sat there, too tired to move. The television was on mute, but I didn't watch it. It was midnight by the time I landed back in the real world again. A text from one of our selectors, D. J. Collins, had flicked back the 'on' switch. He had watched the Cork game twice already. The reigning All-Ireland champions, the greatest team in the history of the game, were waiting for us in an All-Ireland semi-final.

That night, I slept all of two hours.

15

Back to Croker

I WAS ONLY EVER STAR-STRUCK ONCE. IT WAS ST STEPHEN'S DAY 2007, and it was close to freezing outside the Stadium of Light in Sunderland. Myself, Crazy, Martha, Johanna Connolly, Emma Mullin and Avril Robinson had gone over to watch Manchester United hammer the locals.

I was in between two knee operations that winter, and although I wasn't on crutches, it was against good judgement to stand in the piercing cold for five hours just to get a glimpse of Roy Keane. A steward had told us that if we waited long enough he would eventually come out, so we stood there and we shivered. To pass the time we took the piss out of each other, and laid bets on whether Keane would be in wicked form or not. The girls weren't too bothered if they saw him, but they stuck it out for me.

Like Keane, I know people have perceptions of me. And, like Keane, it's probably a cranky one. But he proved us wrong – he couldn't have been nicer. As a player, I loved his no-nonsense attitude, and how straight up he was. He might not have been the most talented player, but he worked his arse off, and was passionate about everything he did.

Keane was driven. He didn't care about anything else. He just wanted to go out and perform, and I loved that. He was someone I could relate to.

In 2016, Fiona McHale gave an incoming member of management, Aoife Lane, a copy of Roy Keane's first autobiography and said, 'If you want to see what Cora's like, read that!' Like me, he'd been known to bite the head off someone on the pitch. I know how this can look, but in my defence, my outbursts were always born out of frustration. For a lot of my career I was in limbo. I felt I had to wait for other players to catch up to my thought process. In my head, I had a move drawn out seconds before it happened. Every dummy, every turn, every finish was pre-assembled before I even got my hands on the ball. When others weren't on the same wavelength, that frustration manifested itself – me roaring and pointing to a space where a teammate should have been. As I got older I tried to calm it down, but on big days under pressure it's hard not to revert to old habits. I try to count to five. Sometimes it works. Sometimes it doesn't.

I think I'm right a lot of the time even though I'm sure I'm not. One of the things I love about playing with Carnacon is the fact that they know me so well and accept me as I am. We never fall out over my outbursts. I'm not saying my approach is right, but I don't think I can change it at this point.

Every season, it wouldn't take me long to figure out who could handle the pressure of intercounty football. Who was mentally weak, and who wasn't. Some players can't even take the pressure of training. They're seventeen and eighteen and they're still being mollycoddled by their parents. It may sound unsympathetic, but I don't have much time for parents worrying about their daughter's sore legs or whether they're training too hard. At that age, they need to toughen up.

When I saw girls coming through with a bit of fight in them – players like Doireann Hughes and Orla Conlon – it was a breath of fresh air. If they were made of stronger stuff I didn't let up because I knew they were able for it. Resilience is something you must build in players, and that's a tricky thing to do, now more than ever. They must be able to take criticism. I'm opinionated, and I can't hold my tongue. If there's something eating away at me, I'll say it. Maybe that's a bad trait. Maybe not.

I'll tell a player straight up what I think, and I'll give them advice. Those that want to hear it are the ones that want to learn and improve, like Orla Conlon, for example. She could ask me questions for hours, and you can see she's come on leaps and bounds. I'm not saying that's because of my answers, but because she wants to learn. I'm sure I've blown the head off Orla too at some point, but she understands why I'm doing it: to better her, and the team.

My delivery may not have been the best, so the introduction of mandatory gum shields in 2017 was probably a good thing for the Mayo girls. I did know when I overstepped the mark, and I would always approach the person afterwards. I'm very open and honest that way. If I do something wrong, I address it, or I apologize.

Eight days before the All-Ireland semi-final against Cork, yet another logo drama broke out. Crazy had worn an outdated jersey for the game against Donegal – the navy one she wore for the 2016 Lidl Division 1 National League final. She had worn it because there had been blood on the new, white jersey. The problem was that it had Lidl on the back instead of the championship sponsors,

TG4. It was also missing the new Elverys logo as in 2017 they had updated it to read 'Intersport Elverys'.

After the match, Elverys emailed the County Board insisting that players wear jerseys with the updated logo. Fair enough. They also said that some players hadn't worn the shorts they had supplied with the Mayo crest. The problem was, we had only been given one pair of shorts to last us the entire year. In that time they can fade, rip or go missing.

Jimmy Staunton of Elverys has been incredibly good to me on a personal and professional level for years. We have a great relationship, and anything I ever asked him for, I got. But I was thinking about the girls who I ran alongside week in and week out, who weren't as privileged as me. That one pair of shorts was all they got yet we were all spilling the same amount of sweat in training.

It got us thinking. Out of interest, what gear did the Mayo men's football team get? It didn't take us long to find out. A Mayo senior men's footballer received the following:

- A full tracksuit
- 2 T-shirts
- A gear bag
- 2 pairs of match shorts and socks, one for the league and one at the quarter-final stage
- 2 training tops
- A warm-up top
- Training shorts and socks
- Away gear, shorts and socks
- An €250 voucher

A Mayo senior ladies footballer received the following:

- A full tracksuit
- 2 T-shirts
- 1 pair of match shorts and socks

Around the same time, the Irish senior women's soccer team went public on the humiliation of having to go into public toilets in airports to change into and then out of their tracksuits so that they could be shared with other Irish national teams.

We were so lucky to have Elverys, who responded by providing us with much more kit, but female athletes in general were being overlooked in so many different ways, and if we didn't point out that fact ourselves, then who would?

A week before the 2017 All-Ireland semi-final against Cork, I recorded a #Behindtheplayer video with the WGPA. Fiona McHale was one of the founding members, so she had convinced me to do it. Aoife Lane, the current chairperson of the WGPA, was involved with the Mayo backroom and her eyes were opened to the reality of a county set-up. She saw things daily. She saw when there were no showers after training; when there were only two floodlights turned on for us; the fruit and rice cakes we had for 'post-match meals'; how difficult it was to get a pitch; the commitment from players.

The WGPA don't sit in an office somewhere. They're on the front line, fighting alongside us. *For* us. Look at the work they did in 2016 with the government funding campaign for intercounty ladies footballers and camogie players. They were key members of a steering group that established a two-year funding initiative of €500,000 for each year which was aimed at programmes such as injury prevention and medical cover. It was also aimed at maximizing their members' performance and giving them access to training facilities. Their five-year deal with Pat the Baker was the first of its kind for a women's sporting organization in Ireland. A revenue share arrangement saw a percentage of all sales go towards the WGPA Player Development Programme. Their free twenty-four-hour helpline offers intercounty players advice and support for personal issues that may arise during their careers, and their #Behindtheplayer video campaign plays a huge part in their mission to promote female athletes. It has always been about different people, with different stories. The videos have received a huge response as so many people have been able to relate to those players and their experiences.

According to Fiona McHale, who is the secretary for the WGPA, mine was the most viewed WGPA video online. It seemed to strike a chord, and I couldn't believe the number of people who approached me on the street or at matches to mention it to me afterwards. In truth, it was kind of emotional to hear Fiona, Martha, Doireann, Crazy and Marie speak about what I brought to Carnacon and Mayo football.

But, just like the LGFA, there's obviously so much more the WGPA can do. Their desire to make players' lives better is incredible, and they're on the right track, but it's not something I'd get involved in myself. I'd rather be on the sidelines in the future trying to win battles on the pitch. Thankfully, though, we have the WGPA fighting for us off it.

That summer, life was so hectic. At one point I even found myself Googling 'anxiety'. On top of everything, the Greater Western

Sydney Giants had sent me forms to fill in for the AFLW draft and to obtain a working visa. My head was barely above water, and all the while my real worry was how we were going to beat Cork.

The morning of the All-Ireland semi-final, I went a mile and a half down the road to visit Mam's grave in Burriscarra Cemetery. It's what I did before most games. I'd stay a while and chat, and, depending on who we were playing, I'd ask for a bit of good luck. This time I'd need a lot of it.

A week out from the game, the team had been named. D. J. Collins had put a mountain of effort into the video analysis. I'd say the man didn't do anything else for an entire fortnight. He's a Cork man, but he was too deep in it now, helping us try to dismantle a side going for seven-in-a-row. We knew our match-ups. Sarah Tierney would take Orla Finn. Orla Conlon would have Eimear Scally. Martha Carter would take Aine Terry O'Sullivan, and Rachel Kearns had the doggedness to match Doireann O'Sullivan.

The plan was to go zonal for the kick-outs, bar me. My job was to follow Bríd Stack. And, if there was a short kick-out, then Sarah Rowe was to take her up. The plan was to isolate them around the half-back line. The system went like this. We split the pitch into three, and everyone would work those areas like never before. There always had to be four people to an area, sweeping back and forth, like an accordion. When we attacked, we were wide. When we defended, we were narrow. And then, we'd press the hell out of it.

It worked. At half-time we led by two points (1–7 to 0–8), but we had missed three goal chances. In the dressing room, before management came in, I spoke. Then Crazy, then Tierney. We were animated. Management, however, were calm. Peter told us to keep driving on, and then our statistician, John Gannon, dropped the reality bomb.

'Ye've had eighteen scoring chances, and there's just 1–7 on the board.'

The stats don't lie. We were poor up front.

When we went back out, Cork had the wind with them and moved two points clear. Then, in the forty-second minute, Aileen Gilroy took an assist from Fiona Doherty and buried a goal, before substitute Amy Dowling netted again three minutes later. We weren't in the clear yet, however. We were two points up with four minutes to go when Orla Finn won a penalty for Cork. Eimear Scally stepped up to take it. I couldn't see much from the other end of the pitch, but I didn't want to look either.

Myself and the Cork goalkeeper, Martina O'Brien, were both down on our hunkers. She was praying, I was praying, and neither of us saw Scally plant her left boot to strike the ball. By the sound of the crowd, I knew it didn't go in. There was way more Mayo support that day in Breffni Park, and the noise carried us.

When the whistle blew, I looked to the sky. It was hard to believe that after ten long years we were finally headed back to Croke Park. Or that we had managed to beat Cork in the championship for the first time in thirteen years.

Fiona McHale came running my way, and God was I happy for her. She'd been at it now for fourteen years and still hadn't won an All-Ireland medal, or even played in Croke Park on All-Ireland final day. She had been one of our generals over the last few years, and probably one of the most gifted players I've ever played with. So I was happy for her. I was happy for Doireann too. I was happy for Marie. Finally, they had got there. Myself, Martha and Crazy had all won and lost in Croker, but we'd stuck it out for the last decade to see people like them have their day. And of course I was more than delighted to be back there myself.

Once I let go of Fiona, I dodged the crowd and made my way to the Cork dugout. Bríd Stack popped into my head almost immediately. We had had our battles over the years, but the respect we have for each other is huge. She's by far the best that's ever marked me, and I knew that day that both our careers were at a crossroads. I just happened to be the one taking the high road this time. Annie Walsh wished me luck, as did Cork selector Frank Honahan.

'Go on now and win it,' he said. 'Do yerselves justice.'

A few of the former Cork players sent texts to say congrats. That's what they're like. Genuine people, with genuine respect.

By the time I got back into the dressing room, Crazy was sitting in the corner with a big smile on her face. She stood up, and we hugged. We didn't say a word. We didn't have to. We both knew that everything we had gone through to get to this moment was worth it.

16

Trash Talk

I had it in my head to ring Finbar Egan. Getting back to an All-Ireland final triggers the memories, and the good days all involved winning and Finbar. I hadn't seen him for years, but two weeks out from the 2017 All-Ireland final I called him while driving to Dublin. My timing was intentional. Knowing Finbar, he'd talk, so I knew I'd savour the conversation more alone, in the confines of the car. An hour and a half later we wished each other good luck. It was like we had never been apart. Just as he had always done, he drove the tactics home. His voice brought a reassurance that I had missed ever since his departure in 2005.

As I drove into Dublin city centre, it was like going behind enemy lines. I was buzzing, we all were. The men had also qualified for their All-Ireland final, so the place was smothered in red and green.

A week after our semi-final win against Cork we held a media night in Breaffy House with a training session beforehand in Ballintubber. Lidl delivered bags of food after training, Elverys followed through with a mound of gear, and Fahey's on Main Street in Castlebar went as far as offering to sponsor us with sports bras.

The session itself was excellent, and I stayed on afterwards to do a bit of extra kicking, media night or no media night. If I didn't, it would unsettle me. After most county training sessions I'd kick a scattering of fifty frees or so. In my own time, I'd head down on Ballintubber pitch late in the evening with the aim of taking another 100 to 150 frees, depending on how heavy the week's schedule was. I'd shoot down to Jimmy's first to borrow a bag of twenty footballs, and off I'd go, kicking in blocks of twenty. Right foot, left foot, alternating the blocks. On the excursion back in behind the goalposts on the clubhouse end, I'd calculate the percentages. For close on thirty years, that's how I'd done it. Kicking. Counting. Calculating.

When I finally got to Breaffy House, everyone wanted a word with me. I'm well able to give the lines, but if I had my way, I'd stay away from it. I never sought the attention, but when you've been there so long, it's almost habit – for me and the journalists. They knew I'd give them something, a nugget or a line to latch on to. And if it took the pressure off the others then I was happy to do it.

The body was sore, so I organized to get physio off Caroline every other evening. We were due to have a recovery weekend in Mullingar eight days before the final, so at least the timing was good. On the Saturday morning we had a pool session, and from 4.30 to 11 p.m. our physios, Brendan Fitzpatrick and Angie Hartnett, were flat out fixing body parts on the physio table. We broke for dinner at 7 p.m., then piled into a conference room in the hotel where we were staying. There, we asked the staff to unravel a red carpet that they had in storage. We wanted to show those who hadn't been in Croke Park before how to greet the President of Ireland, Michael D. Higgins.

Brendan, our physio, played Michael D., shaking and nodding as he went, and our captain, Sarah Tierney, did the rest. T (as we call her) was a good captain, and a good leader. But, better than that, she's a great person. When my niece Kate underwent surgery in Crumlin Hospital in Dublin last year, Sarah called to her every day. There weren't many from Mayo around, so her visits and those of Orla Conlon were a godsend to my sister Kathleen.

I'm sure Sarah will be one of the players who will step up another level when we call it quits. She just gets it. She also has an intelligence that will get her places, and politics wouldn't be too far off the list I'd say. Orla won't be far behind her either. There was a time when she didn't understand my way of thinking, or my obsessive drive to succeed. After a seven-day holiday to Portugal – with Martha, Crazy, Marie, Sarah Tierney, Aileen Gilroy, Noirín Moran and Sarah Rowe – her mind was transformed. For the first time she understood the wiring of our minds, and what we perceived as hard work. As a result, her own perceptions and standards rose, and she moved from the end of the substitutes bench to wearing the number 2 jersey in an All-Ireland final.

That night in Mullingar we made the most of standing on the red carpet. We cross-checked the Clár an Lae and the timing of the warm-up and decided on where we would stand for the national anthem. They were the finer details, but we didn't want to be like headless chickens on the day, wasting energy wondering what the hell the protocol was.

D. J. Collins diligently sifted his way through the video analysis, before Frank stood up to name the team. Management selected the same fifteen that beat Cork, and how could they not? Amy Dowling was the only one who could have been hard done by, having come on to score one of the winning goals, but for an eighteen-year-old she absorbed it well. There was no dwelling or sulking. She just got on with it.

The only surprise management threw at us was a video montage of themselves. We sat there waiting for the clip to roll, wondering what they had put together. Their message was simple: they were with us. From the floor, we watched our selector Michael McHale's face light up the screen.

'It's a lot more than just football,' he said.

He was right. It was about Mayo. It was about the people. And it was about us coming together.

I didn't get emotional for that, but what happened next did move me. Sarah Tierney, Orla Conlon, Sarah Rowe, Noirín Moran and Ann Caffrey had conspired with each of our families, and with Jen Murphy Sketches, to create good-luck videos for each of us. It was touching to see those that mattered most speaking to us from the screen. There was a scattering of my family in the clip – Kathleen, Peter, Collette, and all their kids, and even my brother Brian and his family in Sydney.

When we left to go to bed, the mood was good. Our focus at the following morning's training session was visibly sharper too. The plan was to continue as a group to the men's All-Ireland final against Dublin, and it was important that we went together. If we went separately, we would have been hanging around Quinn's and the Big Tree, getting home late or getting carried away chatting to the crowd.

We sat together in the Lower Cusack Stand, taking it all in. For a moment I drifted forward to our All-Ireland final in seven days' time. I pictured myself turning the corner from the dressing room into the tunnel under the Hogan Stand. Building up pace as I went, then exploding up and down the second I hit the turf. But I reined myself in. I had to switch off. If I didn't, it would generate useless, nervous energy.

With seventy-six minutes played, we watched Dean Rock of Dublin stand over the football. He was just metres in front of us. With two deep breaths, I watched him inspect the Davin End goalposts. Then, he nailed the winning free-kick. For him it was the stuff dreams are made of. The same stuff my dreams were made of. For Mayo, it was like a death in the family.

It was Mayo's ninth All-Ireland final defeat since 1951, and the lads fell like dominoes on the pitch with the agony of it all. The following Tuesday I happened to bump into Donal Vaughan in a coffee shop in Castlebar. He had been red-carded with fifteen minutes to go for an uncharacteristic dig against his opponent, and the rest was history. When I caught his eye, I didn't know what to say to him. I could see the heartache in his face.

The lads' defeat put a bit of pressure on us. Now, everyone was talking about our chances. They wanted redemption.

That week I tried to keep a low profile. In Castlebar, I ate my lunch in work to avoid that very talk. Your head would just be done in from it all. It was the only conversation people had that week. Even the weather went out the window. We had lost before, but this wasn't the norm. And I was just crying out for normality. You pray for the build-up to go as smoothly as possible, but it was anything but.

Ten days out from the All-Ireland final I was driving home from training with Lough Carra to my right when the phone beeped.

I had just a mile or so to go, but by the time I pulled into the driveway there was an avalanche of messages on WhatsApp. Mick Bohan, the Dublin manager, had done a radio interview and the link was being shared.

In a nutshell, it was a spiel about how cynical and physical Mayo were. He had counted thirty-six 'incursions' in our All-Ireland semi-final against Cork, and said it was 'overkill'. Then he spoke about the 'use of the head injury, when it's not a head injury', and warned the journalists he was speaking to to watch out for our physicality.

There was no real acknowledgement of what we had done as a team. We had beaten the reigning All-Ireland champions, and let's face it, we did the Dubs a favour. They had never beaten Cork in the seven times they had met in the championship. We did, twice – in 2004 and 2017. But there wasn't a hint that we deserved to be in Croke Park that September.

Sitting on the couch that night, listening to Bohan, I felt he didn't have an ounce of respect for us. And then came the bit about me. He insinuated that I had cheated in the 2017 National League win over Dublin that March in Croke Park, a game in which I scored the winning point with a free 43 metres out from the Davin End. First, he said I took a 13-metre free from the penalty spot. And then, the equalizing free which I correctly won close to the 45-metre line, I took 'two cuts inside the forty-five'.

'Work that out,' he told journalists.

When asked what his plan was for marking me in the All-Ireland final on Sunday week, Bohan laughed and said, 'There is a sniper over there.' But the most insulting bit was yet to come, when he said that I knew how to 'get frees' and 'intimidate referees'. At the end, he referenced the 2003 All-Ireland final. Bohan had managed Dublin that day too, but a late goal by Diane O'Hora had denied the Dubs their first title. He referred to the fact that I didn't score that day and that if you could keep me quiet, opponents would win the game. But, he added, 'I hope she scores everything on Sunday, and we win.'

I had damaged my anterior cruciate in 2003, yet that fact was never noted. My blood was boiling. Did I take offence? Absolutely. Who wouldn't? Intelligent players and teams know when to slow the game down. That's part of the process. It's part of winning. But, to say I intimidated someone? The thing that annoyed me most was the complete lack of respect, for us as a team, and for me. He made it personal when there was no need.

Twenty-four hours after that article appeared on the website The42.ie, our trainer, Peter Leahy, responded with a statement of his own.

'To say the best player who's ever played the game in ladies football intimidates referees,' he began, 'first, it insults referees that they can't officiate properly with someone of her stature, and secondly, it says that being the best player in the country for I don't know how many years now, she needs to intimidate referees. It's a ridiculous statement, it's a very insulting statement.

'He also said that we use head injuries to slow the game down. Now, we had two serious head injuries late on against Cork. Both weren't far off the end of the game. Both of them were serious hits, and they were shown afterwards on TG4 that they were hits on the head. One of them resulted in a player being quite bad for a week, and she went for a brain scan. To insult someone to say that they're faking a head injury is a very, very large statement.'

I learned not to listen to or read things about myself a long time ago. From the age of fourteen I was an absolute villain one week and a hero the next. I know how fast people can turn on you. But this just felt different. It wasn't ignorance. Mick Bohan is an intelligent man, and a very good coach. Afterwards, he said that what he had said was taken out of context; he was 'hurt' that people focused on the negatives. But, what did he expect? He was the one handing out the negatives with his own choice of words – 'intimidating', 'incursions', 'overkill'. The majority of neutrals saw it for what it was – an undertone of digs wrapped up in fake compliments.

Bohan was too proud to admit that he overstepped the mark.

You wouldn't see Eamonn Ryan carrying on like that. He's a gentleman. And I'm saying that about a man who has caused me so much heartache over the years. So, when Ryan's name flashed up on my phone the Tuesday before the All-Ireland final, I smiled.

It was a touch of class.

'Cora, just texting to wish you the best of luck next Sunday. All the best from Pat and myself. You might also convey my best wishes to Yvonne, Fiona and Martha. Don't feel like you have to respond! – Eamonn.'

A few other faces in the GAA world sent messages that week, which was a nice touch.

I didn't want anything to creep into my headspace so I decided to work right up to the Friday. It didn't feel like we were in an All-Ireland final that way, which was good.

A few of the girls claimed to have had niggles, but in truth they didn't. I had seen it all before. It was pressure. Every team has someone who'll start to carry an 'injury' coming up to a big game.

But you know they're absolutely fine. It's in their head. They need a fall-back if things don't go well for them. That's all. I don't judge girls in any way for that. I've seen it hundreds of times over the years, and I know it's pressure manifesting itself.

An All-Ireland final is a massive occasion, and for years Crazy, Martha and myself had talked endlessly about making it happen again. For the girls who had never played in an All-Ireland final in Croke Park, this was surreal. They were trying to deal with that. *God, we're actually in an All-Ireland final!* I knew they'd be all right by the time we got to Croker. And, once I knew everyone else was OK, then I'd be OK.

17

Falling Short

AT 7 A.M., THE ALARM BEEPED. IT WAS D-DAY, BUT THE SKY WAS still blue, and I didn't feel any different. My mindset was the same as it had been for the sixty-six other championship games that preceded this one. And not once did it enter my head that it would possibly be my last.

All week the media had been predicting my retirement. But they didn't know what was in the pipeline. A few days earlier I had sat at my computer and completed the online application for the AFLW Draft. It was official, I was doing it. As I typed, the prospect of being away from the Mayo set-up became more real. Clicking 'send' was confirmation of just how much my life was about to change.

Bar the 'Famous Five' – myself, Crazy, Marie, Martha and Doireann – Christmas Down Under wasn't on anyone else's radar. I hadn't even told Brian that I'd be living with him in Sydney within a few months. On the way to Croke Park I sat at the back of the bus with just my thoughts. Conversations don't happen in moments like these. You search for an inner calmness, but it's a hard thing to find. I drowned out the sirens of the Garda escort by listening to music, but as we neared Jones' Road I reverted to the audio clips of Mick Bohan's interview. That night on the couch when I first heard it, I knew I would hit 'play' again on the afternoon of 24 September 2017 when Croker came into sight.

She knows how to get her frees, knows how to intimidate referees ...

I didn't need motivating, I just wanted to concentrate my mind that fraction more, because any fraction you can get, you'll take.

As we arrived in Croke Park I scanned the vitals of the younger players. They were calm, and ready, as was I. I could hear the hollow hum of the crowd above, but strangely enough, you're more insulated from the atmosphere than you'd think. During the week we had spoken about how the attendance record was likely to be broken, and now 46,000 fans were above us, waiting for the last spectacle of the day. We didn't know it at the time, but it would be the equivalent of playing at a sold-out Stamford Bridge, White Hart Lane or Villa Park.

You could sense there was something different in the air. Both teams would play their part in history regardless of who won, but we were there to win. The only stat that currently mattered was that it was fourteen years since our last All-Ireland title. It felt like an eternity in the wilderness.

I could have given up long ago. The girls, however, needed to experience it. They needed to know what it was like to step off the bus and walk through those double-yellow doors and into the dressing rooms. They needed to reflect on how hard they had worked to get there, because it was never easy. Just ask Dublin. They had lost the last three finals by an accumulated four points, and they too felt that enough was enough.

As I had envisaged the week before, I turned right, around the corner from the dressing room and into the tunnel. The sound of the vuvuzelas hit me first. As we waited in the tunnel, the noise vibrated off the walls. It almost came up through the soles of our boots. It was only then that it became real: this was an All-Ireland final. I had contained everything up until that moment – the hype, the nerves – but there was no holding back now. The energy had to go somewhere.

After the noise came the light. Then the spring of the sod. I hopped twice to test if it had survived the two games beforehand. It had.

For the team photograph, I made sure to stand with Martha to my right and Crazy to my left, and we rattled each other's shoulders for assurance. We had come so far, and hung on for so long. While we waited for President Michael D. Higgins, I spotted Kathleen in the crowd with Aoife, Kate and Chloe. They were wearing their Mayo jerseys, and I gave them the thumbs-up. I didn't smile, because I couldn't. I just wanted the waiting to go away so I could get stuck in.

Dublin got off the mark first, and it took me a few minutes to figure out how they had set up defensively. They played it cute. Sinead Finnegan was marking me, but there was also a 'side marker' tailing us. I was well used to teams playing a sweeper in front of me, but this was new. It was clever, and it was something we hadn't come across before.

I managed to wrangle free and fist the ball over the bar on the Hill 16 end to get our opening score, but chances were few and far between. The others were getting dragged out the pitch, hunting for possession, and I was isolated inside with two blue jerseys.

When the ball did come my way, I found some breathing space but my execution was poor.

I didn't feel more pressure than usual, but it wasn't happening for me. The crowd sensed that too. I didn't want it to get to me, however. I had never shirked my responsibility, no matter how bad things got, and I wasn't going to start now.

In every game there is always a defender in my vicinity shouting, 'She's not going to pass!' I might pass, I might not, but the only way to stick it to them is to put the ball over the bar. On the one hand people are saying you're selfish, and on the other they're saying, 'Get the ball to Cora!' Being called selfish bothered me a little when I was younger, but I quickly learned that any good forward has to have a selfish streak in them. It's your job.

Dublin settled better into it than us, and with nineteen minutes played, Niamh McEvoy managed to hit the net with three of our gang collapsing around her to try to stop the ball. Then five minutes later we lost Crazy to a yellow card. Her trailing leg brought Sinead Aherne down inside the square, and although our substitute goalkeeper, Aisling Tarpey, brilliantly saved Sinead's penalty, sixty seconds later our right wing-back, Rachel Kearns, was also in the sin-bin.

Doireann Hughes and Niamh Kelly dropped back into midfield, and we clogged the middle. It wasn't the best scenario, and we could have folded, but we didn't. Even when we went down to thirteen players we managed well for the remainder of the half, making sure Dublin didn't score again. We hadn't played to our full potential yet, and we were still only a goal down at half-time.

In the dressing room, I tried to recompose myself. I knew I hadn't performed. I had registered seven wides, but at least I had time to wipe the slate clean. Each of us caught our breath and reassured ourselves that we were still in it, which we were.

In the second half, however, we didn't get as many chances. With eleven minutes to go, and ten points on the board, we were still only a goal down, but Dublin switched on and we switched off. Two minutes later, Orla Conlon was sin-binned for a second bookable offence which didn't help either as Noelle Healy then ran riot in the forward line. From there on out they walked through us, with Sarah McCaffrey and Carla Rowe getting three goals between them.

In truth, Dublin were the better team. You could tell they had bottled all the hurt from losing the previous three finals to Cork.

When the hooter went, our girls gradually gathered in our back line as Dublin celebrated. Instead, I hovered on my own down by the Davin Stand. I knew if I went near the girls I'd get emotional. And, with cameras everywhere, I didn't want my pain to be public. Crazy found me, and not long after that I could see Mick Bohan floating across the field in my direction, with a cameraman following him.

I panicked when I saw the camera. It was very well staged. He didn't open his mouth, not even to say hard luck. It was a simple handshake, and he moved off. If you ask whether his comments affected the referee's decisions on the day, you'd have to say, to an extent, they did. But, fair play to Mick Bohan. He played a game, and he succeeded. There has always been pressure on me in any game I've played so his comments didn't add any more or any less. Most of the pressure actually came from people predicting that this was my last game in a Mayo jersey.

Aoife and Chloe made their way on to the pitch, and it was nice to have them sit there and comfort me. Aoife understood, because she has seen us win and lose. But it was hard to see her hurting for me, just as Kathleen and Dad were hurting in the stand. Your family want it so badly for you because they know how much you've sacrificed, and for how long. And it's not easy on them either.

As I made my way back down the tunnel, I heard 'The Rare Ole Times' blasting out through the tannoy for the Dubs. It seemed a little apt. In the dressing room, Frank, Peter, Crazy and Sarah Tierney spoke. Then I followed with a few words.

'There's no point in wasting your talent if you're not going to come back and try again,' I said, doing my best to hold back the tears.

I told them that Mayo ladies football needed strong leaders. We needed people who believed in us to drive the thing forward again in 2018. Even though we were at our lowest, everyone in that room needed to stand up and come back again. I could see that some of the girls were crying so I didn't speak for very long. There's only so much you can say, and only so much you can take in.

I was dragged outside for more interviews, and by the time I came back I was the only one left to shower. Marie had been selected for a drugs test, and the others had headed for the players' lounge. I couldn't face going in there. Instead, I boarded the bus to stay away from it all, and Martha, Marie and Doireann joined me. Crazy knew well enough to bring us each a drink from the bar, and we joked that we were staging a protest against Marie's selection for a drugs test. In reality, we just wanted to crawl away and hide. It was my third time losing an All-Ireland final in Croke Park, and I felt hollow.

Back in the Burlington Hotel, I sat in my room for some time trying to make sense of it all. But there was no point in having a post-mortem. It was over with. We just had to numb the feeling for the night that was in it and see where tomorrow took us.

At the function, I couldn't bear to listen to some of the County Board officials ramble on so I stepped outside for a brief break from it all. Marie came with me, and we found a corner by an emergency door in the foyer. It was peaceful for all of ten minutes, before a group of about twenty players and family filtered out to join us. All I wanted was a bit of peace and quiet. I needed time to decompress, not to have to repeat conversations about where it all went wrong.

My brother's and sister's kids turned out to be a great distraction. Aoife, Kate, Chloe and my nephew Tom were all at the banquet and they entertained me for most of the night, twirling and dancing with all the girls. They were my saving grace. Although I was down about losing, watching them brought a smile to my face when I needed it most. At 6 a.m. I made it back to my bedroom. I was never so happy to climb into bed.

I managed four hours' sleep before I had to get up to go and visit Temple Street Hospital. It was the first time the losing team had been invited and, as much as we all wanted to turn over and go back to sleep, it wasn't about us. A nurse greeted us when we arrived, and her understanding hit me straight off.

'People always say it could be worse, and that's very true,' she said. 'But, you all put your lives on hold trying to win an All-Ireland medal. I know yesterday's defeat is the worst thing at the moment, but it'll get better.'

She was right. And when we visited the children and met their parents, it put everything in perspective. As we were leaving the Dublin team arrived, but thankfully we didn't cross paths – we're very old-fashioned in that regard. I don't know how I feel about the losing team going to the hospital. Don't get me wrong, it's a wonderful thing to do, but it's a winning tradition, not a losing one.

Back in the hotel, Marie and myself sat in the corner of the bar and had a drink. My sisters and nieces were in the lobby, but we finally had time to ourselves. We texted Crazy to come down and then it was just the three of us there, content to be in our own space.

We're a bit clannish like that, but it's something the other Mayo players were always aware of, and respected.

It was the same when we headed back west for the homecoming in Castlebar on the Monday. When the night moved on to Bally-haunis, myself and Crazy snuck away to meet her mam, Margaret, and her Aunty Joan in the Corner Bar. It was nice to just get a bit of normality amid the madness.

Afterwards we joined the rest of the team in Mac's Pub, and within twenty minutes of our arrival we had them all brought back to life, hopping on bar stools. We might like our own space, but we'd always start the craic. Crazy, of course, was the life and soul of the party, but we'd all be good stickers and are always the last ones standing at the end of the night.

At 5 a.m., twenty of us or so strolled down the road to Margaret and Pat Byrne's house in the middle of the town. Three made do with a bed in the bathtub, but the Byrnes looked after us again, just as they did after our first All-Ireland win eighteen long years earlier.

During Tuesday's drinking session, I told a few of the girls about Australia. The Giants had given me a bit of breathing space after the defeat, but in the next few weeks I'd have to board a plane to Melbourne for the AFLW Draft. The timing wasn't great because emotions were running high, and personally, I still didn't know how I felt about it.

My body was tired, and I didn't know how I was going to cope playing a professional sport for four months. I was as stiff as a poker, and a few days of drinking wasn't exactly the recovery session I needed.

The Thursday after the All-Ireland I saw a call coming in from Mike Finnerty of the *Mayo News*. I didn't answer. Thirty seconds later, Angelina Nugent from Midwest Radio flashed up on the screen. To have them both ring at the same time was odd. I listened to Angelina's voicemail. She had the story about me going to the Giants. I hadn't yet told my family or colleagues so I asked her not to say anything just yet. I did the same with Mike, and they both promised to keep quiet until I had spoken to certain people and I knew I could trust them.

When I hung up, Rachel Kearns, our wing-back, just looked at me from across the table and said, 'I'd hate to have your life. Everyone wants a piece of you. How do you cope with it all?' Well, you just do. There have been good and bad things said about me for years so I've never really wasted my time worrying about what people thought of me. If I'd worried about it too much it would have eaten me up long ago. When it came to family, however, that was a different ball game.

As it got closer to going-home time, we got quieter. We all knew that once we walked out the door, another year was over for Mayo ladies football. It was hard. You get separation anxiety, and you wonder how you'll all survive without each other. It's like we were breaking up with each other. For the last eight months, most of us had spent six nights of the week together, and here we were, finally going our separate ways.

That can be a lonely place, but just as the nurse in Temple Street Hospital said, 'It'll get better.'

18

The Draft

FOR THE NEXT FEW DAYS I WAS A FULL-TIME MAM. THE TIMING was perfect because it helped focus my mind elsewhere. It was also a bit of normality – making packed lunches, doing school runs, and tucking Aoife and Chloe into bed at night. Their sister, Kate, was in Crumlin Hospital for an operation to have a cyst removed from her ribs. The pressure of it caused them to crack each time she had a growth spurt, but there wasn't a bother on her. Kate's a strong girl, and she has Mary Staunton's mental toughness, and stubbornness.

Most of my nieces and nephews do. They're good kids, and they appreciate what they have. Any chance I get, however, I stress the importance of hard work. I've always been realistic with them. I never wanted them to be wrapped up in cotton wool, or to lack resilience, like I sometimes see with young players nowadays. That's important to me, so I never mollycoddle them.

Some day I'd like to be a mother myself. I love kids, and I knew I'd miss my eight nieces and nephews like hell when I went to Australia. But I had to put all of that to the back of my mind. It suited me not to think about it because when it came to it, I would have no other choice but to cope.

Two weeks out from the AFLW Draft, Kathleen told the rest of the family that I was heading to Australia to play footy with the Greater Western Sydney Giants. It was easier that she told them for me. It took the pressure off. She told the kids that I would only be gone for six weeks, when in truth it would be four months. Looking back, Kathleen's tactics also helped fool me into thinking I wasn't going for as long as I was. It was much easier to think of it as six weeks. Even though my first trip to Sydney would be a short one to take care of formalities before the draft announcement in Melbourne, once I had gotten through that I would then be leaving as soon as the club football season ended.

I dragged it out longer than I should have with work, especially given that the news had leaked, but I was nervous. There I was out of the blue, asking my boss, Pippa Daniel, for time off to jet to Sydney for a week to go to the AFLW Draft. Then in the next breath I asked for five months' unpaid leave to pursue a potential career in a professional sport on the other side of the planet, all things going well. I knew Pippa would support me because she always did. It was a relief to have that bit over with, and playing house with Aoife and Chloe while Kate was recovering well after her operation was a great distraction.

In the meantime we had beaten Knockmore to win our nineteenth senior club championship title with Carnacon. It was the third time in twenty years that I had captained Carnacon to a senior county title and it was a long road since I'd lifted our first in 1998 as a sixteen-year-old.

Now that I think about it, there weren't that many games that I lost with Carnacon. At underage level we were only ever beaten once – by a point in an U16 final against Kiltane. Every day

Carnacon went out we were expected to win, and win we did. But, maybe we took things for granted, and forgot to celebrate to the extent we should have. So this time around, when we played Knockmore in the final, I made sure the young ones celebrated and savoured it. It can all end in a heartbeat, so you have to make the most of it.

The weekend after the county final win we were due to play Kilbride of Roscommon in the Connacht semi-final. At the same time I was supposed to be on a plane to Australia. I rang Beatrice a few weeks before the county final and told her about Oz because I could foresee my departure for the draft causing problems with fixtures. And, just as I expected, Beatrice was pure level-headed about it. There was no drama. There never was with Beatrice, and that's why we get on. She was thrilled to see me being given such an opportunity, and if this was the situation, then she'd find a solution. End of.

We needed Kilbride to change the game to the Friday night before I flew out and I knew I could trust Beatrice to be discreet and get the job done. Sharon McGing's hen party was on the same weekend, so as it turned out it suited everyone to move it. For months I had done well to keep my secret under wraps. I'd told only a select few and they had passed with flying colours.

However, the day before the Kilbride game, it all unravelled fairly rapidly. I had a missed call from an unknown number on my lunchbreak. An Irish journalist, Marie Crowe, had the story and would be breaking it on RTE News later that day. She said she had it from a number of sources that I'd signed with the Giants. I played dumb and said I had no idea what she was talking about. I refused to corroborate the story. Two hours later, an article surfaced online stating that I was linked to a move Down Under.

I was playing a Connacht semi-final in less than twenty-four hours and instead of being focused on the game I was rehearsing lines in my head to deny the news to people's faces. People I cared about. I had told my family, my close friends and work, but there were still people in my life I wanted to be the first to tell, face to face. I owed them that. But someone broke my trust, and it affected other people in my life when it shouldn't have.

On 13 October we beat Kilbride in Roscommon, and celebrated the win at Sharon McGing's hen party in Athlone. At midnight, I ran out of the place like Cinderella because I had to be up at 5.30 a.m. to leave for Dublin Airport. I couldn't sleep a wink. I'd been going non-stop for the last few weeks. My head was constantly racing, and my body had yet to catch up with itself. I was apprehensive, second-guessing what was ahead of me. But when Crazy, Fiona, Martha, Marie and Aoife Loftus, a former teammate, came back to mine at 4 a.m., any chance of getting a few winks went completely out the window. The lack of sleep, however, would be the least of my problems over the next forty-eight hours.

At 5.30 a.m. the following morning I loaded my suitcase into the boot of my car and left for the airport. The girls herded themselves into the porch and waved me out the driveway. Then, I was on my own. That's the way I wanted it. It meant fewer goodbyes, and less emotion.

By the time I got to the Etihad Airlines check-in desk, I had talked myself around a hundred times as to why I was doing this. It was something that was literally thousands of miles outside my comfort zone. I had nothing to prove to anyone, but to myself, I did. I wanted to find out if I was up to it, and if my body could go another round, another season, if I simply put my mind to it.

I wanted to prove that I could adapt to an entirely new sport. The prospect scared me, absolutely, yet the energy I got from even thinking about it excited me equally. It was like the addiction I'd felt as a young girl taking hold of me all over again.

The first roadblock of the day surfaced with the lady at the check-in desk. There was a problem with my visa, so I was rescheduled to the 7.10 p.m. flight that night to give Alan McConnell and the Giants time to rectify the paperwork. The waiting around didn't help my anxiety.

At 4 p.m. I walked back to the check-in desk for round two. This time my name didn't show on the system. I started to think it was a sign that I shouldn't be going, and I began to seriously question my decision. By now I was agitated. I was alone, tired and on the verge of tears. For the next two hours I stood at the desk and watched an Etihad staff member ring everyone he knew to try to reinstate the booking. Eventually he succeeded, and I was fast-tracked through security. The plane had already begun boarding but I managed to make it with a few minutes to spare.

I was officially on my way. I had gone beyond the stage of tiredness, but even so, my mind wouldn't sit still. All the talking I had done in the car to convince myself that I was doing this for the right reasons had evaporated at the check-in desk. I felt bothered by it all, and a long-haul flight is the worst place you can be when your mind is wandering.

While I knew that this trip was just the precursor and I had to make it through a medical before the contract became official, it was still the first time that everything felt real. And then the worry set in. I worried if I could handle being away from home for four months. I worried about Kathleen, the kids, and how Aoife would

Left: In action during the 2006 Connaught final. There was always huge rivalry between Mayo and Galway.

Below: Crazy, Martha Carter, Triona McNicholas and myself celebrating our FAI Senior Cup final win with Mayo League in December 2006. I loved playing soccer in the off-season as there was a lot less pressure.

Below: With sisters and clubmates Sharon and Caroline McGing after putting an end to Cork's winning streak in the 2007 league semi-final.

Above: Winning our fourth All-Ireland Senior Club Championship with Carnacon in November 2011. We beat Na Fianna from Dublin in the final.

Above: In 2011 we won the club All-Ireland and also celebrated twenty-five years of the club. *Front, left to right*: the four captains of our All-Ireland winning teams: Caroline McGing, me, Michelle McGing and Fiona McHale.

Left: Receiving my 2011 All-Ireland club medal from the legend Páidí Ó Sé.

Left: Delighted to win a 2013 All-Star award alongside my best friend, Crazy. She deserved it so much after years of hard work.

Below: The 2014 All-Star trip to Hong Kong with Crazy and Fiona McHale was one to remember.

Bottom: A training session with Cork's Angela Walsh during the 2016 All-Star trip to San Diego. These trips were a great way of getting to know players from other counties.

Above: In action against Dublin's Deirdre Murphy and Martha Byrne during the 2017 All-Ireland final.

Left: Celebrating with clubmate Fiona McHale after defeating Cork in September 2017 to reach our first All-Ireland final in ten years.

Above: With my nieces Chloe and Aoife in Croke Park after our 2017 defeat to Dublin. There's no worse place to be when you lose. I hope I'll see the girls play in Croke Park themselves someday.

Above: This picture says it all. Feeling both joy and relief to win our sixth All-Ireland club final with Carnacon in November 2017. I left for Oz two days later.

Below: One of my first training sessions with the Sydney Giants – you can tell by my white legs. Also pictured is our inspirational captain, Amanda Farrugia.

Above: Sharing a joke with Al. He is one of the best coaches I have worked with. I learned so much from him.

Below: February 2017: looking a bit worse for wear when Sonia O'Sullivan comes to watch me play against Collingwood in Melbourne. I sustained a broken nose in the second quarter of the game but was determined to play on. Our physio, Claire, gave me unusual strapping to stop the bleeding.

Above: Signing autographs in Canberra for some young Giants fans.

Left: Two of my Giants teammates, Alex Saundry and Nicola Barr, really helped me settle into the club. I was the butt of their jokes on most occasions!

Below: Celebrating our round 6 win against the Western Bulldogs with Elle Bennetts. It was probably our best win of the season.

Above: The AFLW Best and Fairest Awards in Melbourne. *Left to right*: Alex Saundry, me, Louise Stephenson and Alicia Eva.

Above: Spending time with my two nephews, Jack and Cian, in Sydney. It was great to have family over there and it made my move to Australia a lot easier.

Below: I've been asked to do a lot of media work lately alongside some brilliant footballers and analysts and I love doing it.

take it all. I worried about the Famous Five, and missing out on milestones like my friend Aoife Loftus's wedding, Sharon McGing's wedding and Marie's thirtieth birthday.

Then, what if something happened to someone while I was away? I thought of Dad. I thought of my neighbour, Gerry Biggins, who had been sick for fifteen years or so, his wife Una and their four children Rachel, Gerald, Luke and Katie, who I used to babysit. And I thought of Crazy's dad, Pat. In recent years Parkinson's had slowly taken hold of him, and as a family they'd been through the mill. I couldn't get them out of my head. If something happened to Pat, or Dad, or anyone while I was in Oz, I didn't think I could forgive myself. It felt like I was leaving them at the very time I should have been there for them.

On the second flight, from Abu Dhabi to Sydney, I pulled up the calendar on my iPhone and counted how many weeks I would be away. Sixteen. I counted again, just to make sure. It did the trick. Slowly, I drifted off to sleep.

At 6.30 a.m. on Tuesday, 16 October, I walked through the sliding doors at the arrivals hall in Sydney International Airport. There waiting for me with a wide smile was Alan. It was great finally to meet the man who believed in me and who had worked so hard to make this happen. We drove for thirty minutes to the club's training base at Sydney Olympic Park, and the brightness and heat were the first things to hit me. On the dash of Alan's car it read 28°C, but it felt much more stifling than that.

When we arrived, Alan gave me a tour of the facilities. The place was unreal. The nearest comparison I have is the Munster set-up at the University of Limerick. But this place was even light years ahead of that. Everything was located in one building, and it was all shared between the men's and women's teams. There was no divide. All my career I had fought for parity, in one form or another, so this was like finding the holy grail.

In the gym, the Giants netball team were powering through a strength and conditioning session. Other than that there weren't many around, with the AFL men's team not starting pre-season until November.

Alan was deep in conversation with the administration staff, so I wandered freely and Snapchatted the girls back home pictures of my new world. Never-ending rows of machines lined the floor. The weights were individually branded with a Giants 'G' logo, and an AstroTurf area off to the side had every sports gadget you could think of. But it was the huge orange block lettering looking down on all of it that caught my eye: 'We accept the standards we walk past'. That was exactly why I was here.

Over the years, people have said that maybe in another lifetime I would have made it as a professional athlete. But, this was it. It was happening in this lifetime. It might have come later than I had expected, at the age of thirty-five, but I was going to give it my best shot regardless. Plus, I had everything at my disposal to help me be the best professional I could be.

The locker room was something you'd see in a Disney movie, but it was ours. No matter which way you looked, an inspirational quote lined the walls, and in that moment I had an overwhelming feeling that I would be among a group of people who would comprehend me. And I them.

The following morning I showered and freshened up before meeting Alan and Nicholas Walsh for breakfast in a coffee shop in the Olympic Park. The last time I'd seen Nick was almost twelve months to the day at the 2016 Fexco Asian Games when he joked to me about playing in the AFLW. And now here I was alongside him, eating bacon and eggs and talking footy!

Afterwards, we went outside and did a skills session for ninety minutes. I enjoyed it, soaking up everything the lads said. However, I felt that I was struggling a little, especially with the kick-passing. It was easy for me to hide at sunset down in Clogher pitch, but out here in Sydney, not so much.

The heat and tiredness weighed on me too, and there was pressure to perform because the session was being recorded for technical purposes. To add to all of that, the head coach of the men's team, Leon Cameron, was watching. In the middle of the session I heard him shout across to Alan, 'Hey, Al! You'd be mad not to sign her, mate!' That gave me a boost. Leon was a legend in footy circles having played 256 games in the AFL, and I pretty much knew then that they had it in their heads to sign me.

In the afternoon we talked contracts, and that's where Nick came into his own. It was great having another Irish person there, and better still to have an 'insider' who knew the business. There were figures flying everywhere, talk of relocation costs and all sorts, but Nick broke it down and got the best deal. I would earn an honest wage. They would give me an apartment close to my brother in Randwick and a car to get me from A to B. I didn't really need anything else. I was there to learn, so I was content with the deal.

To put a stamp on things, I had a medical exam with the team doctor and physio. And when all that was done, I signed on the dotted line.

It felt good. It felt surreal. I was floating on air to think that I had actually gone ahead and done this. That evening I had a celebration dinner with Brian, his wife Denise and my nephew Cian. Before bed, I rang Kathleen and the kids to tell them the good news. It was a trial run for what was to come, and for now we were all coping OK.

The following day was D-Day – Draft Day. It was the first time since I'd got to Australia that my nerves triggered to a higher level. I flew to Melbourne with Alan, the manager of the Giants' women's programme Libby Sadler, and Alison Zell, the Giants' AFLW media manager. Before boarding the plane I caught sight of the *Sydney Daily Telegraph* on a newspaper stand. The headline read GIANTS' IRISH LASS KICKER, and next to it was a photograph of me swinging my leg at an O'Neills ball in the All-Ireland final. Life was about to change.

We spent the day at the headquarters of the National Australia Bank (NAB) in the docklands area of Melbourne, and I met some of the other players the Giants had drafted. As we chatted, I wondered to myself, *How many Up and Downs would they each last under Finbar?*

The day was long. There was a lot of hanging around, and only so much small talk I could handle. It was hard, too, to know what to make of the other players. We were all in the same boat, but I felt myself recoil. I tried to hide it, but as you know, my shyness multiplies in unfamiliar territory. It was like being back in secondary school, making small talk to make friends.

I was the last pick of six for the Giants, and forty-seventh out of a total of forty-nine. It didn't bother me that I was at the bottom of the pile. The Giants had taken a chance on me as the league's first international draft signing, and that was enough. I hadn't played the sport a day in my life. I was coming to the end of my career and was the second oldest player in the draft. It was a substantial risk for them. But I knew I had more to offer than just my skills as a forward. They needed leadership. They needed someone who'd been there, done that, and whose work ethic aligned with the culture the Giants wanted to create. In their inaugural season in 2017 the team had finished bottom of the table, twenty points behind the Brisbane Lions. They pocketed just one win, and they needed toughening up mentally. That's where I came into the equation for Alan, and there was no going back now.

Overnight, the news broke back home in Ireland. I woke to a barrage of notifications on my phone, including messages from Kieran Donaghy, Zac Tuohy, Colm Cooper, Steven McDonnell and Tomás O Sé. They were all great footballers that I looked up to and their words of encouragement made me realize that I was doing the right thing.

All I wanted to do was get back out on to the pitch. I wanted to get better, much better. In the brief time I had spent with Alan and Nick I saw an obvious improvement, but I wanted to practise any chance I got, so Alan arranged two kicking sessions, the first in the morning at the training ground and the second in the afternoon at the Giants' home ground in Spotless Stadium. I got much more comfortable holding the ball, standing over it, and spreading my hands evenly around its sides. My straight kick-passing was getting there too, now that I had tidied up my technique, while my around-the-corner kicking style complemented things already. Though really, as long as I was putting the ball between the posts, the guys didn't really care which way I did it. They arranged for me to study some video footage of key opposing forwards. I watched their runs, their jumps, and I noted the tackles, the velocity and ferociousness of each hit. And with every goal I saw, I wanted the chance to prove I could do the same.

That session in Spotless Stadium was the icing on the cake. It had been a venue for the 2000 Sydney Olympics, and although it was 13,000 seats shy of MacHale Park, it felt surprisingly special. There was something very Irish about that Friday. For a start, it was raining. It was the first time in three months that the Aussies had felt raindrops in Sydney, and secretly I was delighted.

The next day, after an 8.30 a.m. skills session, Alan and I headed to the Royal Botanic Garden to have lunch with the President of Ireland, Michael D. Higgins, his wife Sabina, and Tánaiste Frances Fitzgerald, who happened to be in town on state business. It had been only a few weeks since I shook Michael D's hand in Croke Park, and here I was now presenting him with a Giants singlet, and he wished me good luck all over again.

Back at Alan and his partner Susie's house, I watched a couple of men's games, with Alan narrating tactics by my side. The various game plans fascinated me and took me back to my days of running offence on the basketball court in Carnacon Community Centre with Art Ó Súilleabháin telling me which plays to call. This time it was Alan's turn, and I left his house with a hard drive full of games to study and dissect.

That night we had a send-off barbecue at Brian and Denise's, with Alan, Nick and Susie. It was a lovely evening, and it gave me a sense of what life would be like when I returned.

The following morning at 6 a.m., Cian clambered on top of me. I took him to the coffee shop around the corner to give Brian and Denise a lie-in as Denise was due their second child in just a few weeks. It was nice to spend time with Cian. He's full of beans and there wouldn't be a bother on him if you threw him into a pen with all the gang back in Mayo. They'd all be as mad as each other.

That afternoon, Brian dropped me to Sydney Airport. It would be another twenty-three hours before I got home, but I was glad I had made the journey.

On Sunday, 21 October, I landed into Dublin at 8.30 a.m. and drove the three hours home to make club training in Clogher at 1 p.m. For the next seven weeks the Giants and Australia would be no more. They understood my commitment to Carnacon, and the starting date on my contract was open until Carnacon were finished in the championship. So from here on out it was all Carnacon.

I was tired after the flight, but I wanted the young ones to see me fighting through it. They had to know that being tired was never an excuse to miss training, even if I had just come halfway across the world. I needed to set the tone because Galway's Kilkerrin-Clonberne were waiting for us in the Connacht SFC club final. We needed to be all in if we were to beat them and keep the dream of another senior All-Ireland club alive.

The provincial final was played in Ballyhaunis, and it was an epic battle that produced eleven goals, five penalties, two red cards, and was level eleven times. At half-time, Kilkerrin-Clonberne were slightly ahead with a score of 2–9 to 4–4, but Fiona McHale, Michelle McGing, Doireann Hughes and Marie Corbett were flying it. They gave me a mountain of ball, and I scored 4–13, which included three penalties and ten points from play. However, Ailish Morrissey scored a point on the sixty-third minute for the Galway champions that saw the game finish deadlocked at 5–17 to 6–14. We'd have to do it all over again the following weekend.

On heavy winter-soaked pitches, games like that take a lot out of you, so for the next few days I did as much recovery and rest as I could. We knew the replay would be just as hectic, and it was too. Kilkerrin-Clonberne led by five points, but midway through the second half we got it together with Fiona playing a stormer in midfield. We drew level, only for Martha to find herself in the sin-bin, and Kilkerrin-Clonberne went four points clear.

The game was as physical as the first day out, and both myself and Louise Ward also found ourselves in the sin-bin for ten minutes after separate incidents. I knew I'd be back on for the final minute or two so at least I had a chance to change the game. When we won a close-range free on the stand-side in the second-last minute, I knew what I needed to do. Float the ball in. Kilkerrin-Clonberne put five bodies in the goalmouth; they should have had more. I aimed just above their heads, and the ball floated between their hands and into the roof of the net. Tie game.

Extra-time loomed, but somehow Amy Dowling found herself one-on-one with the keeper and she rattled the netting. We had won! The final score was 4–10 to 2–13. It was a cracking game, and as captain it felt great to lift the trophy for our sixteenth Connacht SFC club title.

In the All-Ireland semi-final we faced the Ulster champions, St Macartan's of Tyrone. They were coached by former three-time All-Ireland winner Ryan McMenamin and we travelled to Augher expecting a physical game. Surprisingly, we won easily enough and we were through to another final.

The plan was always to leave a legacy. Not me, but us – the older gang in Carnacon. The club made us who we were, and now we had to pay it forward. In 2017, our aim was to win our sixth senior All-Ireland club title, but the plan ran deeper than that. It was only a matter of years before a handful of us would retire and we knew it was time to lay the groundwork.

I've said it before: there's nothing soft about Carnacon. We built an unbelievable work ethic and culture, and success thankfully followed. From the very start we were all in it together. The culture Beatrice, Jimmy and the first generation of players created went beyond the present. Now it was time to make it the future. That's where the likes of Doireann Hughes come in.

I've known Doireann since she first walked through the gates of Clogher pitch as a twelve-year-old girl. For the next decade I drove her to training, and watched her become the competent young woman she is today. I'm like a proud mother when I see how she's turned out. There's no question it's all down to her upbringing, but I'd like to think that myself and the older girls played some part in the type of person Doireann has become.

I knew she would relish being in an All-Ireland club final, and she was excellent when we took on Mourneabbey of Cork in Parnell Park that December. They were no joke. They had contested the 2014 and 2015 finals, and although they had yet to lift the Dolores Tyrrell Memorial Cup, they were experienced. They would be out for redemption and Carnacon would face the brunt of their desire.

We settled well with a point from Martha, and by half-time we were three points in front. In the dressing room I preached to the younger girls not to get carried away, and we didn't. Mourneabbey made the comeback we expected, but we hung on to win by 0–15 to 1–10.

The few seconds at the end of that game were magic. No words can describe it. I was the first captain to lift the Dolores Tyrrell

Memorial Cup for Carnacon in 2002, and fifteen years later it felt just as special.

We had now won nineteen senior county championship titles in twenty years. We had won sixteen Connacht SFC titles, and six of nine All-Ireland club finals. And I couldn't have been happier for the newer generation – the likes of Amy and Louise Dowling, Sadhbh Larkin and Emma Cosgrave – who had never won a national title. That's what winning this time around was all about. They now knew what it took, and that's the legacy we had set out to leave.

19

Becoming a Giant

I DIDN'T HAVE MUCH TIME TO SAVOUR THE WIN OVER MOURNEABBEY. I had to be on a plane to Sydney forty-eight hours after the game, and my phone didn't stop ringing. There wasn't a moment to inhale, or take it all in. Everyone wanted me for something – a television interview, a radio interview, a documentary – when all I wanted to do was spend my last few hours with family and friends. The saddest thing for me was how my departure to Oz took away from the girls' achievement. No one wanted to make a fuss about them, or Carnacon's sixth All-Ireland title. The media made it all about me, and that annoyed me.

The evening before I was due to fly we were still in the thick of touring local parishes with the Dolores Tyrrell Memorial Cup. It was pushing 8 p.m. and I still hadn't had a chance to say goodbye to Dad, Kathleen or the kids. So as we moved to the next parish, I texted Kathleen and asked her for a lift. It was the only way I could get a few minutes in private with my family. And that's how I got to say my goodbyes – in the back of Kathleen's Citroën Picasso in Belcarra, a couple of miles outside my home in Clogher. As I hopped out, I held back the tears. I don't know how I kept it together, but I did.

At 4.30 a.m. we left the Drum Inn in Clogher, and the girls came back to mine to send me off. I didn't go to sleep for fear that I'd miss out on the last bit of banter. That, and I knew my mind wouldn't have settled anyways.

Crazy offered to drive me to Dublin Airport, and I was glad of it this time. On the way we stopped in Ballyhaunis because I wanted to see her parents before I went. It wasn't until I was on my own in the airport that the enormity of leaving for four months hit me. Once I'd got through security, I found a seat in a quiet corner at the end of the terminal. There, all alone, I started to cry.

When I landed in Oz on 7 December, it felt nice to be back on solid ground. It was impossible to get comfortable during the flight. I had badly bruised my ribs in the All-Ireland club final, and no position eased the pain. At the time of the collision I thought I might have broken a rib. Even as I lay on the grass, I convinced myself that whether my ribs were broken or not, I was still getting on the plane. So, when Brian collected me from Sydney Airport at 6.30 a.m., I was happy to stretch, even if it hurt.

I couldn't wait to meet his son Jack, who was born while I was back in Ireland. The plan was to stay with Brian, his wife Denise and their two sons in Randwick until my apartment provided by the club was ready. Randwick is a friendly suburb between Bondi Beach and Coogee Beach with a lot of Irish, so I figured I'd stay there if it suited everyone.

As soon as I was off the plane I was straight into life as an AFLW player. My first session was that evening so Alan McConnell arranged for Rebecca 'Besso' Beeson – one of the small forwards on the team – to collect me at 2 p.m. Training didn't start until 5.15 p.m., but we were expected to be in the club ninety minutes beforehand to get screened and prepped by the physios. When I saw Besso pull up outside the house, I realized I was anxious. I was sixteen years her senior, yet she knew all the right things to say and immediately put me at ease.

But when we arrived at the club, the butterflies really set in. This was it, my first day in the job. I don't think I've ever been as nervous. The situation was so alien to me. I couldn't believe I was walking into a new club, so far away from home, not knowing anyone. I was starting all over again, and that frightened the hell out of me.

Alan introduced me to the coaching staff and to the team, and the first thing they did was congratulate me on Carnacon's All-Ireland win. To be honest, it caught me off guard. I was surprised by how much they knew about me, and about the club. But I sensed that they cared, and I liked that.

A few mornings Nicholas Walsh collected me at 6.45 a.m. I had training at 8.30 but Nick had to be in the club early, so we doubled up. It was nice to see a familiar face, and as we drove, he assured me that I would be just fine. I knew Nick wouldn't plámás me, and that's why I was drawn to him and the Giants. They were honest and up front.

I was allowed to do a little bit during the session but the physio team had my ribs and my jet lag much more in mind than I did. Things went well, but there were times when I felt completely out of my depth. I was a small fish in a big pond and I did that thing where I go into myself. A few of the girls noticed, too. Our vice-captain, Amanda 'The Fridge' Farrugia, Emma 'Swanny' Swanson, Renee Forth, Tanya Hetherington, Courtney 'Gummy' Gum and Maddy Collier all went out of their way to make me feel welcome, and that softened my edginess.

After training, Alan drove me back to Randwick. Usually he didn't drive to work, he scooted, but he had the car that day. It was good that we had some time together. Alan was all questions about the All-Ireland club final, and I could tell he was trying to get a deeper sense of what made me tick. Alan's a shrewd operator. He was subtle, and he took an interest. That's what made him so good. He was the first person hired by the Giants. His job was not only to coach the women's team: as Director of Coaching he oversaw the fifteen other coaches in the club too, including the men's head coach, Leon Cameron.

On the day of a men's game it was Alan's job to observe. During the week, he'd watch the game back from three different angles and at the same time he'd listen to the audio from the coaches' box. Then he'd assess their decisions from what he saw and heard and give feedback. The end goal was that everyone would improve. There are twenty-plus games in the AFL season – that's a lot of games, and a lot of footage to watch. But, Alan McConnell is a workaholic. He's passionate about making Greater Western Sydney Giants one of the best franchises in Australia. He wants it to be the club everyone respects and wants to be a part of. That's Alan's dream, and he's getting there. I could tell that he never missed a trick so I was excited to see how he operated. I couldn't wait to learn from someone who was so respected in the sport, not just within the Giants, but within the AFL.

On 13 December it was my birthday, and I thought I'd got away with it. I hadn't. At the start of the team meeting the girls burst into 'Happy Birthday'. I had turned thirty-six and, bar my sore ribs, life was good. It was great to be able to help Brian and Denise out with baby Jack, or take Cian to Coogee Beach to see Santa

Claus. It was different, I'll give you that, but it was lovely to be with family so far from home. The funny thing was, I never really felt homesick. Every second day I was on the phone to Kathleen and the kids, FaceTiming them at the breakfast table. We were all coping surprisingly well. Life had just moved on.

I was driving myself now too and it was great to have that little bit of freedom. I lived on the opposite side of the city to most of the girls, so I would leave at 12.20 p.m. as it took me an hour to get to the club. That was probably the most stressful thing in Sydney – the traffic!

Gradually I settled into my new life. Every Thursday was Education Evening. Typically, someone came in and spoke to the team – someone like US Olympic gold medallist Helen Maroulis, who had shown the girls a few wrestling tactics the week before I arrived. Another week we had a speaker in from a charity called Ladder, which helps young people aged sixteen to twenty-five who are homeless. Ladder was founded by three AFL players, and each of the men's GWS players donate $25 of their match fee to the charity. It was interesting to hear how the players could volunteer, and it was nice too to get a bit of perspective on life outside my new bubble.

On Education Evenings, Alan also showed us video clips of how we would play and set up. All the information was also available on an app called Game Plan, so everything we discussed was at our fingertips whenever we needed.

The terminology, however, was hard to grasp. It was an entirely new language to me. 'A1, A2, attack 1, attack 2 …' To begin with I didn't have a clue what was happening, but Tanya Hetherington took me under her wing. We were opposite numbers, and Tanya was also trying to impress Alan, yet she was willing to sacrifice her own game to help me improve mine. She was a coach herself, and a good one at that, so I picked her brain any chance I got. I also pestered Courtney 'Gummy' Gum. She was thirty-six too, and the three of us became known as 'The Vets', with Tanya the youngest of us at thirty-two. From day one we formed a great relationship, which wasn't just because of our age. We knew that what each of us was doing at this stage of our careers wasn't easy, and because of that we had huge respect for one another. Our work ethic was the biggest thing we had in common and that's really what drew us closer. I had a lot to learn, and the two girls were a huge support.

As a 'tall forward', it was all about leading patterns – how I ran, and where I ran to. We played with a system of five backs, six midfielders and five forwards, and it was all about creating space. In some ways it is very similar to how you might run in GAA, but in other ways it is very different.

Aussie Rules is based on structures. I had to learn the Giants' structures and how we were going to play, depending on the type and location of a stoppage in the game. The forwards had to play a triangle, a line, or a U-shape formation for stoppages. Defensively, it's all about numbers, and locating players. You don't man-mark. There are six on six, so you push players across the pitch to mark an opponent. It's similar to a zone defence in basketball but over here it's called 'locating'. You count your numbers and go to the nearest player. At the same time, you call your teammates to move one over, so you're constantly handing your opponent off. That takes a lot of communication, a huge amount, and Tanya and Gummy were excellent in helping me get my head around it all.

At the time I still didn't know a lot of players on the squad, and I was still sussing out everyone's personality. My new teammates were still very much strangers. Some had made a huge effort, some hadn't. It actually took an entire week for one player to say hello, but I could tell she was a little bit cagey about me. I was this foreign player who had come in to take up their sport, having never played it. I'd feel the same way if it was the other way around. I'd be cautious. It didn't bother me though because I was there to learn. At the same time, it was interesting figuring out the dynamic of the group.

Alan was figuring us out too. He talked about the importance of being a team, and what the club's values were – family, communication and trust. Then he posed a question that took us all by surprise. He asked us if there was a pecking order in the team. The girls were taken aback by his question, but he was right to ask. There was an undertone there, and we needed to be much closer as a group.

'Cora, I need you to talk more,' Alan continued. 'That's why I brought you over here. You've been here a week now, and you've barely said a thing.'

I didn't feel like I had the right to say anything. I was a newbie trying to fit in. I didn't want to ruffle any feathers, and I certainly didn't want to make any enemies. So I had stayed quiet.

On the way home in the car I couldn't stop thinking about what Alan had said. It annoyed me, but at the same time I didn't want to let him down. He had taken a huge gamble on me, and even though I hardly knew him, I had huge respect for him. I felt a sense of loyalty to Alan, which is strange, because it usually takes me a very long time to trust someone. I had an instant connection with him, and I couldn't tell you the last time that happened to me.

Training was tough, and the heat was a killer, but I sensed that I was getting better with each kick. Everything was so professional, I had no reason not to excel. We were all contracted with the Giants but my visa didn't permit me to work, so that helped. A lot of the girls still had to earn a living, but I was able to swing by the club every day, grab a few bags of balls and practise my kicking in the Cage. The Cage was a huge indoor facility, and being able to practise indoors was a big change from home.

On the days we trained, we were expected to be ready for the pre-training meeting at 5.15 p.m. The team meeting was held in one of the boardrooms and in total, players and staff, there were forty of us in it. There was also a meeting room for the forwards, another for the midfielders, and one for the defenders.

Alan would outline the upcoming session in detail – what the drills were, how we were to do them, for how long, and what groups we were in. Each training session was videoed from two different camera angles so Alan would analyse six to eight clips from the previous session. He'd highlight both the negative and positive aspects so that before we ever stepped foot on the pitch, we all knew what we needed to focus on. Outside on the sideline there was a large digital clock that timed each drill exactly. If Alan stopped, the clock stopped; not a second was wasted. There were fifteen members of the backroom team at every session, including four coaches, videographers, physios, masseurs, the team doctor, first-aiders to do our strapping, water runners and a psychologist. Every possible element was at our disposal.

When we finished on the pitch, we had five minutes to get into our gym gear, and that session would last sixty to ninety minutes. We were allowed to bring in our phones but could only use them for the purpose of following the gym programme, which was uploaded on to TeamBuildr. Each programme was specifically tailored to each player, and the strength and conditioning coach and his two assistants worked their way around the room.

Initially, I tried to impress them. But I had to be very careful. I was lifting weights with my ribs still heavily bruised, so I had to pretend that I was OK. I didn't want to be the one to say that I couldn't do something. My ribs aside, I also had to contend with the heat, my age, and the fact that I had just come off an eleven-month season. But, I had to suck it up!

Afterwards, there was a stretching and recovery session. At the back of the dressing room the dietician had a selection of protein shakes, yoghurts, breads and cereals ready for us. To finish off, you took either an ice bath or a hot-cold bath for ten minutes, before heading home around 9 p.m.

One particular day in the pre-training meeting, Alan approached me. He wanted me to speak to the team about what makes a great club. What made Carnacon so successful? I had fifteen minutes to gather my thoughts, and I'd be lying if I said I wasn't nervous. I barely knew these girls, and I got the vibe too that some of them still weren't happy I was there. This was Alan's way of getting me to tell the girls what I was really all about.

I explained to them all about Carnacon – where my little village was in Ireland, what we had won, and how we weren't all that liked because of our success. I spoke about our winning culture, and our stubbornness. And then I spoke about trust, friendship, family and respect.

'In Carnacon, we treat everyone the same, from the youngest to the oldest. We expect so much of our younger players. We mind them, but we don't give them anything soft. We expect to win every day that we go out and play, but we always respect our opponents, no matter who they are.'

I don't know what the girls got out of that talk, but I think they saw the real me. By putting me on the spot like that, Alan very subtly got me to open up. Everything I spoke about was exactly why he'd taken a gamble on me. He needed the others to see that, but it needed to come from me.

The hardest training I did, both physically and mentally, was probably a week out from Christmas Day. I dropped a few marks that I shouldn't have, and that was supposed to be my strength. I hated it when I wasn't good at something. I was frustrated, but I didn't want to show it. I thought of home, of Mayo football, and I wondered how the AFLW girls would cope if the shoe was on the other foot.

The Mayo gang are just as talented, if not more. We're ahead of them when it comes to catching and movement. They thought I was quick off the mark, but it's just because my footwork is faster from Gaelic. In Australia they call it 'patterns of running'. Our instinct in playing Gaelic football is to go from nought to a hundred miles an hour, whereas in AFL they coast. That's just how the game is played. You kick. You catch. You make ground.

Ladies footballers also train just as professionally as the Aussies but we don't have a third of the resources. The Sydney set-up is so professional; you have a network of support constantly feeding you information to make you a better player. We don't have that at home, but that's exactly what makes ladies footballers a mentally tougher breed. In the past we've had to fight to have a physio, an S&C coach, even a recovery session. So, in that regard, a lot of Irish girls would excel in the AFLW just given their resilience.

That said, it's by no means a walk in the park. It's an entirely different sport. You can hang off your opponent in Aussie Rules. You can push players and block runs. And that's what ladies footballers would struggle with the most – the physicality of the tackle. I can handle that part of the game because throughout my career I had two or three players hanging off me. But these girls take it to a whole other level. That's why I partnered myself with players like Amanda, Swanny and Tanya, because I knew they would push me.

There wasn't much let-up over the holidays. I had five gym sessions, four running sessions, a cross-training session and some extra skills sessions to do while I was off. But I made sure I did more than that. On Christmas Eve, we went to six o'clock Mass, and afterwards Brian and myself headed to the Dogs Hotel pub in Randwick for a few drinks. It was my first time away from home at Christmas, and it felt strange, but at least I was with family. Brian and Denise were so good to me, as were their friends, and that made things easier. Cian was excited for Santa, and on Christmas Day we celebrated with a morning swim at Coogee Beach.

On St Stephen's Day it was back to reality, running in 30°C heat. I didn't want to slack off because I knew I had so much to catch up on. Every day I pounded the footpaths around Queens Park, and took to the Cage in the club to do extra kicking sessions. It was probably the toughest two weeks I've ever put down. So much so, I didn't think I would survive the next few months. My body ached all over, but the challenge was too addictive. Every morning I woke in pain, but I would go again.

To relax, I paddle boarded in Rose Bay, ate pizza at Bondi Beach, and took Cian on day trips to Taronga Zoo, or Sydney Aquatic Centre. For New Year's Eve, the club invited me to watch the fireworks on a boat trip around Sydney Harbour. I was the only player on board, but I knew they wanted to make it a special night for me, being so far away from home. Alan and Susie were there, along with the club's CEO, Dave Matthews, other board members and admin staff. It was a once-in-a-lifetime experience, and I appreciated that those high up in the club were so considerate to ask me to join them.

Over the next few days I picked up my training even more. Alex 'Sauce' Saundry joined me for a few gym sessions, and slowly we got to know each other. She was one half of 'The Sauce Barr' videoblog, with our teammate Nicola Barr. The two of them combined were the Giants' equivalent of Mayo's joker, Crazy. Their constant slagging made me realize that I'd been accepted into the team, and I really appreciated that time over the Christmas break when they made me forget about missing home.

A few mornings, Nick also invited me to help with the men's team. He was working with some of the injured lads doing rehab, and it was a great way to see how the guys operated. I didn't have a clue who any of them were but they always said hello. Some of them even slagged me about my 'swivel' style of kicking, and they were always hugely supportive of the women's set-up. That inclusiveness was massively encouraged in the club, from the top down.

We shared the same facilities as the men, despite the fact that they were full-time and we were semi-professional, contracted to just fourteen hours a week. The men were there more often because it was their job, but that was the only difference. We crossed over a lot, and that opened my eyes to what things could be like. I realized just how far off we were from a set-up like that in Mayo. Fair enough, the money and facilities made it more feasible in Australia. We don't have the same kind of financial backing in Ireland, but money shouldn't be a barrier to equality. For a start, we could all just come together and figure out a way forward.

We returned to training after the holidays with a 2-kilometre time trial at 7.30 a.m. It was 32°C and I was saturated in sweat, but I was happy with my time. The extra work had paid off.

Off the field, the club continued to make us better players too. We had an Education Morning to learn how to use the club's video analysis package, Sportscode, and on our own time we could watch clips of each of our sessions on specially allocated computers in the club's offices. A psychologist also spoke to us about our expectations, and what we stood for as a team. We listed ten things that made us a good team, a good family, and what could derail us. We agreed that we needed trust, support and communication, and it hit home that these were values each of us had to bring if we were to build a winning culture as Giants.

At the end of the meeting, Alan and Susie invited the players and staff to their home for dinner the following day. The CEO, Dave Matthews, the Chief Operating Officer, James Avery, and all the backroom staff – Sim, Claire, Gail, Munty and all the line coaches – joined us.

Personally, I don't use sports psychology. It's not that I don't believe in it – I do. Each person is different, though, and I tend to use my match and life experiences to get me through. But some players get a huge amount from sports psychology, and I think as a group, getting together in Alan's house with senior members of the club, we realized they had our backs. Slowly, but surely, the players were beginning to realize we had each other's backs too.

Some days at training I felt like I was running around like a headless chicken. One particular day I got six shots off but only scored one. It wasn't good enough. We had two challenge games coming up before the season opener and I wanted to be better. I expected to be better. I found it hard to measure my performance. I didn't know what I should be measuring it against, and that was the problem. I measured my performance just as I would in a GAA game, and you can't do that. Ladies football and Aussie Rules don't compare. Initially, my tendency was to make that comparison, and that's where my frustration came from, but gradually I adapted.

After training, I would get a rub-down from one of our physios, Claire. She was lovely, but I tested her patience a little bit. She wanted me to take it easy and recover, but I couldn't. I didn't know how to. I was obsessed with becoming as good a footy player as I could be. And the only way I knew how to do that was to practise. The best thing about being in Australia was also the hardest thing I had to adapt to – the training methods. There was so much focus on recovery, on looking after your body, and not on training. That drove me mad because all I wanted to do was train. Why are we not training on the pitch tonight? Why are we doing another recovery session? I had Claire driven demented. She wanted me to sit down and relax, but kicking a football is what relaxed me. That *was* my mental health time!

I just wanted to get better. I needed to get better. It was in my psyche.

20

Miles Apart

I WASN'T NERVOUS FOR MY FIRST GAME, I WAS MORE APPREHENSIVE. I'm not sure what the difference is between the two, but I know I wasn't nervous. I was ready, I just didn't know what to expect. The Brisbane Lions were in town for a pre-season challenge match on 20 January 2018, and it was officially my first AFLW game. I didn't really know what I was getting into. I wondered what the standard would be like, and if I would survive the 32°C heat.

What I did know was that all eyes were on me. That added a little pressure on Alan too, and I didn't want to let him down. Brian, Denise and the boys were there, and I knew Brian was proud of me. We were never the kind of family to say that straight out to one another, but I knew he was excited.

I kicked two goals, and I managed to get to grips with the physicality of the game too. But, it was tough. Very tough. I had eight contested marks inside 50, and that was a good thing, apparently. The closest way to describe the inside 50 is like the 45-yard line in football. In AFL, the more marks you contest inside 50 – that is the goal area you're attacking – the better. So, the more contested marks, the more scoring opportunities you've created for your team.

I was oblivious to the meaning behind the stats, however. All I wanted to know was what I did wrong, and how I could improve.

Between GPS, video and stats, there's nowhere to hide. I'm not a fan of stats in general because they don't measure work rate. Some of the girls were so fixated on getting as many touches of the ball as they could to drive their stats up. They were content with that. But what mattered most was what you did with the ball. I said it to Alan. They were getting too hooked up on it, and he knew it too. We needed to be more accountable for the possession we did have. Me, I was caught in the tackle a few times. I should have taken a shot, or passed the ball off, and I wasn't long realizing that I needed to be that split second quicker. That said, it wasn't a bad start.

We won 12.4 (76) to 4.2 (26). (For every goal, you register six points, and for every behind, you score a point, and the total score is then tallied in the brackets at the end of the scoreboard.) The dynamic of the group changed after that victory. It came alive. The girls who hadn't spoken to me all that much when I arrived came around. They saw why Alan had brought me over, why he'd invested in me, and the value that I brought. I'd say some of them thought I was mad. Others reckoned I was 'fearless', but I was just being myself. Maybe it was because I never showed emotion. Back in Ireland, people had had twenty-three years to get used to me, but I was new to them. They quickly realized that I was game for a laugh. And the second they did, they didn't stop slagging me – mostly about my accent! But that helped us to bond.

At times they called me 'Big Dog' just to rise me, and a few of the girls even set up a fake Cora Staunton fan page on Instagram.

Secretly, I enjoyed the banter. It reminded me of the craic at home, and slowly we all came to terms with one another. I made a point of bringing one or two of the younger players out with me for extra kicking sessions too, or I'd join them for a cup of coffee in the canteen. That was something I always did with Mayo or Carnacon and I was now comfortable enough to do that with my new teammates.

I didn't think anything of it, but after the Brisbane game our vice-captain Alicia Eva sent me a text message: 'Hey mate, just thought I'd check in and see how you're going this week, and to check in on how you're taking the barrage of teammate social media love (including me!)?! If it's too much and you just want people to chill, let me know. On another note, the way you're galvanizing the group is really, really special. Let's grab a coffee this week if you're free!'

Alicia was a brilliant vice-captain, and an even better teammate. Alan, however, was the glue, and he drove us all. He's a people person. He took an interest in what was happening in our lives outside football, and that created a unique bond with each player. He knew how to manage all thirty of us. And he had me figured out too! He understood how driven I was, and that I wasn't doing it to get in his good books. It was just the way I was. So, after that first win, I was delighted for Alan more than anyone.

From the first day I met him, he never once judged me. I wasn't used to that. During my career, almost every coach I'd played under – and sometimes teammates – had preconceptions of who I was. Alan didn't. He judged me on what he saw in training every day, and that's why I trusted him so quickly. To him, I was just Cora. Someone who wanted to do her best, and win. He's very much a listener too, and I like that in a coach. Having said that, any time he gave me a compliment, I couldn't handle it.

'You're doing very well, Cora.'

'I don't want to hear it, Alan!'

We were like a husband and wife arguing! Every time I'd contradict him. He couldn't understand that side to me. At the same time, Alan knew I wasn't the type of player that needed their ego massaged. More often than not he just laughed at my replies. I'm confident in my own right, but when it comes to compliments, they make me uncomfortable. I'll simply deflect, or make a joke, just to make the awkwardness pass.

Alan understood the difference between compliments and giving a player feedback. There's a fine line between the two. A compliment will never make you a better player. Feedback will. Every day I was learning, and every day I saw something I could bring home. I was so happy I'd had the courage to pack my bags and start all over again. The season hadn't even begun but it had already been such a huge experience. I loved the training, I loved the challenge of trying to improve myself, and I loved going into the club, meeting everyone.

Getting to know the girls and Alan was fun, and then there was Nicholas Walsh. I can't speak highly enough of him. He always looked out for me. He spent his weekend watching footage of the Brisbane game, and on the Monday he called over and talked me through everything I did. The good, the bad and the ugly. He didn't have to do that. But Nick always had my best interests at heart – in the club, and outside it. I could ring him any time of the day, or call to his desk in the office, and he'd be there for me. I met the man only once before I ever got to Australia. He didn't have to put that time and effort in for me, but he did. Those kinds of people don't come around too often, and the Giants are very lucky to have Nicholas Walsh.

I didn't miss football either. In January 2018, Mayo faced West-meath in the opening game of the Division 1 National League. I texted the girls good luck, but other than that I barely looked up the result. It was just the second time in twenty-three years that I didn't feature in the league, but I didn't miss it all. I had a new lease of life with the Giants. Here, I could just play footy. I didn't have to deal with the drama. I turned up to training, made myself a better player, and tried to perform. I wanted the Mayo girls to do well, but it was time they had a go at it without a few of the older gang around to guide them.

It was time I got to grips with my own season opener too, and on the bus to Casey Fields in Melbourne for my first AFLW game, 'A Sky Full of Stars' by Coldplay played through my headphones. It was Round 1 of the 2018 NAB AFLW, and the Giants had much higher hopes this season. The previous year they were awarded the wooden spoon, and when Alan came into the club he had to lay the foundations all over again. We'd already seen how much he and the staff had put into the programme, and we wanted to deliver for the club.

The ground at Casey Fields seemed so much more enclosed. There was a carnival-type atmosphere with fireworks and fan zones, and thankfully there was no booing – which made a change! There were 5,000 in the crowd, so it was somewhat strange. I couldn't compare it to either a Mayo championship match or an All-Ireland final. But I was so engrossed in the game that I didn't have time to take much else in.

Over the previous few weeks I had retrained my brain to a new ball and a new game. This was it, and I soon realized that things had revved up five or six gears since the challenge game. Playing AFLW wasn't as easy as it looked. I was being pushed, punched and shoved in a completely different way. At the same time, I had to remain aware of everything I'd worked on during the week.

The sides were level entering the fourth quarter but with three minutes left Melbourne snuck a goal, and the win. Despite scoring a goal myself, I was disappointed with how I played. I knew what I had to do, but it was strange not knowing in detail about everyone else's role on the pitch. That was alien to me – being the rookie, not the veteran. In football, I knew exactly who the corner-back was marking and what they should be doing. And if they weren't doing it, I'd tell them as much. Here, I wasn't in control of anything. I was barely in control of myself. I couldn't influence the game like I could at home.

Afterwards, I spoke with the coaches and reviewed the footage. Alan said he'd give me a six or seven out of ten. That wasn't bad, but it wasn't great either. I always knew it would be difficult to pick up the game in just eight weeks. But, that was my job. I never wanted that to be an excuse, and I didn't want the coaches to use it either. The reason why I didn't play well was because I didn't play well. End of story.

On the Monday when we returned to training, I was still annoyed with myself. But I had to focus on the next game. I couldn't dwell on my weekend performance. Whether it was brilliant, bad or indifferent, I had to move on. My body was sore, and Claire gave me a bit of a talking to. She banned me from doing any extra kicking until the Wednesday. I asked if I could just do thirty minutes, but she said no. I asked if I could do twenty, but she wasn't having any of it. Every day off, I was in the club doing extra kicking, but it had caused little tears to form in my groin. Claire was right, I needed to rest. The thing was, I needed to practise too. Most of the girls didn't train if they were told not to. I was the opposite. I *had* to train.

Our next game was at the start of February against Carlton at Drummoyne Oval – just six days away. I didn't know if Alan was going to pick me to start or not. At thirty-six, it was the first time in my life that I was worried about whether I would be selected or not. I was seeing it from the other side, and that was humbling. I was doubting myself, and on the Monday night I had a real crisis of confidence. Was I any good at this, or had I made the biggest mistake of my life? Either way, I just had to get on with it.

In my third game, away to Collingwood, I knew my nose was broken the second Sophie Casey's elbow hit me. It happened at the end of the second quarter as we trailed by ten points, and if we lost, our season was pretty much over. Immediately, Claire realized I was in trouble. I did too. It was the fourth time that I had broken my nose, and I was familiar with what came next. 'I'm fine! I'm fine!' I snapped, not wanting to come off, but Claire instructed me that I had no choice with the blood rule. I broke the poor woman's heart. She was an excellent physio, and I had every faith that she would do her best to get me back on the pitch, within reason.

We headed downstairs to the medical room, where the club doctor inspected me and carried out a SCAT test. I knew I wasn't concussed, but the doctor called out a number of letters and I repeated them back. I had to stand on one foot with my eyes closed for thirty seconds and do a few other small tests. Then the doctor compared my results to the baseline SCAT test results I'd done pre-season. I passed, but before I could rejoin my teammates the medical team had to try to put my nose back in place.

On the first attempt I didn't have an injection to numb the pain. I stood there, gritted my teeth, and took it. Nothing. They tried to manoeuvre it into place again, and this time I had an injection. It only numbs the area for ten to fifteen minutes while the bone is manipulated, but that still didn't work. I told Claire that I was fine and that we could fix it after the game, so I could get back out there for the third quarter. We rejoined the team in the dressing room for the half-time talk. As I listened, Claire and Kay, our second physio, tag-teamed in and out, stuffing my nose to stop the bleeding.

Shortly into the third quarter, my nose began to bleed heavily again. And there, on the sideline, the two physios unstuffed and restuffed my nose before wrapping a bandage around my head to keep everything in place this time. The pressure was awful from the swelling, the poking and prodding. My septum was completely pushed over to the left-hand side. I could only breathe through my right nostril, but I was just happy to be back out there.

At the start of the fourth, Gummy flicked over a goal that helped keep our hopes for the season alive. That comeback was great to be a part of, and the girls belted out the Giants' team song – the words to which I didn't have a clue about!

Well there's a big, big sound
From the West of the town –
It's the sound of the mighty GIANTS!

They were crazy for the celebrating. They all had such positive energy, and they had high-fives coming out their ears. They laughed at me for struggling with that, because I never did celebrations, but I didn't mind. I was delighted for them, and for Alan especially. It was his first AFLW win after all his years coaching, and he deserved this moment. As I stood there, he came over, gave me a little hug, and asked me if I was OK. You could see in his smile just how proud he was of all of us for digging so deep.

'It's OK, I'm fine,' I replied as best I could, muffled as I was by the bandage.

He then told me that he thought I had been 'sensational', and I told him that I didn't want to hear it. But my confidence was back up, and to add to the win, one of my sporting idols was in the crowd.

Sonia O'Sullivan won a gold medal for Ireland in the 5,000 metres at the 1995 World Athletics Championship. She also won a silver medal at the Sydney Olympic Games in 2000, and she now lived in Melbourne. If you were growing up in the nineties in Ireland, Sonia was the only athlete that young girls had to look up to. There was no one else that made me think, *God, I want to be like her!* I admired the way she carried herself, and how she stayed so grounded despite all her fame.

We had met briefly at different events over the years, and she'd texted me before the game saying she would be there. She had cycled from her home to the Olympic Park Oval and chatted with Brian, Denise, and other Irish fans who spotted her. After the team sing-song I made my way over to the boundary to say hello. We shared a joke about how lovely my bandage looked, and I introduced her to Alan. He asked if Sonia would join the team and our families in the dressing room to say a few words, and she kindly agreed.

No one on the team knew who she was, bar one of the physios who was a huge athletics fan. Personally, it was an honour to introduce her to the girls.

'Sonia is a superstar back home,' I said, 'and in my eyes she's Ireland's greatest ever athlete. Growing up, she was my sporting idol, and to have her here is really, really special ...'

It was surreal, to be honest. Here I was, introducing my idol to one of the greatest sports clubs on the other side of the planet! I never would have imagined it.

The next job was to go to the hospital. The team doctor was wary of letting me fly because there was a large haematoma, or blood clot, in my nose. There was a risk that it could travel to the brain, so as a precaution I had to get checked out. Thankfully, the consultant cleared me to fly because I didn't want to have to stay the night in Melbourne. The airline held the plane for a few minutes at the request of our team manager, Libby Sadler, and when I arrived the girls clapped me on to the flight. I was mortified, and they knew it too. But, deep down, I didn't care. I was happy that we had turned a corner.

We had our first win, and every day we were growing closer.

The following morning I saw a specialist about my nose at St George Private Hospital in Kogarah. There was no avoiding surgery, but it was all about the timing. If I got the surgery done now, I'd miss the rest of the season, and that was never an option. Waiting just meant things would be a little more complex; they'd have to break my nose before the four-hour surgery. But it was always going to be complex anyway given the scar tissue that was there from the previous breaks.

There were a few risks with delaying the surgery, but I decided to take my chances. Firstly, if I got hit in the nose again, I risked breaking another bone. There would be no deferring surgery then. Secondly, if I got an infection in my sinuses, I'd be in a bit of bother. And thirdly, if I got a belt in my other nostril, I wouldn't be able to breathe – and then I'd definitely be in a spot of bother. I hadn't come all the way here to play just three games, so once the club's chief medical officer signed me off, I deferred my surgery and went back to training.

It was now March, and we were performing OK. We'd drawn with Adelaide, beaten Fremantle, and every weekend we were digging deeper. For me, every day was a school day. Each game I narrowed my focus to doing three things as best I could. That might be attacking the ball, rolling away after a tackle, or lining up a kick, but I kept it simple. And, as the days flew by, I found myself getting more immersed in the sport and invested in my teammates. We sensed that we were part of something special. We had changed the trajectory of the club, and together we were living the work ethic and culture Alan had envisioned.

By the sixth round, we sat in fifth place. We faced the ladder leaders, the Western Bulldogs, and it was going to be a huge challenge. We pulled off a shock win in Canberra to give ourselves a one-game shot at making the Grand Final. Our confidence was at an all-time high. Twelve months before, a lot of the girls had been at rock bottom. They had now turned things around; for the club, and for each other.

The main thing was that I was ruled fit for our final game, the showdown against Brisbane on 16 March. I was carrying a knee injury after the Bulldogs game. The second I landed on my left foot, I knew something was wrong. There was a shooting pain out the front of my knee, and then pins and needles. I didn't let on how bad it was. Instead, I asked the medical team to strap my knee, and out I went.

The following day, an MRI scan showed that I had a medial ligament tear. A ligament attached to my patella tendon was also badly inflamed and I had bruising on the bone itself as well.

'OK, but can I play against Brisbane?' I asked the doctor.

The answer was yes, but my knee would need to be heavily strapped. As it was, it felt like it could go underneath me at any second. I was willing to take that risk, however, if it meant helping the Giants reach their first Grand Final.

For the opening five minutes we took it to them. We scored a goal, and the huge home support got us going. But then it all fell apart. We lost our shape. We were second to the ball. Not one of us took the game on, and there was no going back when the Lions overran us in the first quarter (7–38). For the next three quarters we matched them stats-wise, but it was too late. They trashed us by forty points. It was hugely disappointing. We had come so close. We believed in ourselves and yet when push came to shove, we couldn't deliver.

Despite our disappointment, it was still strictly business in the dressing room afterwards. There were no thank-you speeches, like there would be at home. Instead, the post-mortem was already being laid out on the table. That's how professional this thing was. For ten minutes, Alan broke the game down. He was so strategic about it. We were sitting there devastated yet he was still going through the minute details of where it all went wrong. It was a harsh talk, but we needed it.

'I'm hugely proud of you as people,' he told us, 'but tonight I'm disappointed in you as footballers.'

It was that straightforward. The stats on the board next to him said as much. That's the reality of professional sport. We had played poorly in five of our twenty-eight quarters during the season, and ultimately that's what cost us a chance at making the Grand Final. We had let ourselves, and Al, down.

The season ended there, but for me the entire experience had been incredible. Did it change me? That's hard to answer, but I hope it has. There was a different Cora in Australia. My role within the team had changed, so I changed. It didn't matter what I scored, all I had to do was work hard. At home, I always had to be the scorer, the on-field leader. That was the expectation of me in Mayo. It was the expectation of my teammates, managers, the media, and of myself. That was the responsibility I took on as a young footballer. It was all I knew. Now, I know otherwise.

One of the biggest things too was that Alan McConnell and the Giants didn't judge me. There were no preconceptions. They saw me for who I was. They accepted me. That made me relax more as a player. Maybe it was the environment too, but I don't think so.

I also learned that there are multiple roles within a team, no matter how big or how small. I'd nearly go so far as to say that I learned more about team sport in the four months I spent in Sydney than I did in the twenty-three years I played ladies football. My eyes were opened. I realized that I didn't have to be the best person on the pitch, I just had to be the best person I could be. The Giants made me see that.

I had never imagined it possible to walk into another club and feel at home. Yet, every day I walked in, I felt exactly that – at home. I could easily have been playing for Carnacon, only this was on a much bigger scale. I'd arrived completely outside my comfort zone. I didn't have my close friends to confide in. I didn't have Crazy to soften my social awkwardness. I didn't have Kathleen or the kids to distract me from the pressures of football. It was shit or bust. I just had to be me.

A few days before I flew home, Alan called me into the club.

'We want you, but do you want to come back?' he asked.

'You know I do!' I replied.

Throughout the season I'd sensed that the club wanted me back. Alan had too, and there and then we agreed privately, in principle, that I would wear the Giants jersey again in 2019.

I arrived home on Wednesday, 18 April, and it took some time to reacclimatize to the Irish weather. It was lovely to see everyone, and the girls were playing some good football under the new Mayo coach, Peter Leahy. Peter had been with us the previous year under Frank so there was a bit of continuity, which was good.

On the Sunday, Mayo beat Cork in the Division 1 National League semi-final, and two days later he rang me to see if I had made a decision about coming back or not. Mayo were due to play Dublin in the National League final in eleven days' time, but I had no intention to return then. The girls had done brilliantly to date, and besides, I hadn't really sat down and figured things out in my own head. It would be a twenty-fourth successive season, with a four-month season in a new sport thrown on top of that. So I told Peter I'd come back to him after the National League final, and that for now we'd say nothing. As far as I was concerned, if the media asked, we agreed to both say that we were going to talk after the league.

The following Monday, just five days out from the National League final, a headline in the *Western People* newspaper read STAUNTON'S INTERCOUNTY FUTURE REMAINS UNCERTAIN. Peter had been asked about my future with Mayo and he'd spoken about it when my understanding was that we had agreed not to talk – at least not until after the National League final.

'We haven't spoken,' was the first thing he said. Then, he went on to say, 'The reality is the panel is open to anyone who wants to play for Mayo and she's one of the best players in the country. We have an emphasis in place: it's about the team. It's not about individuals. Cora is a big name but if she comes in she'll be coming in as a team player. Our forwards, at the moment, are shooting the lights out. If that continues, we're quite happy with the forwards we have.'

Was he saying I wasn't committed to Mayo? Was he saying I wasn't a team player? Was he trying to send a message that he didn't need me, or that he didn't want me? I didn't understand. I thought we had agreed that we'd talk after the National League final. We had also agreed to keep my return out of the papers because the girls were getting ready to play in a National League final. It should have been about them, but somehow it was about me, and I hadn't even opened my mouth.

On the Saturday, Mayo lost to Dublin in the final. Forty-eight hours later, Peter Leahy asked me to meet him in Breaffy House Hotel in Castlebar. My mind still wasn't made up, but I couldn't let his comments in the *Western People* go unchallenged. I had to address them and clear the air if I was going to go back.

We met in a quiet corner of the hotel and chatted casually at first about Australia. After a few minutes, I knew he meant business when he pulled out a notepad, as did I. 'Rate your fitness out of ten at the minute,' was the first thing he wanted to know. Why do you want to play with Mayo this year? What role do you see yourself playing in the team? Aside from football, what can you bring to the team this year?

I was basically being interviewed for a position on the Mayo team! I didn't know of any other player who'd had to sit through something like that. Why me? It was so disrespectful, and disappointing. If I could turn back the clock, I'd have walked out of there. After more than two decades of giving my all to my county, my character and commitment were being questioned, prodded and poked. I was so angry, but I managed to stay calm.

When the line of questioning subsided, I told him how disgusted I was with what he had said in the *Western People*. That in itself was hurtful, to me, my club and my family. I had never fallen out with him – I'd had him as a coach twice before, in 2013 and 2016, and he knew how I worked and how I put the team first. We'd had many a good talk about football so he wasn't a stranger coming in, trying to figure me out. He knew me. He knew what I was about, and often praised the winning mentality that Carnacon players had, but now I was getting the impression that he didn't want me back in the squad. So I asked him straight out. Did he want me back on the team or not? He said he did, but he couldn't guarantee me a place.

I didn't expect to be guaranteed a place. I just expected fair treatment, and that in no way should my age be a reason not to play me. If I was good enough, then I was good enough. Peter wanted an answer right there and then about my future, but I told him I'd come back to him in a week with my decision. I thought that when I met him I would come away with a clearer idea, but the opposite was true.

As we stood up to leave, he had one more question. If I wasn't the free-taker this year, how would I feel about it? I said I wouldn't mind if I was the free-taker or not, so long as the best free-taker on the team was the person taking them. That person, I told him, was standing in front of him. And, with that, I turned and walked away.

That was my belief, and in my heart I knew I was good enough to go again. Yet, after all these years, did I really need someone questioning my commitment to Mayo football? I spoke with Crazy and Kathleen, and Beatrice and Jimmy. I made a list of pros and cons about going back – and the cons far outweighed the pros. That said, I made my decision. I was going back. I needed to go back. I was fit and I still had a hunger to win with Mayo. I wasn't ready to hang up my boots just yet.

The day before the team was due to reunite after the League final defeat and revisit Clare Island for a training weekend, I texted Peter Leahy.

I'll be there tomorrow.

From the off, I was cautious. I didn't know how my return would pan out given that I had come back into the team midway through the season. In over twenty years playing for Mayo I had only ever joined the season at such a late stage once before, because of the ACL injury in 2008. I doubted myself. Would I start? Would I be dropped? I didn't have a clue.

It was the first time in my career that I didn't question the stand-ards we had set ourselves as a team. That's what I had always done

273

before – asked questions of management and of ourselves as a team, to make sure we left no stones unturned. This time around, it was different. I made a conscious effort to keep my head down and focus on my own game. I'd work hard and earn the right to wear a jersey in the Connacht final. If I could prove that I was still worthy of a starting place, then I knew I would be fine.

But, things didn't ever really feel fine. Obviously every manager is different, not only in how they coach, pick their team and prepare for big games, but also in how they interact with and motivate players. Peter had a tough approach and I could see that some players weren't thriving in this new dynamic. Some seemed obviously unhappy in themselves, which was worrying at that stage of the season. Others seemed absolutely fine, which proves that what knocks one person will motivate another. Roaring and shouting have always been part of the training process to a greater or lesser degree, depending on the manager. Most intercounty players cope well with that as long as they get some encouragement along the way too. Finbar and Frank were both well able to roar back in their time and I certainly never had a problem with it as they also knew when an encouraging word was needed – and it's not like I haven't been known to shout myself. This just felt different.

In the lead-up to the Connacht final against Galway in June, things seemed to take a turn for the worse. A few of the girls didn't appear to be coping well in the environment and several of us became genuinely concerned for them – I wasn't alone. This was real life, and players have real struggles. As a footballer, as a person, you need a safe place to express yourself. Some didn't feel they had that any more and it was for that reason a number of us – twelve players and two members of the management team – decided to leave the panel after the Connacht final. I can't speak for anyone but myself, but some of the players affected had been teammates for over ten years, so while I was aware of the implications of our actions on the remaining players, I felt loyalty was also owed to friends who needed support, and so I made my decision.

It was extremely difficult to walk away. I didn't take the decision lightly. None of us did. I questioned if I had done the right thing. Why didn't I ignore it? Why didn't I just stay and finish the season? But, I know who I am and what I stand for. I was raised with morals and principles, and even though it probably wasn't always the popular thing to do, I can always say I stood strong for what I believed in. There were rumours around that I was the cause of a collective walkout; that I wasn't happy because there was talk of using me as an impact substitute. I'm used to untrue rumours circulating about me, but this talk was also a hugely disrespectful assumption to make about the other players involved. The likes of Fiona McHale, Sarah Tierney and Marie Corbett are all very strong, independent women who are well able to think for themselves. To suggest for one second that they'd walk away if I just clicked my fingers and said, 'Come on, we're going' . . . it just wouldn't happen.

I knew that I would be the one to take the blame. I was only in the door from Australia and things had gone south – even I could see how that would look. It was the easy story to run with, but as the saying goes, 'It's a long road that has no turning'. It hurt to stay silent but it wasn't about me, it was about protecting my teammates and respecting their privacy. So, if it was easier for a certain quarter to hang it on me, then so be it. For my friends, I would take it.

Those few weeks were some of the most stressful of my life. I couldn't sleep, and at times I found it hard to cope. There were days when I almost felt like I had to go into hiding. I was afraid to walk down town during my lunchbreak because I knew people were talking about me. I was so paranoid that I wouldn't go into certain coffee shops because I was fearful of who I'd see, or what they'd say, all the while knowing the truth. It was an incredibly difficult time, for everyone. But, hand on heart, I knew I had done the right thing.

Epilogue

As this book goes to print, I don't know if I have played my last game. Have I played my last game for Mayo? Who knows? Right now, I can't see myself ever being able to admit that I'm done, but I'm sure there'll come a point in time when I have to make a final decision.

From the age of thirteen, when I first pulled on a Mayo jersey, I knew how blessed I was to be in that position and to feel that connection with my county at such a young age. And, when I think back about how I was thrown into the spotlight so early in my career, I think I handled it fairly well. As well as I knew how, anyway.

The passing of Mam gave me an ability to cope. Overnight, I grew up. I became an adult. I learned how to handle hurt a lot sooner than most, and that made me resilient. Maybe even too resilient. But it meant that I could hack the criticism when it came. Because it did.

I knew I had a talent. I knew I was different. Yet I always understood that talent would only get me so far, so I worked hard. Every day I lived for consistency. Every morning I woke wanting to make myself a better player, and every day I wanted to deliver. I wanted to be the best I could.

I'll miss that when I'm gone; that craving to make myself better. That, and the routine of being part of a team. Sport gave me structure. In a way, it was my crutch, but it was the friendships I made along the way that really got me through. Take Crazy, for instance. She was constantly in my shadow, but not once did she ever get jealous. She knew how much I put into the game and she was only too delighted for me when accolades came my way. None of it would have been possible without her. She was the glue for us all, and I can never thank her enough.

I know I'm not getting any younger and retirement is coming to get me, and when it does, I'll tackle it on my own terms. The ideal ending would have been to just slip quietly away, close the door behind me and move on. For now, I'll escape a second Irish winter and throw myself into another season of footy in Sydney with the Giants, where I'll continue to learn, and continue to compete. Australia has offered me a new lease of life at a time in my career when I should be winding down.

My first season in Sydney was a huge leap of faith. I went out with the aim of becoming the best player I could be, but I was unsure of just how good I could become. Without a deep understanding of the game, I had to simply focus on my own job, my own patch of turf. This was entirely different to how I play football. With football, while I might be in the full-forward line, I'm also fully aware of everyone else's role on the pitch and whether or not they're doing a good job. I can read the game at a glance.

A second season with the Giants gives me an opportunity to grow my understanding of Aussie Rules beyond my role on the pitch. This will help me become a better player and teammate. I've been studying the game and have kept up my fitness programme since coming back to Ireland. I feel fit and I'm still hungry to compete so I see no reason why I can't make a stronger contribution in my second year back. Only time will tell.

You know by now, that's who I am. I only deal in black and white, and I'm driven, incredibly driven. At certain times in my career that was misconstrued, but what you see is what you get. I'm just a proud Mayo woman, a proud Carnacon woman, who cares about winning, and those I love.

Yes, over the years the lows have far outweighed the highs, but when those highs happen there's no better feeling on earth. They've made me keep going longer than I ever expected. If I have played my last game for Mayo, then so be it. It may not be the fairy-tale ending, but that's life. You just pick yourself up, and go again.

Acknowledgements

I'm very grateful to be in this position, and to say thank you publicly to everyone who helped and encouraged me every step of the way. My family, without a doubt, have been the leading force. To Dad and all my brothers and sisters, your never-ending support carried me through; and Kathleen in particular, you always listened, gave me solid advice and had my back.

To my nieces and nephews, my brothers- and sisters-in-law, my aunties, uncles and cousins, thanks for all your support, love and guidance throughout the last thirty-six years. I know I have not been the easiest to deal with at times and football consumed most of my life, but I hope I have made you proud.

To all the special people in my magnificent club, Carnacon. I am so lucky to have come from such a brilliant club. Jimmy and Beatrice, who have been there from the beginning – I will never be able to thank you enough for all you have done for me. You have been there through the good days and the bad, and I don't think I would be where I am today without your support and guidance.

To all my teammates in Carnacon, both past and present, it has been one hell of a journey and I am extremely honoured and privileged to have played with each and every one of you. The memories have been great, and here's to creating a few more.

Aisling, you may be no longer with us, but the years we spent together playing with Carnacon and Mayo I will always cherish.

To all the managers I have had with Mayo (and there've been a few!), especially the ones who stuck by us, thanks for making me the sportsperson I am. A special mention must go to Finbar Egan: you shaped and moulded me into the footballer I am. Thank you so much for the brilliant six years we had with you. You helped me through a very difficult time in my life and for that I shall be forever grateful.

A huge thank you, too, to all the medical staff for keeping me on the pitch and relatively injury-free throughout my career. I realize again that I was not the easiest to deal with at times, but it was all for the love of playing. A special mention must go to my good friend Caroline Brennan who always made herself available whenever I needed a physio appointment, or patching up.

To all my teachers and coaches in Burriscarra National School, Ballinrobe Community School and Athlone Institute of Technology, and to all my teammates and coaches from Castlebar Rugby Club, Ballyglass FC, Kiltimagh Knock Utd, and Mayo FC – thanks for everything.

To my employers, the Mayo Travellers Support Group, and especially to my boss Pippa Daniel, thank you for being so accommodating in every way possible over the years.

To Mary White, who helped me pen this book – to think I didn't really know you before we started this project and now you probably know me as well as anyone! Your professionalism, dedication and foresight were the driving forces in making this book a reality. Thank you for your patience and friendship. It has been a pleasure to work with you and I wish you every success in the future.

To Fiona Murphy of Transworld Ireland, thank you for all your hard work behind the scenes. Your advice and support throughout this project have made it possible.

Margaret and Pat Byrne, you have looked after me since I got to know you both more than twenty years ago. Margaret, you were like a second mother to me at times, and I will never forget that.

To all the GWS Giants, thanks for taking a gamble and bringing me to your amazing club. I am forever indebted to you for what was a wonderful experience. To all my Giants teammates, thank you for making me feel so welcome and for making my time at the club a very special one.

To Alan McConnell and Nicholas Walsh, the two men who made my AFLW journey possible, thank you both from the bottom of my heart. You made my experience in Sydney such an enjoyable one. Alan, you never judged me and you simply accepted me for the person that I am. I will always appreciate that.

Finally, to my close group of friends – Crazy, Martha, Marie, Doireann and Avril. Thanks for always being there, no matter what the situation. I am blessed and honoured to call you my friends. I am so proud of you all and I know no matter what, we will always have each other's backs.

Crazy, where do I start? My best friend and teammate for the best part of twenty years. I will never be able to repay you. I honestly don't know where I would be without you. You stuck by me and always saw the best in me when maybe others didn't. You have made me a better person and I am so lucky to have you as a best friend.

ACKNOWLEDGEMENTS

Sport has been a huge part of my life and I am so grateful that I had a long and successful career, and it's all thanks to you guys. It's been a blast!

Cora

Picture Acknowledgements

Every effort has been made to contact copyright holders where known. Those who have not been acknowledged are invited to get in touch with the publishers. Photos not credited have been kindly supplied by Cora Staunton.

Section One

Page 5: In action, Mayo v. Meath 1999: © Ray Lohan / SPORTS-FILE; First All-Ireland final: © Aoife Rice / SPORTSFILE

Page 6: Meeting the President: © Aoife Rice / SPORTSFILE; Goal!: © Ray McManus / SPORTSFILE; Celebrating with Claire Egan: © Tom Honan / INPHO

Page 7: Laois 2001: © Aoife Rice / SPORTSFILE; Devastated: © David Farrell / Western People; Carnacon All-Ireland title: © Michael Donnelly

Page 8: Coaching with Crazy: © Henry Wills / Western People; Galway 2003: © Lorraine O'Sullivan / INPHO; Running with Sonia: © Michael Donnelly

Section Two

Page 1: 2006 Connaught final: © Ray Ryan / SPORTSFILE; FAI Senior Cup final: © Damien Eagers / SPORTSFILE; With McGing sisters: © Matt Browne / SPORTSFILE

Page 2: Carnacon v. NaFianna: © David Maher / SPORTSFILE; Carnacon captains: © Michael Donnelly; With Páidí Ó Sé: © Michael Donnelly

Page 3: All-Star presentation: © Brendan Moran / SPORTSFILE; All-Star Tour: © Brendan Moran / SPORTSFILE; All-Star training: © Brendan Moran / SPORTSFILE

Page 4: Celebrating with Fiona McHale: © Donal Farmer / INPHO; Battling Dublin: © Ryan Byrne / INPHO; With nieces: © Ryan Byrne / INPHO

Page 5: Club All-Ireland win: © Oisin Kenlry / INPHO; First training session in Australia: © Ryan Miller / Greater Western Sydney Giants

Page 6: Sharing a joke with Al: © Craig Abercrombie / Greater Western Sydney Giants; Meeting Sonia with a broken nose: © Michael Dodge / Getty Images

Page 7: Signing autographs: © Craig Abercrombie / Greater Western Sydney Giants; Celebrating round 6 win: © Ryan Miller / Greater Western Sydney Giants

Page 8: Punditry: © Piaras O Midheach / SPORTSFILE

Index

INDEX

INDEX